The Reporter's Notebook

DENNIS BLOODWORTH

The Reporter's Notebook

DENNIS BLOODWORTH

mc Marshall Cavendish
Editions

Illustrations by Chan Su-Mei
Cover art by Opal Works Co. Limited

Published by Marshall Cavendish Editions
An imprint of Marshall Cavendish International
1 New Industrial Road, Singapore 536196

Other Marshall Cavendish Offices:
Marshall Cavendish International. PO Box 65829 London EC1P 1NY, UK • Marshall Cavendish Corporation. 99 White Plains Road, Tarrytown NY 10591-9001, USA • Marshall Cavendish International (Thailand) Co Ltd. 253 Asoke, 12th Flr, Sukhumvit 21 Road, Klongtoey Nua, Wattana, Bangkok 10110, Thailand • Marshall Cavendish (Malaysia) Sdn Bhd, Times Subang, Lot 46, Subang Hi-Tech Industrial Park, Batu Tiga, 40000 Shah Alam, Selangor Darul Ehsan, Malaysia.

Marshall Cavendish is a trademark of Times Publishing Limited

National Library Board Singapore Cataloguing in Publication Data
Bloodworth, Dennis.
  The reporter's notebook / Dennis Bloodworth. – Singapore : Marshall Cavendish
  Fditions, 2010.
  p. cm.
  ISBN-13 : 978-981-4302-85-2

  1. Bloodworth, Dennis – Anecdotes. 2. Reporters and reporting – Anecdotes.
  3. Press and politics – Southeast Asia – Humor. 4. China – Politics and government –
  1949-1976 – Humor. I. Title.

PN5449
070.4332092 – dc22   OCN657945390

Printed by KWF Printing Pte Ltd

For Malcom Muggeridge and David Astor —
who gave me my chance.

In grateful acknowledgement

ACKNOWLEDGEMENTS

I would like to thank all those of my colleagues who have allowed me to quote them, steal their expertise, or tell stories about them in this book, including Neal Ascherson of *The Observer*, Keyes Beech, formerly of the *Chicago Daily News* and *Los Angeles Times*, Michael Field of the *Daily Telegraph*, Richard Halloran of the *New York Times*, Estelle Holt, formerly of Reuters and Associated Press, Stanley Karnow, formerly of *Time* and the *Washington Post*, Anthony Lawrence of the BBC, Robert Pepper Martin, formerly of *US News and World Report*, Guy Searls, now with the *Hongkong Standard*, Frank Robertson, formerly of the *Daily Telegraph*, Peter Simms, formerly of *Time*, and Gavin Young of *The Observer*.

I am grateful to Prime Minister Lee Kuan Yew, and former deputy premiers Goh Keng Swee and Sinnathamby Rajaratnam of the Singapore government, for permitting me to quote their off-the-record statements; to William E. Colby, former director of the Central Intelligence Agency, for clearing one anecdote for publication; to Windsor Gregory Hackler, formerly of the University of Hawaii at Manoa, for providing the audiotapes of a seminar on journalism held in Honolulu in 1978 at which Keyes Beech, Richard Halloran and I were the speakers; to Christine Sipiére for verifying passages on Vietnam; and to Peter Watson and Geoffrey Murray of the Times Press Foundation School of Journalism in Singapore for reading the manuscript and giving me their professional comments. Above all, I should like to thank Chan Su-Mei for her apt and amusing sketches, which so happily complement the text.

CONTENTS

INTRODUCTION

Asked if she knew who had made her, Topsy gave the immortal reply: 'Nobody as I knows on…I 'spect I growed.' This monograph might have said the same, for like Topsy it, too, just 'growed'. It began as a suggestion for a lecture to a school of journalism, was translated into a limited project for a text that would provide light if minatory extramural reading for the students, and ended as 'another damned, thick, square book' that I have written not only for my fellow journalists but for the general reader — if with some misgivings.

Misgivings because mine was a lopsided career. I spent all but three of the thirty-five years of my professional life as a foreign correspondent, most of them in the Far East. I have never covered a flower show or a divorce case or a cricket match, and have not held an editorial post since I was twenty. It is not for me to instruct the young journalist in all the techniques of the job, or lay down the law to my colleagues, let alone pronounce upon the ethical dilemmas of owners and editors. I must leave that to the experts.

But I may still have something of value for the student of journalism and the experienced reporter, even when it contradicts what others say. For the student, because every man who faces a major operation finds it useful (if not necessarily encouraging) to listen to someone who has already been through it; having heard the doctors describe it in theory, he wants to know what it was like in terms of flesh and blood — and how to cope. And for the veteran, because those who have been operated upon themselves are only too keen to compare notes with a fellow sufferer.

To the exasperation of that bored bystander, the general reader? I hope not. Intelligent people are inquisitive about each other's business, because the odd thing is that one man hardly ever knows how his neighbour does what he does. To me the skills of a stonemason are as fascinating as those of a safebreaker, for I am tantalised by my own ignorance and want to understand more. And that surely applies not only to the reporter, who makes a living out of human curiosity, but to the tinker, tailor, soldier and sailor who may well find the inside story of a journalist's professional life as interesting as it is to another journalist.

This is no school primer, moreover. *Reporter's Notebook* is a collection of essays on the different facets of the trade, but they are enlivened by what I trust are revealing anecdotes set against the tapestry of the times. Some of them may throw new, if incidental, light on events of the recent past in Southeast Asia and China in particular, for I have included now-it-can-be-told material that could not then be disclosed.

The book inevitably switches from country to country and year to year, since the anecdotes are not arranged chronologically to form a pictorial record of modern history, but thematically to illustrate the different kinds of problems and predicaments that beset the reporter. I have rewritten or summarised a few that appeared in two earlier books of mine, *An Eye for the Dragon* and *The Messiah and the Mandarins*, but, by the same token, they are not designed this time to underline the differences between East and West, or the ironies of the Maoist era in China; they are related solely to the journalist and his job.

I have dedicated the book to my mentors, Malcolm Muggeridge and David Astor. It is a poor return, but the least I could do. I owe them my career, I can never repay them, and meanwhile an unfair Oriental philosophy makes them responsible for all that follows (since they were unwise enough to meddle with my destiny). But *Reporter's Notebook* is also for all journalists of both sexes* who try to record the truth before it is burned beyond recognition on the funeral pyre of history, knowing that the closer they get to it, the more are they themselves likely to be singed. For they serve a profession one of whose many salutary qualities is that — at its best — it is the enemy of the cheat, the liar, and all those who have something disreputable to hide.

DB.

Singapore, May 1988.

* *Not being a sexist, I refer to the abstract journalist as 'he' throughout the book.*

'I am myself a gentleman of the Press, and I bear no other scutcheon.'

— Benjamin Disraeli, *to Parliment, February 1863.*

I STORY LINE

'Your turn, Blood. Tell us a yarn.'

'YOUR turn, Blood,' a voice whispered harshly through the darkness. 'Tell us a yarn.' It was to be my first shot at putting words together. I was starting young — the year was 1928, so I must have been about nine — and if I was caught I would be whacked, for it was after lights-out in the dorm, and the deadline for stories past. Perhaps there was an omen there, a warning of what was to come for the next sixty-odd years. But I had been an inmate of Birchington House Preparatory School for Boys for only a few months. The other three men in the room were at least two years senior to me and had intimidating names — Gascoigne, Chetwynd, Rathbone (nephew of the callous and supercilious Basil). I gulped, and obediently hammered out my lead.

There was, I said, this rich English pirate who had a huge fleet of terrifically fast clippers armed to the teeth, when suddenly fifty proud Spanish galleons appeared off the storm-tossed coast…It was a good intro, with the guts of the story in the first par. But when I paused after five minutes in order to think frantically what might come next, there was silence. No one protested that I had left him in an agony of suspense. A horrible suspicion sidled into my mind. I waited a moment and then breathed their names. No one answered. They were all sound asleep. It was an inauspicious beginning to my career as a wordmonger.

But apart from snatching the indigestible leaves we called 'green cheese' from passing hedges and stuffing them into our mouths on a scoff-now-pray-later basis, the only way we could kill boredom during our frequent compulsory walks along the crumbling coast of south-east England was by spinning each other yarns. Nor was this discouraged, for the master in charge was usually a young man in his early twenties called Barker-Smith, whose hobby was the English language. My relationship with Barker-Smith was uneasy, for by the time I was eleven we were both madly in love with the same woman — the 26-year-old music mistress — and while he had been slow to press his suit, I in my impetuous youth had already made a pass at her during a piano lesson, planting a great, fat, wet, sloppy kiss on the side of her head as she bent to correct my arpeggios.

Nothing came of the affair, however (I like to think I quit while I was still ahead), and meanwhile the world of letters became a bond between Barker-Smith and myself. He taught me to listen, until I found I had a better ear for words than music, even when our beauteous inamorata was thumping the old upright piano beside me in the gym. I still see him reading an essay of mine with narrowing eyes, and hear him hiss indignantly, 'They commenced, Bloodworth? *Commenced*? Only the vicar's sermon *commences*.' He made the offending verb sound like the watery mince we had for lunch on Thursdays. I have never used it since, except in fun.

I was hooked on language, and very soon writing my first full-length work of fiction, a fast-paced thriller about a gang boss operating from the penthouse of a skyscraper who could nevertheless drop his victims through a steel trapdoor in the floor of his office when he got tired of shouting at them. It must have seemed a long way down. The setting was New York, a city which I knew only slightly, mainly because I had never travelled beyond Brighton. That was why, perhaps, I was able to put the Chicago Loop in the middle of Fifth Avenue without worrying, as I might have done later in life, about the usual nit-pickers questioning my geographical accuracy and writing disgusted letters to the editor. But this was before the days of the blockbuster, short novels were the rage, and after pushing a steel pen through eleven pages of a lined exercise book, I bowed to fashion and wound the tale up.

Authorship had proved too exhausting. It is best to learn these things when young, and by the time I had moved on to the Upper Fifth at Sevenoaks. I had lowered my sights. I would be a journalist. I would wear a green eyeshade and yell at copy boys. Even better, I would be an ace foreign correspondent like Gary Cooper in *Shanghai Express*, wearing a trenchcoat with a turned-up collar and getting my scoop among all those benighted Chinese while the bombs fell futilely around me. I abandoned my five-finger exercises on the piano in favour of two-finger exercises on a typewriter (not knowing that I would never get beyond them).

To my joy, my stepfather went broke: I could now leave school and go straight into Fleet Street. But the outside world was not quite like that in 1936. Scanning the columns of classified ads in the *Daily Telegraph* every morning, I slowly became aware that the path to the reporter's notebook might prove more devious than I had thought. No London editor wanted a cub who could not pay a premium for his training, or had not cut his teeth on a provincial paper as a junior reporter, obituary writer, sub-editor, proof-reader and tea-maker. (No one asked for a university degree or a diploma from a school of journalism in those days). But I was a penniless Londoner and had to earn a living. When I made my move, therefore, it was not into the sinister black box that housed the *Daily Express* in Fleet Street, but a dismal laboratory near the Elephant and Castle pub which had advertised for a pig food analyst.

The head chemist quickly discovered that I was not much good at pig food analysis, but the pigs — who understand nothing of the art but know what they like — gulped down the fodder I passed fit for them to eat. In consequence. I was able to hang on to my lab coat until a small and ephemeral press photo agency on Ludgate Hill took me on as a dogsbody at one pound a week. This was more like it— if only a little. The two photographers who ran the agency scoured the dailies each morning for news of coming events that might yield saleable pictures — a society wedding, a royal visit, a carnival, a cup final, the Derby or a demonstration. I learned to man the telephone for them, hold their tripods steady while they shot the action, develop their film, print enlargements, write short captions, and then race down Fleet Street, wet pictures in my hand, to beat the competition to the art editors of half a dozen national newspapers (whose offices were always up four flights of stairs, it seemed).

My horizon was widening, and life jerking into focus. On a single day I might wait nervously for Stanley Baldwin outside 10 Downing Street in the morning, and hold a magnesium flash in a sweating hand at Denham Studios while the film star Annabella posed sulkily in her dressing room after lunch. But our subjects were not always so famous, and on another I would be taking down all the names of the numerous offspring of a newly-appointed American ambassador called Kennedy as most of them shuffled into line for a group photograph — 'John F., Robert F., Edward M...' They were the first Americans I had ever spoken to.

And then came my baptism as a reporter. A prominent sportsman named Gandar Dower proposed to race cheetahs in England as a rival attraction to dogs, the agency was to take photographs of this exotic if fleeting craze, and I was to write the accompanying copy. I sat hunched on the edge of a low armchair facing Gandar Dower in an unfairly imposing drawing room, very conscious that a disobliging fate had given me — among other things — a writer as the subject of my first interview. No one had told me how to go about conducting it, and I made up the rules as I went along, leaving my notebook in my pocket, asking the first professional questions of my life, memorising Gandar Dower's answers, and agreeing to let him see my story before it was published. (Faced with a beardless youth of seventeen, he could hardly be blamed for reinsuring). I sent him three pages of single-spaced typing, and he struck out only one line. The story ended up, translated into Hungarian, in a theatrical magazine published in Budapest. I was actually in print, somewhere out there to the south-east.

Later that year the photo agency sank without trace, but I managed to leap to safety at the last minute by joining a magazine publishing combine in Fetter Lane called Cosmopolitan Press. I had to take a cut in salary, of course. I was paid ten shillings a week, and my first job was to cull from about fifty provincial papers dumped on my desk each morning all the unconsidered items of news that might be worth following up. I was on the bottom rung, with nine men above me (among them Lee Howard, who would one day become managing editor of the *Daily Mirror*), but in time I graduated to reporting and sub-editing, writing copy and proof-reading. Our main weekly, moreover, was *World's Press News*, a journal for journalists, so that I became a looking-glass learner, absorbing my trade from the very material I was working on. And that taught me not only about takeover bids and Fleet Street tycoons, those hired and those fired, but offset printing, the price and composition of newsprint, the latest typeface (Peignot), layout and make-up and three-tone colour, the difference between a linotype and a monotype, and just what a 36-point Century Condensed triple-deck flower pot agglutinate headline was and would look like on the front page.

By nineteen, I had earned my green eyeshade. I knew more than I would ever know again about the nuts and bolts of the business, and could talk technicalities out of the side of my mouth (the one not juggling with a cigarette) that would sound like gibberish to me today. But I was still being paid only thirty shillings a week, and after about fifteen months I was lured away by a seductive advertisement in the *Daily Telegraph* offering three times as much to a suitable young journalist who could write and edit a newsletter about the Far East. When I got the job, I felt as if I had won the Irish Sweep. *Four-pounds-ten a week* — and as if that were not enough, I was free every afternoon except when we went to press. With time on my hands, I wrote the draft of a novel almost eerily similar to Evelyn Waugh's recently published *Scoop,* and in deference to my new-found field of work paid a shilling for a second-hand copy of a little pocketbook called *The Hundred Best Characters.* I was, I fondly imagined, going to add Chinese to my schoolboy French.

Shortly after war broke out in September 1939, I was called up and drafted to an infantry regiment. (I still have my paybook, in which a semi-literate corporal described me with the right touch of equivocacy as a 'jourlinist'). But given my dubious linguistic attainments I was soon transferred to Intelligence. This did not, as I had hoped, plunge me immediately into the shadow-world of the secret agent. By Christmas I was a lance-corporal polishing the brass buttons on a uniform in a snowbound army hut near Aldershot when a new recruit, wearing a tomato-coloured sports coat and an almost demonic gleam in his sapphire eyes, pushed his way through the door and slammed it against the winter outside. I said my name was Bloodworth, and he said his was Muggeridge. Over a cup of cocoa and a slice of home-made fruit cake he told me, to my hushed astonishment, not only that he was a correspondent on the *Daily Telegraph* but that he had written a Book Society Choice called *The Thirties.* He had a proof copy with him, and would lend it to me. Awed, but not to be outdone, I asked him if he would skim through the typescript of my novel. He read it and even sent it to his literary agent, who very sensibly threw it straight back at him. 'Don't be discouraged,' said Malcolm Muggeridge, unconcerned. 'Remember, whatever you do, you must write.'

When I left the army seven years later, there was standing room only in Fleet Street, just as there had been when I had left school ten years before. Instead of fudging results in a pig food laboratory near the Elephant and Castle, I found myself mismanaging a sheet metal works in Peckham and flogging its products around the provinces. But destiny seemed to have ordained that my winding path to the reporter's notebook be paved with broken businesses. Like my stepfather and the press photo agency, the sheet metal works went under. Suppressing any passing fancy that this was too much of a coincidence, I went to Malcolm Muggeridge for help.

He was as delighted by the news of this latest disaster as I had been by my stepfather's financial failure, and for precisely the same reason. 'Now we can get you back into journalism,' he said. He introduced me to David Astor, editor of *The Observer*, and Astor asked me to write a 1,600-word profile to show what I could (or could not) do. I gave it to him a week later. He read it through a little sadly, but suddenly brightened, his finger on one line. 'I quite like this,' he said, surprised, and I was in.

That was typical of *The Observer*. Bewildered pros who joined the paper from the sweatshops of Fleet Street would find themselves surrounded by gifted amateurs in what appeared to be a political club, its ancient premises a warren of cubbyholes bearing no resemblance to the sort of newspaper office that employed Clark Gable. (Years later a colleague would describe it as being 'like a continuous seminar, a convention of disputatious Talmudic scholars, a joint session of the Fabian Society and the Second International...') But by the same token, this was no place for the beginner. There were no handholds, no technical guides, no house rules about style, comment, or the length of a lead, no instructional memos, no basic papers on libel and contempt. It was assumed that those who came here had already learned the grammar of the trade and were fluent in the language. For the rest, *The Observer* itself was the newcomer's stylebook. This was the deep end. (And deeper for some than it was for others. In 1952 Muggeridge in all innocence asked Astor if he had a job for another wartime friend who said he was 'anxious to get back into journalism', his 'regular profession from 1935 to 1940'. But our paths never crossed. His name was Kim Philby, and he pursued a rather different career.)

****

By March 1949 I was in Paris, legman to the chief correspondent and feeling my way cautiously into the Byzantine politics of the Fourth Republic. At Cosmopolitan Press I might have riffled confidently through the English provincial dailies, but now I was construing alien newspapers whose idea of a riveting front-page lead was an enigmatic question phrased in the conditional — 'What is it that would be passing itself at rue Saint-Dominique?' There were new-techniques to learn — how to talk a story out of a frigid Foreign Ministry in basic French, where best to stand while the *flics* were breaking up a fist fight in the fractured Assemblée Nationale, or beating left-wing rioters into breathless docility in the Place de la Concorde (out of the way: you let them hit first, and asked questions afterwards).

And there were other arts to acquire: filing stories in telephonese to a copytaker in London, cannibalising the output of a chattering Agence France Presse teleprinter, covering the crowded conferences of international organisations — NATO, UNESCO, OECD, the General Assembly of the UN itself (one short season only), and communist marionettes like the World Peace Council. The foreign ministers of the Big Four convened, to niggle endlessly in an upper chamber of the Quai d'Orsay while a hundred correspondents waited below for their eight striped-trousered legs to appear through the ceiling. (An open lift brought them down feet first, and the symbolism was irresistible).

I started writing background copy, then my first feature, then think pieces, finally a syndicated column, a Paris Letter in which I was at last allowed to make my own jokes. I was standing in for my often absent chief, and was myself sent to Trieste to cover anti-British riots, to Rome to gatecrash the Italian Communist Party and do a profile of the socialist leader Pietro Nenni, to Geneva (briefly) for the international conference to end the fighting in Korea and Vietnam. I was beginning very tentatively to think that I might after all belong in the same world as Gary Cooper in *Shanghai Express* (I had nearly been beaten up for a British cop while wearing a trenchcoat with a turned-up collar in Trieste), but I did not know how close I was to dreaming my own tomorrow.

By May 1954 the Indochina War — the eight-year-long struggle between the French colonialists and the 'Vietminh' liberation movement under the communist leader Ho Chi Minh — was drawing towards the foreseeable future, and my editor asked me for a profile of General de Castries. De Castries was the gallant hero of the battle of Dienbienphu who, having dug himself into an obvious trap on the orders of his superior, had named the redoubts of his surrounded strongpoint after his girl friends, while waiting for 'Uncle Ho' to mate him in one. I had been writing news stories about Indochina for some time, acting as back stop for our man in Saigon who, like all correspondents who were not French, was often kept further away from the war than we were in Paris. In consequence I had cultivated officials of the French colonial service anxious to make their point, and Vietnamese on both sides of the conflict equally anxious to make theirs, and by the time I was in a position to match a profile of de Castries with a profile of Ho Chi Minh, *The Observer* was ready to send me to Saigon.

Vietnam was theoretically at peace. Two months after the inevitable defeat at Dienbienphu, where the breastworks of 'Isabelle' and similar redoubts had failed to keep the Vietminh at bay, the Geneva Agreement had brought the war to an end. The country was divided into two zones at the 17th Parallel, the north under the communist Ho Chi Minh, the south under the anti-communist Ngo Dinh Diem (who was theoretically responsible to the absentee Emperor Bao Dai). General elections were to be held in both zones in July 1956, so that they could be joined together again as one Vietnam under one government. The magicians at Geneva, in short, had sawn the lady in half at the waist, promising to produce her in one piece later. But since they were not very good magicians, the trick was to go wrong and leave only a revolting mess.

I was supposed to go to the Far East for four months only, and then be brought back to Rome to take over the Mediterranean. I never returned. Yet the rest of my life began badly. Forty-five hours out of Paris, the Air France Constellation landed at Saigon in darkness and torrential rain. I had no Vietnamese piastres, and when I finally reached my hotel after making the last lap of my journey in a streaming trishaw, I dripped across the foyer to be told that my cabled reservation had arrived but there was simply no room for me — there, or anywhere else. The few hotels in Saigon had been taken over by members of the International Control Commission appointed to supervise the armistice negotiated at Geneva, and by an army of correspondents who had come to watch them do it.

I called the duty officer at the British Embassy, and eventually a charitable diplomat gave me a room with a broken shower for one night only, and fed me my first meal in Southeast Asia — bacon and baked beans on toast. But by noon the next day I was eating a vegetarian lunch served by shaven-headed bonzes of the Cao Dai sect who were celebrating the Mid-Autumn Festival at the Great Temple at Tay Ninh. This was more like it, I thought, as I gazed at the riot of gaudy dragons entwining its pillars, listened to the gongs, sniffed the incense, and watched the private army of the Cao Dai Pope march past. My first twenty-four hours in the exotic Orient were not over, however. By four o'clock, a French doctor was putting stitches in my nose after I had made an over-exuberant dive into a small private swimming pool. But I was able to cadge a bed for my second night in Saigon from the Reuter correspondent, and another for my third from the Australian military attache. If the Far East was making its mark on me, I was making my mark on the Far East.

I forgot about my appointment with Rome. For the next two years my base was to be a cool, tiled room in the Hotel Continental Palace. The room had no telephone, I had no radio and no files, Saigon had no reliable local press, and (at first) no other resident correspondent from a British newspaper. Covering Indochina was to be reporting in the raw. Fresh from France, an air-flown journalist with none of the usual additives, I shuttled between North and South Vietnam via Cambodia and Laos in a miscellany of second-hand aircraft to get a miscellany of first-hand stories. In Vietnam these included Ho Chi Minh's triumphant entry into Hanoi with the sneaker-shod Vietminh in November 1954, and the exodus of the first 'boat people' — the hazardous flight of more than half a million anti-communist Vietnamese Catholics to the South; the violent sect rebellion against Ngo Dinh Diem in Saigon in which a quarter of the capital burned down; and the palace revolution in 1955 that ended the reign of the Emperor Bao Dai and — one year later — made Diem president. For the South Vietnamese (and the Americans behind them) had not signed the Geneva Agreement, the general elections to unite the country were therefore never held, and by 1956 the two halves of Vietnam had solidified into two independent republics that were heading, inevitably, towards another war.

But I was not confined to Indochina. In the summer of 1955 I was granted a visa to Beijing, and felt like a philatelist in paradise once that rarest of stamps was safely in my passport. Only a handful of Western correspondents had been allowed into Mao's tender young republic, and no Americans. I made a lone tour of China that lasted seven weeks, and in the Hall of Magnanimity in Beijing heard Premier Zhou Enlai tell the National People's Congress that the number of farming cooperatives must be drastically cut — while behind his back Chairman Mao was saying it must be doubled. It was an early lesson in 'party solidarity'. And Mao Zedong.

In October 1956 I covered riots in Hong Kong, only to be sent to the other end of Southeast Asia the same month to cover more riots in Singapore. For my territory was expanding. I was appointed chief Far East correspondent of *The Observer*, and Singapore was to be my base for the next twenty-five years. I was not often there. The riots were symptomatic of a post-war era in which disillusioned Southeast Asians, awakened by the proven ability of small yellow men from Japan to give a whipping to big white chiefs from the West, were impatiently shaking themselves free of the tight-fitting bonds of the colonial past — the Indochinese from the French, the Indonesians from the Dutch, the Malayans from the British — often to find that they had fallen into the hands of even more autocratic bosses, communist and anti-communist.

In consequence, the Far East correspondent was geared to a twisting kaleidoscope of events that had him flitting incontinently from communist terrorism in Malaya to a crisis in Rangoon and a coup in Bangkok, from civil war in Sumatra to the Great Leap Forward in China, from student riots in Tokyo to student rebellion against President Syngman Rhee in Seoul. And that takes us only to 1960. I was back in Vietnam, Laos and Cambodia in the years that followed, as communist guerrillas took to the jungle again in a new bid for the mastery of all three Indochina states; switched intermittently to the friable fringes of Malaysia in mid-decade when President Sukarno of Indonesia declared armed *Konfrontasi* against the new federation; and commuted to Hong Kong, Taiwan, Macao and finally China itself to monitor the madness of Mao's Cultural Revolution as we moved towards the seventies. In a self-governing Singapore, meanwhile. Prime Minister Lee Kuan Yew had closed with the communists in a catch-as-catch-can struggle for power, and then taken the island into Malaysia — only to see it thrown out again in a charged atmosphere of racial distrust between Malays and Chinese that would explode into more bloody rioting in Kuala Lumpur in 1969.

After the Tet Offensive in Vietnam in 1968, I stopped covering the ground in Southeast Asia. I continued to write pieces about the region as a whole, but concentrated mainly on the last agonies of the Maoist era, the Gothic horrors of a China in the grip of the Gang of Four, and the new dawn under Deng Xiaoping. I toured the People's Republic for the last time in 1980, and retired from journalism at the beginning of 1981.

I had forgotten what an exhausting business it had proved to finish my first book, to write off that gangster in the New York penthouse who had the long drop on his rivals. I had published nine others by then, and was under the absurd delusion that a deadline for 100,000 words in a year's time would always mean less nailbiting than a deadline for a thousand words tomorrow. I should have known better. I should have quietly tipped my typewriter into the nearest mangrove swamp and taken up pottery or stamps or orchids or tea-tasting. But there was no escaping destiny. 'Your turn, Blood,' the voice had whispered through the darkness. 'Tell us a yarn.' And it was still whispering.

2 GOA OR BUST

It was the last car left in Belgaum.

JOURNALISM is not a science, but an art. Each newspaper develops its own distinctive style, and may change it as readily as Picasso when it falls out of fashion and does not pay. (Every tabloid certainly goes through its own 'Blue Period'). But whether the reporter in the field is linked in the public mind with the orotund profundities of the *New York Times* or the slam-bam-thank-you-ma'am tactics of the London *Daily Mirror*, he is always a joker in the pack. As a comment, 'jourlinist' was as subtle as it was unconscious.

The reporter has no fixed status. One day he will be drinking Pol Roger with a friendly prime minister (who is anxious to sell him a bill of goods); on the next he will be tartly snubbed by the teenage receptionist in a fifth-rate bucket shop, or bawled out by a sweating sentry at the trademan's entrance to a police barracks. His feet never quite touch solid ground. For he is no executive ensconced behind a desk in an ergonomic swivel chair under the protection of a purring secretary with retractable claws, but out in the street at the mercy of all mankind. And his only two-edged talisman — God help him — is the name of a newspaper that may be taken by some as a password, by others as a proof of guilt.

If he is a correspondent in the Far East, his workaday life calls for him to absorb something of the pious resignation of the more devout Asians around him, to strive between drinks for that perception of the Infinite that alone can enable him to view the changing cosmos with equanimity. Otherwise he will be sixty by the time he is thirty. For a start, he is engaged in the maddening business of collecting perishable news against Western deadlines in the timeless East, and in the face of placid officials keenly aware of the comic side of Caucasian impatience. It may be less timeless than it was, but in President Sukarno's day, for example, a visa to Indonesia could cost him twenty-five dollars and three weeks of waiting while the world forgot whatever it was that he was supposed to have gone there for in the first place.

And wherever he travels, he is fighting a conspiracy among political leaders to sweep the dirt under the gorgeous Oriental rug. There may be famine in Bangladesh, mayhem in the Philippines, chicanery in Malaysia and corruption in Thailand, but somehow the reporter is supposed to be tactful about it all and still keep his job. Otherwise he is an unscrupulous sensationalist, a scurrilous scribbler whose mischief-making distortions of the official truth are deliberately designed to foment strife and multiply all man's miseries.

True, few of our detractors go so far as the Burmese rebels who in 1969 offered rewards for journalists (and at a poor penny-a-line rate at that: S725 alive, S360 dead), but like most correspondents in the region I have at one time and another been denied visas for

China, North Vietnam, South Vietnam, North Korea, Indonesia, Cambodia and Burma, publicly attacked in Kuala Lumpur, Taipei, Bangkok and Phnom Penh, deprived of my passport in Saigon, and threatened with expulsion from Malaysia (when my home in Singapore was part of it). These are my references.

The destiny — not to say the luck — of the reporter can fluctuate so wildly that he is left with nothing but his fatalism and sense of fun to keep him sane, even sober. But never have I been caught without a seat belt and thrown about so hilariously as when the Indians annexed Goa in December 1961, cutting easily into the tiny Portuguese settlement which lay half-way down the west coast of their subcontinent like a small, soft bruise on a pear. At least, that was where I finally found it in my school atlas, for India was not my beat and I only knew the uninspiring insides of its international airports. I was at home in Singapore and looking forward to Christmas with my family. I could confidently dismiss the Goa story — a cloud no bigger than Pandit Nehru's hand — as someone else's headache, for I was happily unaware that our man in New Delhi had had the gall to go sick.

The first cable from my foreign news editor in London swung in like a ranging shot at about 9.30 at night:

COULDST FLY BOMBAY PROCEED GOA FOR
COVERAGE INDIAN MILITARY TAKEOVER
SWEEKEND QUERY etc.

I found that all flights to Bombay were fully booked, rang the private number of a BOAC manager I did not know, caught him before he went to bed, and begged him for a seat. He rang back later, obligingly offering to squeeze me on to a plane going as far as Colombo the following morning, from where I might steal a connection to Bombay. Great. But two hours later a second cable arrived from London:

ON REFLECTION PREFER YOU GO DELHI
FIRST FILE COMPREHENSIVE CURTAINRAISER
GOA INVASION GIVING NEHRUS MOTIVES
POLITICAL BACKGROUND RELEVANCE
SINOINDIAN FRONTIER DISPUTE BOMBAY
ELECTIONS INDIAN REACTIONS ETC FOR
THIS WEEKS PAPER THEN PROCEED GOA FOR
NEXT WEEKS COVERAGE.

Or words to that effect.

I caught the BOAC manager in bed this time, but although I grovelled suitably, he was fresh out of aircraft. However, by breakfast he had me booked on a flight to Calcutta the same evening with a wait-listed connection to New Delhi from there. It was now Wednesday, and *The Observer*, being a Sunday newspaper, wanted the think-piece about Goa in London by Friday night, plus front page news follow-up on Saturday. I bought tickets and money, cabled the Imperial Hotel in New Delhi for a room as from Thursday night, packed, wished my wife a Merry Christmas, and caught my plane.

The turbo-prop snored off into the night, and coughed its way up to the apron in Calcutta at 2.30 on Thursday morning. Dum Dum Airport was a clacking mill of Indian passengers, but the New Delhi connection took off full an hour later without me, and the barrack of a building was suddenly empty, lightless, and bitterly cold. I sat down to wait for a bus or a taxi to take me into Calcutta, or a plane that would take me to New Delhi, whichever came first. The bus won at dawn. I rented an attic room full of hot-water pipes and cockroaches in a crumbling museum of a hotel, and slept. It had been a long yesterday.

By 9.30 in the morning I was back on my feet and climbing over and around a jumble of beggars to book a flight to New Delhi and change some traveller's cheques. The best I could get was a seat on an aircraft leaving early in the evening. I improved the wilting hours of waiting by stropping my ignorance on local experts, lunching with an Old India Hand, and talking to the editor of *The Statesman*. By dusk the airline bus was swerving and jouncing its way between the high hovels of the old city to connect with the plane due to put me down in New Delhi at 10.30 that night. It was Thursday. My piece would have to be written and cabled within thirty hours, after I had first found my way around the unknown capital of India (still some 750 miles to my north-west) and dug a story out of it. I could just manage, I calculated. I shouldn't have done. At this point, as if on cue, a delicious little sing-song voice came over the loudspeaker advising passengers that owing to fog at New Delhi airport, the plane had been diverted to Lucknow, where we would all spend a comfortable night. Any inconvenience was regretted.

At Lucknow, some 250 miles south-east of New Delhi, huge bonfires burned in the public squares to keep the poor from freezing, and I shared a double room in the ancient airport hotel with a Mr Gupta. There was no heating. We slept side by side on little single cots, wrapped in our overcoats and all the bedclothes available, including the curtains.

At eight the next morning there was a bang on the door (Good grief, I thought, Friday!) and an Indian pilot strolled in bearing news as stunning as his moustache: New Delhi airport was free of fog.

'So when do we take off?' I asked, my skin crawling with impatience.

'I'm sorry,' he replied with an engaging grin, 'but we don't.'

Calm settled over me like a block of ice on which someone had scratched the words, 'I hate Asia'. 'I wonder if I might enquire,' I began in the frigid idiom of those who write scathing letters of complaint to my editor, 'I wonder if I might enquire, why the hell not?'

'You'd better look out of the window,' he answered gently. I did, and saw nothing. The fog had shifted to Lucknow.

It lifted parallel with the sun, and by lunchtime I was walking jauntily up to the reception desk of the Imperial Hotel in New Delhi with India and my typewriter in my grasp, and perhaps seven hours in which to find myself a story about Goa and Nehru and the Sino-Indian problem and the Bombay elections and — what Bombay elections, anyway? '…but your room was for last night,' the odious fellow behind the counter was protesting. 'I'm afraid it has gone.'

'Well, give me another.'

'I'm afraid we are full.'

'Then book me into another hotel.'

'I'm afraid they also are all full.' At that I began to rave in an ill-mannered way, and this evidently gave him confidence in my probity and financial standing. 'Well, there *is* the royal bridal suite,' he began doubtfully, and before he could say more, I had grabbed it.

It was all gold and ivory and ormolu and buhl and sun-clocks and satin sofas. It ran to four big rooms upholstered in imperial yellow, including a great salon hung with gorgeous drapes, the whole floating on a sea of soft pile carpeting. I dropped my battered bag and travel-stained typewriter beside an orgiastic double bed, stripped off my sweat-stained jacket, and felt like a burglar in Buckingham Palace.

Now what? When in a corner and up against the clock, aim low. My first telephone call was to the public relations officer at the British High Commission, my second to the press section of the Indian Foreign Ministry, and only my third to the dynamic editor of the Hindustan Times…By one o'clock in the morning I was typing the last take of my 1,200-word collect cable on a marble-topped console, having talked a curtain-raiser out of a scratch list of contacts during the afternoon and early evening. A late finish on Lap One.

The next problem was to get into Goa (nearly 900 miles SSW of me by now) and out again within precisely one week, since there would be no chance of cabling from the nobbled Portuguese enclave itself. To do this I had first to fly to Bombay, and from there to the jumping-off point at Belgaum, the nearest town to the border on the Indian side. But, I was assured in every quarter, there were now no flights from Bombay to Belgaum. I would have to do a round trip by air, finally approaching it from Madras in the *south-east*.

By the time I had laid this persistent canard and booked a ticket for Bombay on a plane leaving at noon the next day, I realised that what with the royal bridal suite and other complications, I was going to run low in funds. It was Saturday. It was also two days before Christmas. Even if I cabled *The Observer* for cash, the banks would be closed. I tried tapping a British colleague. He was broke, but he would take me to a rather smart reception that evening to which I had not been invited but where we might be able to pick up something, old boy.

I went back to my royal bridal suite to cable Saturday's spot news to London, bathe and change. The key I had been given at the reception desk would not open the door. Not only that, but I heard loud manly voices on the other side of it. I banged sharply, someone said 'must be the ice', and a strapping young fellow in an undervest and jeans looked out at me, scratching himself wonderingly.

'I'm sorry,' I said in my apologetic British way. 'I'm afraid there's some mistake. This is my — my suite. I've got my gear in there.'

'No mistake,' he said mildly, 'but come in and look around anyway.'

It was a dream sequence. There was no sign of my belongings. Instead, the entire crew of a giant American military transport plane were strewn across the yellow satin in various stages of negligé, purposefully imbibing vodka. On a vast marble sideboard stood a long, thin line of bottles to console men not acclimatized to Indian liquor laws. They all stared at me for a bit, while I stared at the bottles. Then one said slowly, 'I'd say what you need is a drink.' My luck was running after all.

I learned in due course that the hotel receptionist had switched me to a single room with bath which had become available while I was out chasing tickets, money, and the news, and had moved my bag and typewriter into it during the afternoon in view of the sudden transatlantic demand for royal bridal suites. At the evening reception I borrowed fifty pounds in cash from a rich Parsee lady with a capacious handbag whom I had never seen in my life, and set off in good spirits for Bombay on a fine crisp Sunday morning. I was in business again.

In Bombay I ate a solitary Christmas dinner in the dining room of the Taj Mahal Hotel — a vast, echoing hangar for the hungry, completely empty but for a family of three fellow-Britons, who ignored me and nibbled and whispered their way through the meal as if in mortal fear of breaking the monumental silence and being charged for it. The intimidating Indian waiters were magnificently accoutred and turbanned, and served tepid turkey and plum pudding with great panache. But I was refused a liquor permit. Journalists, it seemed, did not qualify as bona fide travellers.

On the next day I flew down to Belgaum in a venerable Dakota which jerked about unsteadily in the capricious Indian air like a stage drunk on a tightrope, and then landed on a sandy patch of grass near a clump of peepul trees but otherwise nowhere in particular, as far as I could make out. However, an old, slightly dented bus stood in the shade, and this eventually dropped me at Green's Hotel — a little rest house, all verandas and cane chairs and jalousies, mosquito nets and meat-safe doors — where I asked with spurious confidence for lunch and a car to take me to Panjim, capital of Goa. The lunch shook the confidence, but almost immediately after it two grinning bandits in off-white turned up in a badly buckled Buick with MYX 1913 on the licence plates, which could have been both the number and the year of manufacture. It was the last car left in Belgaum, the manager assured me. The bandits — Messrs G. S. Kanbargi and Visnu Ramchandara Karkatka — would take me to Panjim, drive me around while I was there, and bring me back to Belgaum for forty pounds, I was told (but not by them, for they spoke no language known to me).

The car was good vintage stuff. All four doors and the boot had been secured with string to stop them from flying open, and after fifteen minutes of driving with his foot on the floorboard the first grinning bandit prevailed, and the engine expired. The second bandit then tried blowing petrol into the carburettor from the filler at the back, swallowed about half a pint of it, and nearly died in his turn.

After some wheezing and throat-clearing, both co-driver and car recovered, and we roared off menacingly through dank Indian jungle overhung with creepers.

The road was cut into short lengths by neat transverse trenches, and sown with mines. But the mines were marked with little flags which the retreating Portuguese troops had forgotten to remove, and were covered by no machine guns. The dilatory ferries were also undefended. After 451 years of Portuguese rule, the little enclave of Goa had fallen. By nightfall we had reached the hither bank of the Mandovi River, across which lay palm-fringed Panjim with its narrow twisting streets of stucco-fronted houses. Screened by lateen-sailed craft, it looked like the original 400-year-old block from which all the mottled prints of trading posts in the Indies had been run off.

We crossed the river on the ferry, to find that my attempt to cable the one recognisable hotel from Bombay had failed. The Mandovi was full, and for a bed for the night I was directed to what appeared to be the colonial poorhouse, though I seem to recollect that a sign said 'Hotel Central'. I pushed open a narrow door to enter a damp stone passageway half-blocked by two recumbent figures in rags and lit by a single oil lamp encrusted with dead insects and dust. A slattern appeared, and took me down a corridor from which cement-floored rooms with black iron beds and barred windows led off like cells. I was shown into one of these, and left with two candles.

I put my suitcase on one of the beds and opened it. My clothes were covered with a thick coating of red dust which had seeped into the rattling boot of the Buick, but I found one shirt at the bottom that was fit to wear. Grimy and parched, I called out through the door to ask for some water. At this an irate mongrel rushed at me, and when I kicked him away, poised momentarily in that rather nervous way dogs have and delivered himself in the very middle of the room, watching me out of the corner of one eye. Before I could utter, a young maid, blinded by the mound of grey cotton sheets and pillows in her arms, walked straight into the mess and trod it over to the bed. 'Agua,' I croaked, rather as they do in films about unfortunate men lured into the desert to die. She pointed to a wash-house across the way. It contained one mugful of dirty water, and was otherwise as dry as a disused bone.

I rubbed down with a towel, put on my clean shirt, and walked out to breathe fresh air, as if on parole. The two bandits, who had sensibly indicated that they would rather sleep in the car than in my dungeon, drove me to the Mandovi. On an open terrace upstairs I drank the three most enchanting whiskies of my life, slowly and blissfully, with the knowledge that I did not have to go back to my cell for at least two hours.

At the next table were a group of Indian journalists, but when I introduced myself, they ignored me. Fortunately. For on the other side of me were three bearded men of a faintly piratical air who had observed this rebuff with a sympathetic eye, and we fell into amicable conversation. They were Goan nationalists of some standing, supporters of Laura de Souza, the strident Boadicea who was making a name for herself by fearlessly shaking her fist in the face of the Indians (as she had shaken it in the face of the Portuguese), and demanding independence — or at least autonomy — from both. We should all go off to dinner somewhere quiet along the coast and talk sedition seriously, they said, but to be fair, I should perhaps first introduce myself to G. K. Handoo, the special adviser from Bombay who was the grey eminence behind the rape of Goa. Where would I find him? Just over there, at the end the terrace.

One minute later I was arranging an interview for the next day with a tall, drawling Indian with a languid air whose throw-away comments on the need to 'educate' the Goans in order to 'persuade' them of the 'real meaning' of being part of India (autonomy would be 'absurd', of course), pronounced in the accents of Eton and Ascot, were to give me chilling copy. That meeting, moreover, would lead me to the general commanding the operation, and so on to others equally eager to tell it their way. It was two hours since I had arrived, a lost soul with not a name to his name to look up, but now I had leads to both sides in my hands. Certain politicians, and lamentable Philistines who know no better, accuse journalists of getting all their news while propping up bars. But like all people who are wildly wrong most of the time, once in a while the Philistines are right.

I went back to my rebels, smiling. Where was I staying, they asked, promptly knocking me off Cloud Nine. My answer caused a sensation. 'But you can't live there,' one of them protested, 'you must take a room in this hotel.' 'It's full,' I replied. 'Nonsense,' they said, and insisted that we troop down to the office and talk to the manager. The ensuing conversation in crackling Goanese English could have been written into the script for the *Son of Dracula*.

'I am sorry,' said the manager, spreading his hands. 'But regrettably there is no room. As I said.'

'But this is our friend. You must do something.'

'How can I do something when the hotel is packed tight with Indian officers. There is nowhere.'

'There is always the fourth floor.'

It came out artlessly, but the manager started. '*The fourth floor?*' he echoed, almost in a whisper, his eyes narrowing as he swung his head to see if others were listening. 'For the love of God, man,

I cannot put anyone here.'

'But it is empty?'

'Of course it is empty, but…but, no, it is impossible. You know I cannot.' His voice took on a new urgency. 'Stop talking about it, I beg you.' But they did not stop, and in the end the manager threw up his hands and surrendered.

After a dinner by the sea at which I fought to memorise an avalanche of fact and fiction that I must later transmute into a few well-chosen words, we picked up my things at the poorhouse and returned to the hotel. The manager glanced around quickly and ushered me towards the passenger lift. I stepped in. 'Not that one,' he hissed, and I then saw that next to it was a narrow box like an upright coffin that I had not noticed before. The buttons revealed that it went to the fourth floor only. 'It is closed to the public, you understand?' he warned. 'It has been closed ever since…' We rose slowly, and I swallowed, tightening my grip on my typewriter and myself. At least we were going up, not down.

Very suitably. For the fourth floor was a miniature paradise, a nightclub shut down by the righteous invader. A comfortable bed had been set up for me in the middle of the dance floor, and enclosed by screens on castors. The ballroom was lit by sixty-seven soft lights controlled by a huge switchboard, and looked out upon a roof garden the size of a badminton court, pleasantly embellished with potted plants. For my modest ablutions, I disposed of facilities designed to meet — separately yet simultaneously — the nocturnal needs of up to a dozen men and women. Having made a tour of this splendid suite, I showed the manager to my private lift and sent him down with a word of thanks.

The next morning I was able to move into a comfortable

double room with a wholly endearing colleague, a religious affairs correspondent of the *Daily Express* named Redfern who had been diverted from an ecumenical congress in New Delhi and was carrying around with him a virgin bottle of scotch, because it had inspired him to go on the wagon. After four days of hard news-gathering we drove back together to Belgaum in the Buick, and took the same drunken Dakota to Bombay. We arrived on Friday evening, and it was time for me to file my main story again. But I was too exhausted to write a word. My luck had held, I thought idiotically. I can sleep now, be called at 2.30 in the morning, and write through the rest of the night. At this, the lips of fate moved so slightly that I did not notice.

Hardly had I begun pounding out the tentative lead for my article at the ungodly hour I had chosen, when insomniacs in the next room banged on the wall and reminded me in emotional and threatening language just how ungodly it was. I went back to bed and rose again at 6.30. But I began to perceive, on the very edge of my understanding, the jaws of a trap. It was already Saturday. Even given a special indulgence, major background copy for London would have to leave by lunchtime at the latest, and I seemed to have heard that the telegraph office closed at midday. I had about five hours in which to summarise a week's work, sort out the intricacies of the situation, throw out the dross, throw in the colour, put it all into reasonably readable form, and then cut and polish it, retype it in cablese (INDTPS CUMTANKS SMORNING PENETRATED SFARS OLDGOA POSTFAILUREF PORTUGUESE ADDEFEND STROPICAL ENCLAVE EXATTACK, as we used to say in those days), correct it, and finally feed it over the counter at the telegraph office, wherever that might be.

By 11.30 I was shouting for a taxi and exhorting the driver quite needlessly to make even greater efforts to break the speed limit and the law of the left. By 11.40, in consequence, I was listening to a clerk in the telegraph office telling me, as if in a dream, that my collect account for charging the cost of my cables to London was valid in New Delhi but not Bombay. I would have to pay cash. And, yes, they did close at midday.

Cash? I looked down at the fifteen hundred words of copy in my hands as a cripple might look at his club foot. 'But I don't have enough cash on me,' I said. 'I shall have to go to the bank.' I glanced at my watch, and felt a cry of despair sink into a whisper in my throat. 'Quick,' I shouted. 'The Chartered Bank. For God's sake, where is it?' I had cabled London for another hundred pounds before flying to Belgaum in order to be able to repay my Parsee benefactress, and if I could not lay my hands on it now the whole trip would have been a waste of time.

The Indian pointed to a noble, faintly ecclesiastical frontage just across the huge square and I rushed out, maniacally hopping and skipping and jumping my way through the rush-hour traffic. The bank was closed. It was not the Saturday before Christmas Eve this time. It was the Saturday before New Year's Eve.

I ran around the building until I found a side entrance, hammered on a door until it was reluctantly opened, and thrust my way past expostulating messengers and guards to stumble like some dazed and exhausted sinner into the cool sanctuary of money. Intent upon their devotions to ledger and calculator, those still present at first paid no attention to the mouthings of this wild, gasping intruder. Then a young acolyte with a small but heavenly smile on his face and benediction in his eyes came forward to murmur reassurances, and bring me salvation at the going rate.

As the minutes dribbled away like pearls from a broken string, the familiar ritual of slips and signatures was performed, and the cash drawn. Another demonic dash across the seething square, and I had paid for the cable as the clock struck twelve. It had all taken less than a fortnight, and now I had nothing to do but go home a year or two older.

3 THE PAPER CHASE

The metal monster he had contrived grew until it filled all the available space.

TELL the story in the lead, they say, and as a hardened hack I seem to have wasted little time in establishing myself firmly as the feckless, irresponsible and ignorant scribbler that is the image of the average reporter treasured by all who are not reporters. I arrive in Saigon with no money, no home, no files — nothing but a thirst, a disintegrating typewriter, and the clothes I impudently propose to stand up in; I arrive in India almost identically ill-equipped with the intention of wrapping up in ten days and two or three thousand words of authoritative copy a crisis on which my mind is almost a perfect blank. Who could be more unprepared for the task his boss has so foolishly confided to him (other than a newly-appointed cabinet minister)?

That is a skin-deep syllogism, however. The do-it-yourself correspondent cannot anticipate the more freakish calls made upon him in his career, and he is therefore paid for his skill in shooting unknown rapids without a map or a moment's forethought if the need arises ('Look, Murdoch, no paddle'). But he is paid even more for anticipating most surprises by equipping himself in advance to meet them head on. A bank manager may appear as solid as he is sedentary, and the journalist an insubstantial, untrustworthy credit risk at best. But the journalist has to be all the more reliable precisely because he deals in a more unreliable medium. He is not handling paper money, but that even more evanescent commodity, paper news. He seeks the truth in an untruthful world, and must pursue it with patience in the most impatient of professions. And he must be more sure-footed because he must move faster.

If the banker behind the bifocals and the bevel-edged desk must be unfailingly systematic in his work, the rootless tumbleweed of a reporter blown here and there by a fickle fate and the follies of capricious strangers — politicians, generals, fanatics, film stars — must be doubly so. For the greater the madness, the greater the need for method. If news breaks suddenly in Saigon or Bangkok or Taipei and his editor yells 'scramble', he must run for his plane already mentally and materially armed for any challenge that may greet him at the other end.

The arming begins at home and never ends, for the more unpredictable the enterprise, the more meticulously must plans be laid ahead to meet all possible contingencies. On one hand, that calls for a network of contacts, and it was through contacts that I was able to gear myself to the Goa story in the few hours before take-off. After breathlessly importuning the Indian High Commission in Singapore and a pair of resident Indian colleagues, the *Straits Times* librarian, the Reuter bureau chief and the British Commissioner General, I had what airlines used to call 'a reasonable amount of reading matter' to peruse on the plane. This was a Manilla file containing a potted history of Goa, maps of the Portuguese enclave, a voluminous document outlining the Indian argument for seizing it, background articles and agency reports that could put me in the slightly surrealistic picture, and the names of the next circle of contacts I would need on the ground in New Delhi. My mind might still be a blank, but I had a file. It might be a poor thing, and none of it my own, but I was now in a position to write a book about Goa without even going there. Except that I was a reporter.

It is a truism that since it is easier to pull information out of a filing system than one's own head, the important thing is not to know, but to know where to look in order to know. When I first made Singapore my base camp at the end of October 1956, I went downtown and stocked up with all the stationery I thought I would need to start a one-man regional crisis centre. By the time I retired twenty-five years later, my records ran to a room of their own. They took up twenty-eight drawers of hanging files in seven steel cabinets, a twelve-foot row of hard-backed punch files, and an overflow of twenty cardboard boxes brimming with miscellaneous cuttings. The office had long since expanded to include a part-time minder to look atter the proliferating bumph as well as the growing library of reference works on the history, politics, philosophy, literature, personalities and customs of all the countries in the Far East.

I had cause for alarm, for I have known this sort of thing to get dangerously out of hand. An American Chinawatcher in Hong Kong once reached the stage where he had to employ two full-time girls and four casual auxiliaries to keep his ominously multiplying filing cabinets in their place. Even then, he was fighting a losing battle. By the time there were more than eighteen of them, they had become unmanageable, and the day arrived when he lost control and they took over. Visiting him shortly afterwards, I found that he had been forced to rent a second, and then a third adjoining flat in order to accommodate them and still have enough room in one corner for himself and his hamsters (which fortunately bred more slowly).

There he would sit, a dry-mouthed Frankenstein, while the metal monster he had contrived grew until it filled all the available space, its pistoning steel drawers relentlessly pumping paper day after day as the press cuttings and monitoring reports and commentaries on China poured into its insatiable maw. It became increasingly difficult for its creator to find time to talk to living sources at all, or even write copy, and meanwhile the very omniscience of the gleaminglifesupport system into which he was plugged betrayed him. When he asked one foreign consular official a question about China, she replied coolly that she would be prepared to oblige anyone else, but…

'But why not me?'

'Because if anyone else asked me that question, the first thing I would do would be to ring you up for the answer.'

Struggling to cope while the thing screamed insanely every morning for more and more paper, more files, more drawers, more cabinets, he was finally rescued by his landlord, who repossessed all three flats (renting one of them to a nunnery). Deprived of its lair, his terrible brainchild slowly disintegrated, and its master lived to tell the tale.

He was a perfectionist, anxious to follow every trend in China, however stealthy (his files foresaw the Tibetan uprising in 1959 two years before it happened). But this meant that he had to throw the beast every scrap of information that he could lay hands on if his records were to be complete. Guilty of stimulating its gargantuan appetite, striving to keep pace with its galloping bulimia, he paid dearly for his failure to limit its diet, and provided a tragic lesson for us all.

But he was also a specialist. For the ordinary correspondent, the secret of taming a filing system was to discipline it from the outset by feeding it only what should be preserved for posterity. The daily ephemera that arrived in my office was not allowed anywhere near my steel cabinets, but relegated to a set of flimsy cardboard sleeves, one for each country. The material in these was sifted once a month, everything that had failed to stand the test of time was resolutely discarded, and only a few durable cuttings made it to the permanent files. That left the running stories. Shaken by my colleague's fate, I kept all cuttings on any running story on a temporary clip (one of a row on the wall above my desk) to be added to each day until it dropped dead from exhaustion. I would then save from the clip and put on permanent file no more than a small selection of key articles that would act as its shroud, wrapping it up for the record.

To report today, however, one must watch not only yesterday but tomorrow, and on my desk was a diary of coming events that must be covered. These ranged from projected conferences and visits of VIPs to the dangerous anniversaries that make the calendar look like a political minefield. Among them were national days (on which a megalomaniac President Sukarno might threaten to annihilate his neighbours, or a senile Chairman Mao proclaim a second Cultural Revolution), and the dates of past exercises in bloodletting that could inspire the mob to honour the sacred memory of one riot by starting another a year later.

Then there were the hardy annuals, like the article that wrote itself at the end of the year on what Asian astrologers and soothsayers predicted for the next twelve months. This I would shamelessly fish out of my files 365 days later in order to write a second piece that checked the accuracy of their prophecies against a future that had by then slid unfairly into the past. I was prompted by the feeling that in a subcontinent overpopulated with seers and visionaries, the prudent observer should keep a careful record not only of what the stars foretell, but what the stars had foretold, if he was to learn whom he could trust with his destiny. The fortune-tellers might have the first laugh, but with this underhand practice I made sure my readers had the last.

Clips and files were one's memory bank, putting a story into its correct perspective by setting it against the backdrop of what had gone before, and enabling one to quote the past against the present. Did a disgruntled Cambodian airman try to remove President Lon Nol from office by dropping 250-pound bombs on his palace in Phnom Penh in 1973? I was ready to remind readers not only that this was the second time in eight months that a flying Khmer had attempted that spectacularly inaccurate method of assassination, but that Lon Nol had joined the select club of Oriental leaders whose own pilots had ineffectually plotted to blow them out of existence from above. An Indonesian flyer had tried to obliterate President Sukarno in 1960, two Vietnamese had tried to obliterate President Ngo Dinh Diem in 1962, and the iniquitous Lin Biao, heir-designate of Mao Zedong, had reputedly conspired to mount a personalised air-raid on the Chairman of China that would have left him master of the People's Republic. Five strikes, no hits. Men have done better with blowpipes.

The device could enliven any story, and sometimes give it depth. In 1957 Tunku Abdul Rahman, the Prime Minister of Malaya, had declared emotionally, 'Britain will ever find us her best friend.' Some ten years afterwards his Finance Minister was calling their best friend 'a toothless old lion', and fifteen years after that Dr Mahathir Mohamad, the latest successor of the Tunku, ordered all government agencies to 'Buy British Last' (which was the peg on which to hang this sad tale of alienated affections).

But the paper chase did not stop there. I needed copies of my own copy to remind me what I had already written, to save me from the twin sins of repeating myself and contradicting myself, and to protect me from those that misquoted me, and the vile accusations of those that quoted the misquotations against me. And while I therefore kept carbons of every article I wrote, I was even more careful to keep all my notebooks, for they were the original seams from which most of that copy had been mined. Methodically labelled, they could always refute the scoffer who challenged my statements by providing chapter and verse to confound him, ensuring that my first word on the subject gave me the last.

And not only the scoffer, for the memories even of friends can fade faster than ink. In 1987 I sent an old colleague in Washington an extract from the draft of this book and asked him to confirm it. The extract described how he had told me in Saigon twenty-three years before that one of the two top Americans in South Vietnam had confided to him that they were going to recommend an 'intensification of operations' that might include using small nuclear weapons against North Vietnam. He wrote back, perplexed. He had absolutely no recollection of hearing any such proposal. It seemed inconceivable that the man should have been so rash as to let him into the secret — or that he himself should have failed to use the story at the time. Accordingly, he had checked with three reliable contacts who had been close to the supposed (but now dead) source — his secretary, his political counsellor Philip Habib, and the then Deputy Undersecretary of State Alexis Johnson — and 'none of them remembered anything like that'. It was my turn to be perplexed, and I still sometimes wonder how it got there. But if I turn up my Saigon notebook for 4 March 1964, there it is, a page of scrawl like a witness stolidly sticking to his story under cross-examination. (There was nothing improbable about it. It was disclosed only in 1988 that President Eisenhower had considered using 'small nuclear weapons' against the Chinese communists ten years before that.)

Old notebooks could also yield long-buried facts and figures, and vintage quotations that had never seen the printed page but could strikingly confirm or illumine a story written twenty years after they were first taken down. An anecdote about the coyly concealed animosity between Chinese and Vietnamese communists, lifted from a notebook dating back to 1955 when they were fiercely protesting their 'unbreakable fraternal friendship', would add spice to an article about their unabashed, full-frontal war in 1979. Five others filled during a tour of China in 1955 would provide piquant comparisons a quarter of a century later when I toured the same places — even visited the same housing estate and the same steel works — in 1980.

I once lost two full notebooks in a taxi while caught in a traffic jam during a military coup in Saigon. It was like a little death, as if ten days had simply dropped out of my life, leaving a black hole for eternity. A colleague who mislaid all of his at the end of a long trip to Indonesia went into a mental depression, became incapable of putting two sentences together on paper, and finally had to retire.

And that was a double tragedy. For if, when the sands run out and the hour glass is turned, the reporter becomes a writer, his notes will bring the past back to life in his books, as old black-and-white newsreel clips do in television documentaries.

Add to the records and the notebooks of the correspondent instruments of instant information like his short-wave radio, his daily news service from Reuters, his BBC monitoring reports, his voluminous telephone index of contacts, and how foolproof it all sounds. But it is not proof against the fool within. Organised, methodical, systematic, the news at his fingertips and the news behind the news in his files, the correspondent may be tempted to look around his office and smugly assume that that is all there is to it, that good housekeeping has put him in an impregnable position to cover everything almost before it happens without moving from his chair. If so, the more fool he.

It was about 6.30 Singapore time when London came on the line on 9 September 1976, and I was pouring my first drink of the day. I was going to need it.

'The appreciation is OK,' said the foreign editor without preamble, 'but you'll have to update it. The chronology...'

'Hold on,' I interrupted unwisely (I should have kept silent and pretended I knew what was coming). 'What's this all about?'

'You mean you *don't know*?' he exclaimed, going into shock. 'Mao's died.'

My stomach felt as if I had lost two more notebooks. I saw it all coming now, all right — the reshaping of the 2,000-word appreciation I had written four years back, the updating of the chronological account of the Chairman's eighty-two years on this earth, the 900-word syndication piece that subscribers were already screaming for from Des Moines to Delhi (since everyone but the ace China-watcher of *The Observer* had heard the news), the 700-word draft for the first leader, the analytical masterpiece for the facing page on what would happen to China now…It was Thursday evening, it was all required within thirty-six hours, and it was as if I were on my way to Goa all over again.

Having let me down, the system hastened to make amends. The files stood up to the challenge, and the deadlines were duly met. But nothing could blot out the shame of my having to be told by my own foreign editor 7,000 miles away that the most important political death in a decade had just taken place in my own back yard. Still, it was all in the family. I was among friends. And did I say my own back yard?

On a fine afternoon on 31 January 1974, the telephone rang and a faint, slightly asthmatic female said, 'Mr Bloodworth? This is the Voice of America in Washington and we wondered if you could give us a run-down on the bombing…Mr Bloodworth, are you still there?'

'Yes — er, but — the bombing?'

'Sure, you know, these Japanese Red Army and Palestinian terrorists who've just tried to blow up one of your oil refineries there in Singapore. As we have it, they've now hijacked a harbour ferry with five hostages aboard and are threatening…you mean you *didn't know*?'

It was the ultimate humiliation. Had it not been for the hoarse rattle of my equally asthmatic air-conditioner, I would have heard the explosions where I sat. But I had to be told about them by an anonymous caller on almost exactly the opposite side of the world.

I could make excuses. The bombers had disobligingly chosen a Thursday to break their story. My paper appeared only on Sunday, and the syndication service sold only background articles.

My intensive spot news checks — with Reuters, Radio Singapore, government offices, my local stringer — were therefore geared to *Observer* deadlines for copy on Fridays and Saturdays.

But although I did not run to an agency teleprinter in my Singapore office, I should have picked up the first flash on the bombing from a newscast. No correspondent can afford to leave a gap in his warning system, because even when it is not about terrorists, news is a terrorist itself. A journalist is like a general who must present a solid defence against an attack that may come from any direction at any moment, and his resources are therefore spread thin on the ground. For the front page story is a stealthy guerrilla, striking suddenly and unexpectedly, enjoying the element of surprise, and the overconfident hack lolling in his paper tower presents it with — quite literally — a sitting target.

All my elaborate precautions proved irrelevant when the bombers struck in Singapore. I would have been better off with nothing but my thirst and my disintegrating typewriter in Saigon. For my room in the Hotel Continental was not air-conditioned, and I would at least have heard the bangs. (Never write them off as routine: a *Daily Mail* correspondent who drank his way straight through two shattering explosions in Saigon in 1965 learned too late that the Vietcong had blown a floating restaurant at the business end of the city into a charnel house while he continued to make light conversation at a diplomatic reception).

The reporter cannot wait passively for the news to come to him, but must go out and get it. At first this may mean no more than putting out patrols in the shape of regular telephone checks, but once first contact is made he must be poised for instant pursuit. This is particularly true of the regional correspondent who covers several countries, and who must be ready to rush to the other end of a subcontinent immediately if that is where the action is. And that is when he picks up his next load of problems. For news may be like a guerrilla, but he is no general with an entire army under command.

'When a soldier moves,' says Ivansong in my novel *Any Number Can Play*, 'all his basic needs are looked after by a vast administrative tail that gives him leave, clothes him, feeds him, transports him to where he has to go, arranges where he will sleep, tells him what to do next, and supplies him with doctors and drugs if he gets hurt or falls sick'.

'Now take the correspondent. A war or civil war or a riot or a coup d'etat in some Godforsaken hole he may never have been to before brings an urgent cable from his editor saying "go". He has his camera, his typewriter, and such money as he prudently keeps on hand for these hilarious occasions and he just takes off. He starts without transport, and if he gets a seat on a plane, it may not be able to land him because of the crisis, whatever it is. If he lands, he may not even be able to get out of the airport because of the shooting. He has no logistical backing, nothing faintly resembling the pillow-breasted nanny of an organisation that every GI Joe Soap can count on'.

'He is in stiff competition with his colleagues, and he takes risks not for Queen and Country or Old Glory and the American Way of Life, but for getting the story and seeing five hundred words of copy on page three. If somewhere along this accident-prone line he slips, and it never reaches his paper, then he has done it all for nothing.'

I apologise for quoting a character from one of my own books, but I could not have put it better myself.

4 TRAVELLING LIGHT

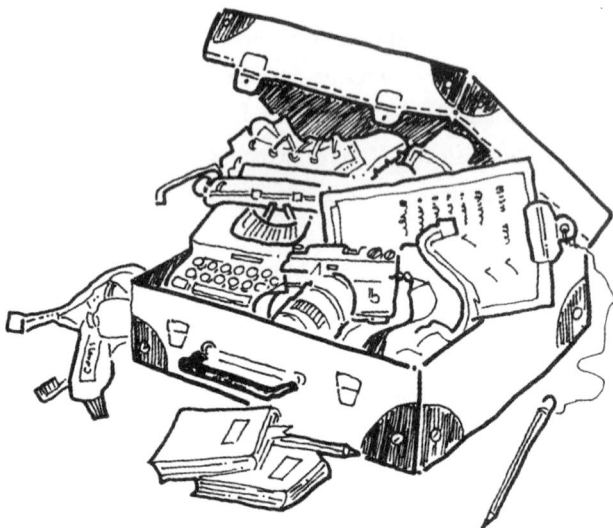

Camping culery? Can-opener? Camera bag? Water purifier? Mosquito repellent? Jungle boots? Dark glasses? Mini-recorder? Alka-seltzer? My own brand of eyewash?

THE reporter's lone flight into the field that Ivansong so ominously traces is really a form of bliss, for there is nothing more exhilarating than to take off solo and escape from all the gravity that pins one down when on the ground — the paperwork and the filing system, the admin and the in-tray, the bills and the bores. London on the line…It is a little like dying, without (given reasonable luck) death itself. And it can be as sudden — the local reporter is on his own and down to his notebook and ballpoint pen the moment he steps out of the office on an assignment. The foreign correspondent has farther to go, but strips off the encumbrances one by one as he gets closer to the action, like a man happily shedding his clothes as he heads for the beckoning sea. He knows that once he reaches the scene of the crime in some forgotten corner of his beat he can stop shuffling papers and reading agency reports and even (for a blessed spell) writing copy, for he will be out there living the news, not hearing it from others. The world and all its woes — except the one he is covering — will be behind him.

But the price of freedom being eternal vigilance, he must be ready when the call comes, and at the outset he will need more than something to scribble on. I would be mentally tapping my pockets from the moment I got the message to go, ticking off a check list of about 120 items stuck to a piece of stiff cardboard that I kept in my old-fashioned grip (I distrusted soft holdalls). The list was divided into sections, starting with things to take — clothes (hot or cold, city or jungle), medicines, documents, gadgetry, and indispensable odds and ends from a whisky flask to washing powder. The grip also contained a ready packed toilet bag, a typewriter, and my 'travel office' — a box with everything I might want on my desk in some remote hotel, from typing paper and spare notebooks to a pocket dictionary and a pocket radio.

There were three good reasons for listening to news bulletins before I filed. The first was to know what was happening on my doorstep — like the ferry hijacking in Singapore that I alone missed. The second was to make sure that my own story had not been killed by another somewhere else — like a White House decision to pull out of Vietnam. The third was to assess how much space, if any, it would rate in competition with the rest of the alarums and excursions around the world that were going to make the morning papers. In October 1962 an outraged foreign editor, faced with an unusable 800-word backgrounder from Laos cabled at urgent rates (one pound sterling for every four words) just as he was splashing the confrontation between Kennedy and Khrushchev over Cuba, shamed me into offering to pay for its transmission. No evening has gone by since without my listening to the news on the BBC World Service.

My inventory reminded me to take address books, traveller's cheques, cable and air credit cards, health papers, passport, and relevant press cuttings about the story I was flying into for me to read on the plane. For each country in the region I kept in my Singapore office a box file from which I would scoop local maps and guides, local cash left over from my last trip (at least enough for a taxi into town from the airport), a list of local contacts, and background documents (a brief history, the names of government ministers, the military hierarchy, the main economic miseries). I would also take the notebooks of my previous visit, and, of course, about thirty passport photographs. A fuss-budget? But it is better to be an old maid than an old hand who never makes it at all. Of two veteran Australian correspondents from Europe who once stopped off to see me in Singapore within a few months of each other on their way to Sydney, the one from Paris carried a passport that was six months out of date, and the one from London had lost the tickets for his onward flight. Yet by that time they had eighty years in the business between them.

Why thirty passport photographs? I have never discovered what Asian bureaucracies do with all the snaps they collect. Having handed in five at the Indonesian Embassy in Singapore when applying for a visa, I was once dunned for three more at Kemajoran airport on arrival in Jakarta. As I protested in my futile Caucasian fashion, a Garuda Airways hostess leaned over the shoulder of the immigration officer, squinted at my vacuous black-and-white image, and said sweetly, 'May I have one too?' I was at once disarmed, but it was not the beginning of a beautiful friendship. I can only think that she must have needed it to complete a hand in some gruesome variation of Happy Families they play when their last victim has staggered off into the night. Tearful Travellers, perhaps? Was she short of Master Spike the Scribbler's Son?

'What shall I wear?' Imelda Marcos may have wailed in Manila, echoing every woman since Eve (who got it wrong) as she surveyed the thousand glad rags on those notorious hangers in the Malacanang Palace, before she flew off into exile in 1986. But how much more poignant was the question when asked by a reporter like me, most of whose twenty kilograms of economy class luggage would be taken up by his professional impedimenta, thanks to his anxiety to be ready for anything (Camping cutlery? Can-opener? Camera bag?). Did I overreact to the hazards of the Mekong Delta (Water purifier? Mosquito repellent? Jungle boots?) or of the White House Annex (Dark glasses? Mini-recorder? Alka-seltzer? My own brand of eyewash?). No, the reporter cannot travel light to first base in that hotel bedroom in Mandalay or Mombasa or Massachusetts Avenue. It is to be his headquarters for the safaris to come, until it is time to go home to the paper tigers that have been lying in wait for him on his desk during those carefree weeks away.

But clothes? The more glamorous correspondents boast that they 'keep a bag ready packed'. It is an intriguing claim. I have often wondered what they did with all those creased Hawaiian shirts they found when they opened their suitcases in Archangelsk in December, the anoraks and furlined boots that confronted them in Timbuktu in July. It is beyond the wit of man to master the art of packing, even if he knows where he is going — with the possible exception of the moon. And the Far East correspondent has to be a quick change artist who can dress for all occasions almost simultaneously, for he may have to rush from an untidy riot to a ministerial *vin d'honneur* without time even to gnash his teeth. In the tropics, a safari suit and ankle-length boots may cover a multitude of sins, and answer most challenges from a battle to a bun-fight; for the rest, as long as he sends no more than one day's laundry to be washed at a time, the reporter will not run out of the basic necessities of life if he has to move suddenly. But that still leaves one small sartorial tripwire that can floor a man at the door: the lack of a tie.

The nearest thing to an all-purpose outfit that I could devise to meet every contingency combined drip-dry underwear and socks, a short-sleeved nylon shirt worn open at the neck, one of those non-crease suits made of petrochemical waste, and suede boots. Unlike leather, sodden suede merely looked darker, not discoloured, while perspiration remained invisible on a sombre synthetic suit, and gave a saturated nylon shirt a new sheen, as if it had just been ironed.

In the pockets of the suit I would carry not only the paraphernalia of my trade, but a comb and — above all — a clip-on bow tie. These accoutrements could transform me in two minutes from a sweating hack just back from the wilds into an immaculate if slightly steaming dude fit to be passed through the most august portals. The whole vile get-up might then freeze stiff in the sub-zero air-conditioning within, but that would only add to the dignified effect.

And that spurious distinction was important. Sober dress alone imparts to a man the air of responsibility that makes other men take him seriously, inspiring confidence and (on a good day) even confidences. Straightening my one Yves Saint Laurent tie while waiting with two cuff-shooting colleagues to meet Chairman Hua Guofeng in Beijing in 1980, I was therefore dismayed to see join us in his anteroom a yawning apparition wearing frayed jeans and scuffed sandals, followed by an equally unshaven sidekick sporting a single pear-shaped earring. But the sidekick was also carrying a mess of cameras, for the apparition was the renowned photographer David Bailey. While David Bailey could get away with looking like a designer tramp with a two-day hangover, however, the humble reporter looking even more humble in a tee-shirt and denim shorts would risk being ignored, even ejected, as an interloping nonentity and an insult to the esteem of whoever had agreed to see him.

No system is foolproof, if only because not everyone is chasing the news: to the reporter the rest of the human race often appear to have inexplicable social priorities whose irrelevance can be quite breathtaking. In the middle of one of the many military coups that ruffled Saigon, the British ambassador evidently thought that the best way to keep me out of mischief was to invite me to a formal dinner with a visiting Brazilian cardinal ('black tie, of course'). Anxious to be about my business, for there were generals and politicians to interview, and tank-ridden streets to be dodged through to get at them, I told the astonished diplomat with some relief (a *Brazilian cardinal?* — wasn't that some kind of bird?) that, actually, I 'did not usually pack' a dinner jacket and had none with me.

But he was not at the peak of his career for nothing. Quickly recovering from his amazement, he said I could borrow a spare one of his, and I was ushered into his dressing room to try on the offending garment. To my great joy, the trousers were two inches too wide and two inches too short. Before he could say 'Moss Bros', the tuxedo was back on the hook, and I was off it. Perspiring journalists enjoyed a sly revenge, however, when Prince Norodom Sihanouk invited the diplomatic corps in Cambodia to a function that required their excellencies from the doyen downwards to wear something they normally 'did not usually pack' — *tenue de travail*: working clothes. For he had asked their countries to help him build a railway, and since their governments had declined to contribute any money, their ambassadors were to contribute their manual labour.

In trying to decide what to pack, the correspondent was caught between the sweat in the streets and the frost in the air-conditioned offices, the dress protocol of dandified Asian god-kings and the dreary garb that was *de rigueur* in communist capitals. To make sure, meanwhile, that his dilemma would always be finger-tight, he was frequently forced to observe the light diet of baggage prescribed for aircraft of minor Oriental airlines that had to watch their weight carefully with advancing age. And if he overcame these difficulties, it seemed, a smiling fate could always intervene to see that he did not win.

At least, that was my impression in 1955, just after Sihanouk put his father on the Cambodian throne in his place in a back-to-front accession, and I was invited to the coronation in Phnom Penh. When in 1941 the Prince had become hereditary monarch of the Khmers, whose tombs and temples at Angkor bore stony witness to the cruel but magnificent past of his forebears, the ancient kingdom of Cambodia had been a French 'protectorate' for nearly eighty years. But by 1954 the French had reluctantly agreed to withdraw. Cambodia was once more to be a sovereign state, and in consequence Sihanouk now proposed to pass on to his parent the bit part of chessboard king, while he himself played the real ruler and shaped the destiny of his country as its autocratic prime minister. (There would, of course, be no rival candidates for the job).

It was therefore an historic occasion. There were to be week-long festivities, and this time Sihanouk was not in an impish mood —

or perhaps he was: correspondents were required to wear dinner jackets to all functions whatever the time of day. These were doubtless appropriate for some, like the gala performance of the Royal Cambodian Ballet in which his daughter danced the lead, but mine infuriated a gaudily caparisoned elephant in the royal procession that preceded it in the morning, and but for a lusty mahout I would have been flattened in all my finery there and then.

In theory, a suit for all seasons was the reporter's dream, however bizarre, but I still had to pack humbler garments, even if I was not to be allowed to wear them in public. For my flight from Saigon to Phnom Penh in a flatulent old Bristol transport was only the first leg of a round trip that would take me on to Hanoi. Like a woman, a reporter should dress to please. Accordingly, I had thrown into my expandable suitcase not only my senile tuxedo, but — for the comrades in North Vietnam — a rather nasty dacron suit in faded lavender that could conceivably have been run up in Magnitogorsk. For less formal wear, I had added a few bush shirts, which I favoured for their four spacious pockets, and a pair of grey slacks.

Once King Norodom Surarnarit was safely enthroned, I was invited to a cocktail party by a secretary of the British Embassy in Phnom Penh, dress casual. Arriving early, I was asked to open a bottle of Cinzano, and handed a combination can-opener and corkscrew. I have always distrusted (with one obvious exception) tools that have more than one function, but I took hold of this gadget, twisted the corkscrew into the bottle, set it against my thigh for purchase, and pulled hard. The cork came out of the bottle smartly enough and the point of the can-opener tore a jagged six-inch slit in my grey slacks at a strategic junction, almost unmanning me at the same time.

On the following morning I took off for Hanoi in my lavender suit and the company of two fellow journalists, the Australian communist Wilfred Burchett and a convivial *Pravda* reporter named Yuri Grischenko. But when we put down in Vientiane on our way north, we were told that the plane would not be able to leave again until the following day. After a gruelling dinner consisting mainly of vodka offered by some hospitable Poles, my two colleagues suggested that we go to a nightclub or so, and we set off in two of the somewhat gaudy trishaws they then affected in Laos. As I leaped down light-heartedly enough on arrival at the Hawaii Bar, however, some small, even infinitessimal projection on the body of this particular *cyclo* treacherously engaged with the seat of my dacron trousers. There was a genteel ripping sound, and a great flap of material fell away from my right buttock.

One cannot trust communists. The other two treated the whole business as an exquisite joke, could produce only one inadequate pin between them, yet insisted that we go into the Hawaii just the same. I managed to sidle through the door, hand on hip as if I were about to draw a gun, and sat down at a corner table with my back to the wall. I had hoped that it would be one of those cosy little clip joints lit only by a sprinkling of small red lamps where the darkness goes on the bill, but it turned out to be a great barn of a place bathed in daylight from a battery of fluorescent strips.

We ordered drinks and were at once accosted by three taxi-girls asking for the usual pineapple juice and a turn on the floor. The two comrades rushed eagerly into the cha-cha with their escorts, leaving me with a rather large, wet-eyed Metisse who wriggled about on her chair amid the heavy fumes of some cloying scent. '*Pourquoi m'sieur n'aimer pas danser avec moi?*' she asked in a tinny little Indochinese voice. '*Peut-et' m'sieur trouver pas j'suis jolie, eh?*' The music stopped suddenly in the middle of this, her voice carried, people began to look, and she began to sound perilously tearful. No, I protested, she was quite wrong; I loved to dance, I found her terribly *jolie*, and nothing would be nicer than to dance with her, only — I made sure the solitary pin was in place — only I had pulled a muscle in my…'Show me,' she commanded with professional interest, leaning over and peering around my back. 'Show me.' And then — 'But… but *you've torn your trousers!* Look! *He's — torn — his — trousers!* *Ça, alors, par example!* Didn't you realise?' And she threw out one of those hard, high laughs that can crack a bedside water jug.

The next day we flew up to Hanoi — Burchett and Grischenko in bush shirts and slacks, myself in a rather eye-catching confection made up of a lavender dacron jacket that might have come from Magnitogorsk, and a pair of black evening trousers with silk braiding down the sides. The communists were visibly startled, but polite. I stayed two weeks, and had a striped cotton suit run up for me by a local tailor called Phuc My.

All went well after that until I prepared to fly from Saigon to Singapore on my way to London for home leave. Clad in the same striped suit and all paid up, I packed the rest of my clothes in my suitcase and deposited it at the nearby Pan-American Airways office for delivery to the airport. Returning to the empty room in the Hotel Continental that had been my home and headquarters for the previous two years, I opened all the cupboards and drawers to see if I had forgotten anything. Nothing — except in one drawer of the desk, where I found a bottle of ink. I picked the bottle up by the cap to make sure it was empty. It was full. I knew this at once because at that moment the bottle parted from the cap in my hand and poured its entire contents down my trousers.

Blasphemously invoking the name of the maker — not of myself, but the suit — I tore off the trousers, threw them into the bath, and turned on the taps. Twenty minutes later I had a shapeless mass of soggy, parti-coloured cotton on my hands. And soon my legs. For there was still no telephone in the room, I was due at the airport in forty minutes, and my one attempt to yell for help from the window to a friend (and a sea of upturned Vietnamese faces) in the square below — 'Look, this is urgent, I've messed up my trousers, could you go across to…' — petered out as soon as I started listening to what I was saying. I caught the plane, and I was dry by the time we reached Singapore. But my seat was not, and I fielded some dirty looks. Quite apart from anything else, the Asian sense of propriety is offended by men caught with their pants down. And I was not just one pair down, but three.

Preparing to move was more than a question of packing the right clothes and the right cuttings, however. It demanded foresight. I tried to keep my passport ready stamped with visas for the countries I visited frequently, so that when the next story broke, I could fly to it at once, wherever it was. It could take a sensitive government a week to grant me a visa, even when the last article I had written about it was officially designated 'responsible and objective reporting' (a favourable write-up). But that was the time to apply for one against the day when a later story would be classified as 'scurrilous lies and distortions' (the ugly truth), and any application from me would automatically be flung to the shredder.

I found it paid, moreover, to ask for a visa for a one-month visit, but to say on arrival that I might be able to stay no more than four or five days. This would inspire those unfortunate bureaucrats deputed to handle the foreign press to arrange whatever interviews or trips I wanted without delay. For it is a fact of life that governments pander to the caprices of foreign journalists in inverse ratio to the time they spend in their country. Go for a week, and the President will see you tomorrow; stay for a year, and you will never get near him again. From being a moving target able to fly away and file at will another day, you have become a captive whom there is no need to court. This idiosyncrasy was particularly marked in communist states, and frustrated correspondents permanently based in Beijing were left to grind their teeth in the foreigner's ghetto, while transient colleagues light-heartedly quartered the country.

I was also careful to keep my inoculations up to date, my stock of traveller's cheques topped up, and in later years a first class travel agent on hand ready to snap to when I wanted to be booked on the next flight to trouble, and — almost equally important — into a hotel where the trouble was to be found.

In halcyon days of overbuilding and underbooking, any fool can drop unannounced into the air-conditioned palace of his choice and demand a double room and a discount. But a wise man will befriend the reception desk while business is bad so that he can be sure of a bed when business is good. For smiling reservation clerks eager to please when a hundred rooms are empty can suddenly become distant and unfeeling when ninety-nine are full, their lips pursed over a mouthful of negatives. Every wet and weary traveller since Joseph and Mary has run into that look. At the height of the Vietnam War, correspondents begging for a bed in the Caravelle Hotel in Saigon would bribe the haughty flunkeys behind the counter with placatory offerings from Hong Kong or Singapore ranging from cinecameras to stereo systems (to be flogged on a fickle black market), and take notes obsequiously — as if interviewing God himself — when told what to bring next time if they wanted their rooms back.

In my early years in Asia, before the crops of Hiltons and Hyatts and Holiday Inns were sown, I was dogged by fears of finding myself sleeping in the street as a hundred correspondents converged with me on the limited houseroom in Saigon or Goa, Hanoi or Rangoon, Vientiane or Luang Prabang. I have dossed down on wooden floors and in tin baths, washed and shaved in public lavatories, and hammered out copy in airport lounges. I have passed the night in an empty brothel in Hanoi, and a full one in Phnom Penh. I have lain awake in opium dens and sleazy Asian inns where the girls, too, bang on your door all night begging to share your bed at almost any price, and you know just how they feel.

I have been reduced to a cubicle next to the latrines in a flop house in Hue, where the olfactory nerves could only be calmed by putting a handkerchief soaked in after-shave lotion over the standing tan and blowing the effluvium back at the loos. If the Taj Mahal in Bombay was 'dry', the waterless, dust-laden Bungalow in Vientiane was drier, and the guests showered at prodigious expense in bottled Perrier. In Taipei, the only approved accommodation for a foreign correspondent was at the Friends of China Club, and Chiang Kai-shek evidently had as firm views about his friends as he did about his enemies. But at least all the 'bugs' in the rooms I slept in were in quotes for once.

Staying with friends could be a mistake, however tempting the prospect of a home from home might seem to a wandering reporter bored with hotel bars and bedrooms, cafeterias and the company of his colleagues. The hotel might be without a soul, but it was the nearest thing he had to Ivansong's pillow-breasted nanny. It would give him a bedroom with a desk and a shower, and wash his dirty clothes every morning without complaint. It would serve him all the food and drink he could consume at any hour of the day, answer the phone for him, and take garbled messages while he was out. It would be totally indifferent to all his maddening last-minute changes of plan, would tolerate his noisy and argumentative colleagues, and not even blink if he suddenly brought four dubious contacts back for drinks and a late dinner.

He could burst in unheralded, rush out at dawn, miss all meals, totter back in the smallest hours of the morning, and never have to apologise to anybody for working twenty-four hours a day. It would leave him to get on with his capricious existence, and ask nothing of him but his money. And it was easy to find for the official messenger bringing advance warning of an imminent press conference, or the unofficial one bringing warning of an imminent bloodbath. What hostess could match that — or would want to? Only the wife of another reporter, on the principle that two can live as hectically as one. Perhaps.

5 FOLLOW THAT STORY

The pilot chain-smoked Gauloise cigarettes throughout the flight, the ash and sparks from which streamed back to the load of leaking cans behind us.

GETTING from A to B, catching a plane in Singapore to pick up a room at the Hotel Continental in Saigon, might be as easy as turning your hand, as the Chinese say. But the trouble with turning your hand was that it left you staring at the lines of your palm. And too often the lines of a reporter's palm told him that he would now have to find some way of getting from B to Z. The story would not be in Saigon, but in some village in the Mekong Delta or the Annamite Range approachable only by pirogue or chopper. And to reach it his basic principle was perforce the hitchhiker's rule of thumb — he had to take the first thing going his way.

The biggest mistake he could make would be to turn down

anything from a pirate taxi to a private plane as a matter of pride because he felt he was being ripped off. If I had the money, I would pay, be cheated, and get where I wanted to go. There was no more pitiful sight than a correspondent left on his two flat feet at the roadside after haggling futilely with a driver over five dollars, while the competition disappeared into the distance and dust where the action was. Did I lay out an iniquitous forty pounds in 1961 for an expiring Buick to take me to Goa? I thought it cheap at the price, the driver was laughing up his cheese-cloth sleeve, and everyone was happy. (The accounts department of *The Observer* was still far away in space and time).

Beyond a decent show of bargaining to ensure a proper respect all round, a few dollars more or less could not be allowed to matter. The books balanced in the end, for so much of one's travelling was free in any case. I could offset the cost of riding in a buckled jalopy from Belgaum to Goa by lolling for nothing in an immaculate Rolls Royce on my way from Phnom Penh to Saigon a few weeks later, after the Australian ambassador to Cambodia had offered me a lift. I believed that when someone said 'Jump in', the journalist should jump. It was an instinct acquired in an era in which the lack of beds in far-off places was matched by the lack of any means to reach them — at least until the Americans moved in in force.

Laos was no exception to this rule. Like Cambodia, it was a sleepy Indochinese kingdom before the French shook it awake and established a 'protectorate' over it at the end of the 19th century. And both needed protecting, for both were the weak prey of their rapacious neighbours, the Thais and the Vietnamese. But after the Geneva Agreement of 1954, which ended the anti-colonial Indochina War and French suzerainty over all three states —Vietnam, Cambodia and Laos — Laos was split by an armed struggle between successive Royal Governments in Vientiane and the pro-communist Pathet Lao insurgents in the provinces. The first were led (more often than not) by the 'neutralist' Prince Souvanna Phouma, and the second by his swaggering half-brother, the 'Red' Prince Souphannouvong. But they were never to be allowed to get on with things by themselves. The Americans, of course, backed the boss-of-the-day in Vientiane, the Vietnamese communists the Pathet Lao.

The problem of the correspondent, pathetically keen to explain to an indifferent world this convoluted vendetta in a mountainous back-of-beyond few in Bognor or Brooklyn had even heard of, was compounded most of the time by a simple inability to get beyond Vientiane once he had got that far. In these circumstances the reporter cannot pass up a chance to be on the spot because he is improperly dressed, or has forgotten his pencil, or does not like the driver's face, or is not sure how he will return to his cable head. And Laos was the best of training grounds for improvised bumming, for learning how to move around the walls without touching the floor, for it had no railway, no more than a spare tracery of decaying roads, no visible means of transport outside the capital, and a civil war that had carelessly torn the country in two. Whenever, therefore, a freight carrier — or better, a Sikorsky helicopter — of 'Air America' dropped into Vientiane from the wilderness and was prepared to take me, I seized the chance to fly back to the front with it, tactfully resisting the temptation to ask the pilot how much the CIA paid him.

Almost once too often. For in the winter of 1961 my sartorial system let me down. I was wearing the paper-thin petrochemical suit and nylon shirt I have said I favoured for all occasions, but this should not have been one of them. It was steaming in Vientiane when we took off, but freezing at night up in the mountains at the regimental headquarters of the Royal Laotian Army, where I slept with no covering on wooden slats in an empty, open-sided barn. I nearly died of cold even after I had put on my bow tie. But at five the next morning I was off to the battlefront in a truck carrying a few drums of water to the thirsty soldiery, and later was able to write an exclusive story — meaning a piece that was contradicted by all my colleagues in Vientiane, who had been fed a purely imaginary account of the action by the Laotian Ministry of Information. Shivering compulsively, I had survived, I sincerely believe, thanks to a bottle of powerful Lao rice wine, and thereafter I never moved without a flask of whisky, a liquid overcoat against the day when — on an impulse of fate — I would again be lifted 5,000 feet and dropped 50 degrees in the same hour.

But while he was often obliged to fall back on interested parties like the CIA for lifts, there was one purely commercial airline that would sometimes take the wandering correspondent where he wanted to go, and no questions asked. Certain bars in Vientiane seemed to be perpetually graced by the presence of a small, sweaty group of laughing, carefree, unshaven children of nature — French, Corsican, Sicilian, Chinese and Metis — who were either drinking Pernod or playing an endless hand of greasy cards or both. The unappetising leftovers of yesterday's wars, they were the pilots of 'Air Opium', which ran the drug or its derivatives in aerial rattletraps held together by wire and will, dropping their cargo at rendezvous in Vietnam, or Thailand, or the South China Sea (where it would be retrieved by fortuitously passing junks).

These genial aviators ferried other miscellaneous freight, including the occasional reporter, but flying with them meant flying without frills. They would rarely agree to carry more than an overnight bag, and that was only fair, for no sane passenger would agree to carry any package for them, however small. But they had other limitations. My colleague, Estelle Holt, stringing for Associated Press and stumped for a flight from Luang Prabang to Vientiane, once approached a voluminous Madagascan pilot of Air Opium felicitously named Babal Angelbal in a local cafe and asked him for a lift. Babal said that would be no problem, and having washed down a vast lunch with two bottles of French plonk, drove her out to a little Piper Cherokee at the airfield. After take-off, she settled down to enjoy the view, not realising that Babal had settled down to enjoy a nap — until the quiet engine became altogether too quiet. Deciding at last that it had died in his sleep, she shook Babal's arm, and asked him apologetically it this was normal procedure. He started up, grunted '*il ne marche pas*', fiddled with the controls, waggled the wings, and the engine came to life again just in time for the plane to clear the next hill. He had forgotten to switch fuel tanks before dropping off. It made everyone's day.

The hairy Corsican who in 1961 flew me from Vientiane to the Plain of Jars in a flimsy crate reeking of kerosene did not repeat the joke. But he chain-smoked Gauloise cigarettes throughout the flight, the ash and sparks from which streamed back to the load of leaking cans behind us that we were taking to the left-wing rebels. More fearful of a snub than sudden death (as most cowards are on these occasions), I failed to ask him, even apologetically, if this was normal procedure. But we arrived intact, and I was already preoccupied with the next leg of my problem, which was how to get to the rebel headquarters in the old fort at Khang Khay, where a disgusted Souvanna Phouma had joined his Pathet Lao half-brother.

The neutralist Prime Minister had switched sides when the Americans shifted their support from him to a right-wing general in Vientiane, so that the nameplate of that weeks Laotian leader appeared to have been turned back to front: instead of spelling 'Souvanna Phouma', the letters had been rescrabbled to read 'Phoumi Nosavan'.

Lightning changes like this might bring tears to the eyes of correspondents obliged to rewrite the Laos script yet again in a few plain words, but they sometimes made for a very civil war indeed, since today's enemy could be tomorrow's friend. No one in Vientiane, it seemed, thought it necessary to stop Air Opium from flying fuel into rebel territory. And the tolerance worked both ways. In the wooden shack on stilts that served as a control tower at Xieng Khouang on the Plain of Iars I heard a Russian 'adviser' to the Pathet Lao chivalrously giving a met. report over the air to an American pilot flying arms to his enemy. That could happen only in Laos; but whether the met. report was accurate was another matter.

I remembered how startled a newcomer had been on hearing the controller in another shack at Vientiane airport announce over the Tannoy that an Air Vietnam plane from Saigon was coming in at 4,000 feet on a bearing of 130 degrees. 'But it's more like 2,000 feet at 220 degrees,' he gabbled as we watched it approach. 'Of course,' agreed some old hand testily, 'but he's giving what's *supposed* to be its height and bearing — how would he know it wasn't?' And did it matter anyway? It was sometimes best not to ask questions. After Air Opium had left me stranded on the rough grass of the airfield at Xieng Khouang, some Poles gave me a lift to Khang Khay. That solved my immediate problem. There was no point in asking how I was going to get back from there. That was going to be tomorrow's worry, and I had never missed a deadline through being marooned.

A reporter was more likely to be stuck in a crowded city like Saigon than in a lonely corner of Laos. Even in his home town he might run into the rush hour and stand about impotently in the rain, flagging full buses and taken taxis while the sands ran out of his story. In a strange capital the dangers of relying on public transport were greater, for correspondents are birds of omen, and their presence often meant that a conference or a crisis was overloading or dislocating communications. A revolution could either clear the streets or block them as the tanks and troops took over. A royal wedding would do much the same.

At such times, the slowest vehicle could be the fastest, and a bicycle better than a BMW. In the East, a prudent reporter took a trishaw, which could worm its way through miles of blaring metal work fused together in a traffic jam, or steal silently through side streets and back alleys to avoid the mob and get him where he wanted to go. Riding a pedicab during massive anti-British demonstrations in Beijing in 1958 involving a million artificially infuriated Chinese (we had just sent troops into Lebanon), I was able to pass through the city peacefully until I reached the British Embassy itself. At the gates, indignant students chased away my pedicab driver after giving him a lecture on the evils of hauling a bloodthirsty imperialist in order to feed his family, and I had no choice but to walk when I came out of the embassy afterwards. But the pedicab driver was waiting for me at the entrance of my hotel when I arrived. For I had not been hiring him by the trip, but by the week.

The correspondent could only make sure he had wheels at all times by renting them for the duration, instead of fecklessly imagining he could pick them up on the street whenever he suddenly, even frantically, needed them. For in an imperfect world, that would be the moment he would not find them. In a Beijing without private taxis, I would sometimes take on a pedicab the day I arrived on the understanding that the driver would stay with me to the end of my visit. In Jakarta, I found a pirate taxi chauffeured by an elderly chief clerk from an insurance company who told me he made more money moonlighting that way, and employed him off and on for several years during routine visits, cabling him in advance from Singapore so that he would be at Kemajoran Airport to meet me. If he ran into trouble — or just could not park — I could still take off on my own. As a Javanese, he was far better equipped to cope with a local hazard than I was, and I never drove myself.

In about 1960, I graduated from a pirate taxi to a minibus, hiring the driver and his mate on the same basis. Kept away from Jakarta's horrendous traffic jams, the bus was an even better answer to the problem of mobility. I could not only move in it, but work in it and sleep in it if the need arose, like a general in his caravan. In a crisis. I was independent wherever I went. And if I did not want to bear the full expense of a long trip to the other end of Java, I could share the bus and the cost with one or two other correspondents, and be doing them a service at the same time.

Covering Indonesia demanded careful thought. The republic was like a broken series of stepping stones that one had to work out a way of crossing from bank to bank without getting marooned by the waters between. President Sukarno himself had good reason to see it in much the same way. Embracing an archipelago that straggled across 3,000 miles from the Indian Ocean to the backwaters of Australia, it was the home of more than 100 million heads of population. But that was its weakness. Once independence had been wrested from the Dutch after two centuries of colonial rule, Sukarno quickly found that his main problem was holding together this string of assorted islands and peoples arbitrarily assembled into a modern geopolitical artifact labelled 'Indonesia'.

Fragmentation threatened to become a way of life. First the Christian Amboinese rebelled in the Moluccas, while fanatical Muslims of the Darul Islam movement raised ramshackle armies that impartially terrorised much of Sumatra, Sulawesi, Kalimantan, and Java itself because Sukarno had refused to declare Indonesia an Islamic state. Then, in 1958, regional military commanders in the island provinces (who had fought for independence and therefore claimed a say in the running of the republic) mounted an armed revolt against the hegemony of Jakarta. The profligacy of Sukarno and the poverty of overpopulated Java were at the source of their disloyalty. The profligacy aggravated the poverty, which gave disproportionate clout to the communists in capital, and prompted the government to milk the other islands of their natural riches in order to devote an unfair share of the national income to the needy but distrusted Javanese cuckoos in the nest.

A variety of vehicles were needed to cover this 'Colonels' Rebellion', which had attracted some of the best political and military brains in Indonesia and was conducted with ludicrous incompetence against the left-wing President. Three of us sailed from Singapore to Palembang in South Sumatra in a poky little coaster, and then rode 600 miles through the mountains to the rebel zone, travelling the first leg hidden in the back of a truck, and the second crammed into an overloaded bus built for midgets, one of whom drove. Once with the rebels, we moved up to the front in an army lorry to whose tailboard we had tied dining chairs borrowed from a rest house in Bukit Tinggi, because most of the space inside was filled by a vast drum of petrol.

But after we had filed all the copy the story would take, we hired a private bus and drove another 600 miles to North Sumatra. With a whole bench each, and room to spare for a dining and working area, we felt completely in control of our destiny wherever we went. It was (in a modest way) like flying in Air Force One.

6 ONE OF OUR FILES IS MISSING

The fix that takes the knots out of the foreign correspondent's nerves is the moment when is copy is safely on its way.

BUT note that casual 'after we had filed', for there was nothing casual about it. The reporter may anticipate every need, exploit every opening, take every precaution and every risk and everything on wheels to cover the story, but it will all have been a waste of time and money if he cannot then get it to his editor. Others may have their opiates, but the fix that takes the knots out of the foreign correspondent's nerves is the moment when his copy is safely on its way. And the trouble in this case was that any facility for filing from the isolated rebel stronghold in Central Sumatra seemed likely to be about as swift and sure as putting a cable into a corked bottle and throwing it into the sea. In a chancy business, however, chance can work both ways.

On leaving Singapore, I had done the only thing I could to solve the problem, which was to arrange with the local bureau of Agence France Presse that they would intercept any copy of mine transmitted by radio on the rebel wavelength, and pass it on to London. But any faith I had placed in this absurdly fragile link when in Singapore faded miserably in the mountain mists above Bukit Tinggi. There was only one way of sending out messages, and that was through an army signals corporal who was reputedly holed up with a transmitter in a hut on some peak above the town. I say 'reputedly' because we were not allowed to approach his eyrie. Instead, we were compelled to hand our stories to a sullen rebel captain who promptly disappeared with them, leaving us to wonder whether the transmitter existed at all, and, if so, whether he would nevertheless find it more convenient simply to tear up our copy once out of sight, and cast it to the winds.

At best, he was likely to censor it — and the trouble with that was that, in the hands of a censor with high school English, copy as pure as snow could not escape calumny. At one point in the political Jacuzzi that passes for Laotian history the Minister of Information in Vientiane personally vetted all press cables, using a pocket dictionary to plough through despatches whose text was framed in cablese and whose punctuation was spelled out in full. It is a matter or record that he blue-pencilled one story which began

PRINCE SOUVANNA PHOUMA DASH
NEUTRALIST PRIME MINISTER OF LAOS DASH
TODAY UPSUMMED…

because, as he later explained, he had looked up 'dash' in the dictionary, found that it meant 'shatter, throw away, dilute, discourage or damn', and decided this was hostile copy that must not be allowed to go any further. Nearly twenty years later South Korean censors firmly struck out a prophecy that their government's new policy would be a 'shot in the arm' for the economy. There were evidently to be no drugs on the market in Seoul.

And even if he passed the prophecies along with the punctuation, how long would it take a Sumatran army officer just to fight his way through the cablese? For those were the days when a lead beginning 'The failure of Indonesian rebel troops to capture Lubukdjambi this morning and advance as far as Taluk without loss before noon' might read:

FAILUREF INDONREB TPS ADCAPTURE
LUBUKDJAMBI ETADVANCE SFARS TALUK
SANSLOSS ANTENOON…

No one could blame him if he did fling the stuff away in disgust.

This odious suspicion worried like a shaggy dog at my mind in particular, for I recalled the act of Gallic treachery that had given me my first grey hair at the end of the Indochina War. Under the Geneva Agreement of July 1954, the French were to yield Hanoi to the communist-led forces of Ho Chi Minh that had defeated General de Castries at the battle of Dienbienphu, but could keep the port of Haiphong until April 1955. I had been in Hanoi the day the Vietminh marched into the city as the French marched out. The telegraph office was shut, we were in the hands of the communists, and foreign correspondents who elected to stay behind therefore entrusted their last-minute copy to a French army press liaison officer named Delassus. Delassus was leaving in a jeep for Haiphong, and swore that he would despatch their cables as soon as he got there that afternoon.

But Delassus was not the ideal courier, for we had often spoken harshly to him of the marvellous propensity of the French military for keeping the truth, the whole truth, and nothing but the truth from all correspondents who were not their compatriots. We had no choice, however. It was already Saturday, but I could still expect my 900 words of breakneck prose immortalising this moment of triumph for Ho Chi Minh to reach *The Observer* in time, since we were eight hours ahead of London. I should have known better. My story made the desk of the foreign news editor, as limp as it was late, the following Tuesday. Delassus had sat on the sheaf of cables confided to him by a dozen correspondents for forty-eight hours.

It was an unwelcome memory at that moment in Sumatra, for the spruce French lieutenant bowling down the main road to Haiphong had looked like winged Mercury himself compared with our hypothetical Indonesian signals corporal somewhere up there in the darkness with his little Morse key. And it was already Friday night. But I need not have worried. The captain passed on the copy untouched, the corporal tapped it into the air waves, AFP fielded it neatly in Singapore and transmitted it to their office in London, and from there it was rushed across to *The Observer* in good time to sprawl across three columns on the main foreign *background* page — for it had arrived well ahead of the news.

The reporter abroad had to trust his luck, but he also had to know the local form. Two correspondents who seized a chance to fly up to Sam Neua in the far north of Laos, and had the good fortune to run into a minor battle, took their cables to the postmaster afterwards and asked him in their best French it he could send them off at once.

Of course, replied the Lao in *his* best French, since it did not include the word 'no'. But they were unaware of this, and walked away down the street filled with that weightless sense of catharsis that afflicts the euphoric who have just filed — until he ran after them waving a piece of paper. 'Perhaps you could tell me what I should with this,' he said. It was a cable apparently handed in by another euphoric correspondent the week before, and it began: 'Today I watched as Pathet Lao guerrillas mortared defence positions...'

Even when telegraph offices knew what to do with a press cable, filing could be a nail-biting business. In Jakarta and Vientiane the clerks would count the number of words twice, and slowly enough to give any fool who tried to hustle the East enough time to walk round the block if he was not to go round the bend. In Saigon and Phnom Penh they went to sleep from noon to three, in Djakarta and Kowloon they pulled down the shutters at nine in the evening and moved the operation elsewhere. The wise reporter made sure he was familiar with these idiosyncracies, and wrote his cables in clear language except when repeating figures (39 RPT 39 STEPS, TEN RPT TEN COMMANDMENTS) which he was also well advised to do. To sabotage one's own communications by trying to save money with gobbledygook like CABLING SWEEEKS COPY LONDON-WARDS SOONEST in a country where English was not even the second language could be as silly as turning down a taxi to save five dollars.

But it was an understandable mistake, for cable charges could take your breath away along with any temptation to be turgid. The leisurely pace-of normal communications induced frenzy when it did not induce apathy, and in Laos Western journalists goaded into expressing themselves in the language of the free world had to be officially requested to talk politely to post office staff. It was useless for a correspondent to send copy from Vientiane at anything less than 'urgent' rates if he wanted it to reach the foreign desk in London or Los Angeles in less than twenty-four hours, and the obliging Laotians therefore invented 'double urgent' rates to part the fool from even more of his money (to which I might add — strictly between these parentheses — a going price for persuading the counter clerk to shift his takes to the top of the pile awaiting transmission). In consequence, so it was said, the press telegrams of foreign correspondents were at one time the biggest single source of revenue in the kingdom (after opium, which was unlisted), and the more cynical suspected that the Laotians were deliberately fabricating coups and other crises just to bring the suckers in.

The suckers, accordingly, did well to use their wits, especially in Indochina, where almost any means was cheaper than cabling. If deadlines allowed, they could air freight their stories to Hong Kong for forwarding. If that was not feasible, they could pay for one of their number to fly them to the British crown colony. If they could find a friendly pilot or a willing passenger, they could give him their copy and ask him to drop it into the telegraph office at the other end — it was easy to discover from airline offices or the reception desks of the main hotels who was a likely 'pigeon' leaving that day for Hong Kong or Singapore. Why just those two? The correspondent had not only to keep a careful note of local rates, but to aim his copy at the nearest Commonwealth terminal. For within the Commonwealth, press cables cost only a penny a word, and even Tass filed to London via Singapore for onward transmission to Moscow. Small wonder; 'urgent press' in the Indochina states moved a story no faster, but cost sixty-one times as much.

In the more sophisticated age of the ubiquitous telex and

the audible telephone, of telefax, satellites, speedpost and special delivery services, much of the hilarity has been taken out of the problem of getting the message across to an editor on the other side of the map. More than thirty years ago I could telephone my stories from Paris to London, observing a few simple rules: open with dateline and byline, spell out names in the alphabet code, repeat figures, put in punctuation and paragraphs, and finally ask the copytaker to read back anything he was unhappy about. Now a correspondent can do the same from almost anywhere in the world. But some of the rules have not changed. In later years I filed through the local bureaux of Reuters, but until I retired I kept my international cabling card up to date, and made sure I had a note of any special regulations that the more ingenious countries devised to complicate the life of the correspondent. I was not to forget that a collect card issued in New Delhi had been tossed back at me in Bombay. And with a similar nightmare in mind, I paid my bills.

This may seem a small point. But I learned before Goa that an unpaid cabling account could stop a correspondent in mid-charge (in more senses than one) as effectively as a dum-dum bullet. And he could not afford the added delay when chasing a deadline, for he was already torn between two kinds of time — the priceless stuff jealously hoarded by his editors in the impatient West, and the cheap, throw-away variety favoured by bureaucrats in the eternal East. I owed the lesson to the Darul Islam rebels, whose thugs picked the fag end of a Saturday afternoon in November 1957 to try to assassinate President Sukarno with a shower of five hand grenades as he came out of the Tjikini School in Jakarta, but succeeded only in killing and wounding fifty-seven other people, most of them women and children.

Painfully ignorant of the 'Tjikini incident', as history was to call it, I was unwisely breaking an unbreakable rule by throwing a joint party that evening with James Wilde of Associated Press in the glorified garage which, thanks to his warm hospitality, I shared with him whenever I was in Jakarta. This 'pavilion' was in a quiet suburb far from the centre of town, and well out of earshot of the news — until the last guest to arrive glanced around and remarked approvingly, 'So glad you didn't have to cancel the party on account of the Tjikini business.' I suddenly remembered it was Saturday as Wilde grabbed the man by the shoulder and swung him back again to face us. 'What Tjikini business?' he demanded, his blue eyes and nose and teeth sharp with professional suspicion. Wilde was competing against three international agencies, and in London the first edition of my paper — like a lady of easy virtue — was just being made up for bed. Told what had happened, we were out of the party and into Wilde's Land-Rover in thirty seconds, leaving twenty-five open-mouthed guests in the smoke haze behind us to give themselves a good time.

It was by then after nine in the evening and raining hard. Troops and armoured cars had already cordoned off surrounding streets as police hunted for the killers, and we found ourselves dodging about in a desperate quest for details in a city that had abruptly become a maze of dead ends. The main cable office was already closed, but a night bureau — a hut at the end of a muddy lane — remained open, and having finally assembled the bones of the story, we fell on its ancient typewriters. The words counted, checked, and doubtless censored, my takes were finally cleared to London by two o'clock on Sunday morning in time to catch the last three editions of *The Observer*. I could collapse contentedly with a bottle of warm Coke, not knowing that my exclusive — there were no other Sunday 'specials' in Jakarta — would rate only three column inches below the belt on

Page One. (The killers had missed, hadn't they?)

Wilde's fine frenzy first started to approach panic when kind colleagues told him that his rival on AFP had got his copy away at least six hours before, having beaten all others to the story. But that was only the beginning. His first takes typed, feverishly scanned and signed, he rushed over to the counter to hand them in, to be informed by a friendly, smiling Indonesian official that under a new ruling he would have to pay cash to send them, as he had not settled his cabling account at the end of the previous month. It proved useless to argue, and going through our pockets with trembling fingers, we found we needed several thousand more rupiahs than we could muster between us if Wilde was to file.

We stumbled out into the night to get the money, followed by a yawn and a warning from the counter that the office would shortly close. Driving half-blind through pelting rain and unhurried army checkpoints, we reached the AP office after a run of maddening delays, dashed up the rickety wooden staircase and into Wilde's room, and converged on the safe in which he kept his float. I glanced at my watch, and assured him that we could make it —just as he shook out his last pocket and discovered he had left the safe key in another suit on the other side of the muscle-bound city.

Outside it was darker, wetter, crawling more than ever with dripping soldiery demanding to see our identity papers by torchlight. After a tormented journey, we found the key in the now deserted pavilion, struggled back to the AP office, grabbed several bricks of rupiahs from the safe, and hurtled over the slippery roads to the cable hut to find that it was just closing. At first the solitary Javanese on duty refused to accept Wilde's copy, let alone wait while he typed more takes, protesting — with some point — that it was too late anyway. But a second look at his shark-like countenance, the taut, agonised flesh streaming back from the predatory nose as it it were in a wind-tunnel, made the clerk change his mind. He counted the words, Wilde counted the money, and we left. It was 3.30 a.m.

Much later that day we rose to hear that a service message had arrived from Wilde's head office. He opened it with shaking fingers to read:

CONGRATULATIONS…WORLD BEAT…
SUKARNO ASSASSINATION ATTEMPT…

The AFP story had been held up by a technical hitch after reaching Amsterdam for onward transmission. Other agency bureau chiefs had been non-starters: we might have risked throwing a party, but they had risked going away to the hills for the weekend, leaving Jakarta to the mercy of their stringers. But just as the Goa experience had put a year or two on me, so the Tjikini incident had aged Wilde far more than it aged Sukarno.

7 HIS EXCELLENCY AND OTHERS

The ignorant reporter can best get a quick fix from his own embassy.

THE late guest who told us of the Tjikini incident in half a dozen words thrown negligently over his shoulder was a third secretary at the British Embassy in Jakarta named Braithwaite. But while his almost criminally careless handling of hot news may seem to reveal the distance of the diplomat's mind from the demands of the journalist's job — a distance that can trap the unwary reporter into kissing the ring of a cardinal when he should be kicking a crisis into shape (at least on paper) — it also reveals the exact opposite. For both are in the business of collecting information, and the difference is only in the deadlines of the day, since diplomats also have to entertain peripatetic prelates from Brazil, whereas correspondents do not. The point was not that

Braithwaite was blind to our ignorance, but that he had beaten us to the story, which had obviously reached the Foreign Office in London before we had even heard it.

Wounding things have been said about the gilded life of the diplomat, but journalists cannot be squeamish. On arriving in a foreign capital, I always called at the British Embassy and signed in. It was a principle dictated by both protocol and prudence. It was a matter of courtesy to let the Queen's agent on the ground know that he had another liability on his hands, for it was to my embassy that I would turn if a malevolent fate or my own folly landed me in trouble. In an emergency, an embassy might find me a bed (I owed my first night's sleep in the Far East to a second secretary in Saigon); it would intercede for me if I was arrested or expelled by a government outraged by my errors or accuracy; it would send me a doctor if I was sick (in Saigon, an immortal Frenchman who told me I had rhenal colic because I *did not drink enough*); it could repatriate me as a 'Distressed British Subject' if I was sacked on the spot and stranded without a penny; and it might even send out my copy when all other channels were closed — in Laos the British Embassy radio transmitted pooled stories for the isolated correspondents in Vientiane every day for a week during one destructive struggle for control of the capital.

But there was more to it than that. When I was abruptly told to cover the seizure of Goa, my immediate problem was to find the beginning of a thread that I could pull to unravel the plot. One obvious move was to badger diplomats I knew in Singapore for introductions to diplomats I did not know in India, since a name to quote is like a password when crashing the gates of any institution from a palace to a prison. Armed with the right shibboleths, I called the British High Commission in New Delhi as soon as I reached my royal bridal suite, for on flying into unknown territory with a strange political landscape, the ignorant reporter can best get a quick fix from his own embassy, even if he has to allow for magnetic variation. With its political, military, commercial, consular and, of course, press sections among others, a diplomatic mission can sketch in the general background for the newcomer, point to the questions that need answers, supply the names of prominent natives who might do the answering (and so unreel a second string of introductions), and warn him of all the hurdles and technical hitches ahead.

Or lack of them. Sent to Rome for the first time in 1953 to write a feature on the Italian communists, I was misled by what I knew of their secretive and conspiratorial French comrades, whose headquarters in Paris was then an almost impregnable fortress. In consequence, I was resigned to a devious, time-wasting flank attack through a series of delicate huddles with left-wing intermediaries. It was a second secretary at the British Embassy who gave me the key to a short-cut by pointing out that no key was needed. Unlike the French, the Italians ran an 'open' organisation. Why not just walk up and bang on the door? I did— and saved myself a week's work. Apparently, no one had thought of doing it before, for my full page on 'Velvet Glove Communism' was described as 'breaching the gates of capitalism'— by the Italian communists themselves.

Even when I was experienced enough to delude myself that I knew my own way about a country like China or Indonesia (but not yet experienced enough to know that I did not), I would still sound out the British Embassy (as well as foreign and local colleagues) before doing my own digging. Second-hand sources? The irony about truth is that to get a balanced picture of a street accident, let alone a crime, it is best to talk to the witnesses first, and the actors themselves only when one knows what has happened. For the horse's mouth can too often turn out to be the horse's ass. And that can make it difficult to decide whom to see when.

About to fly off to a corner of my beat where I had no stringer to lean on, I would be tempted to cable one or two local political contacts in advance from Singapore, warning them of my coming, so that I could be sure of having brains to pick from the moment I touched down. I was driven by a neurotic urge to get the story fast, and above all not to find myself kicking my heels in a hotel bedroom with no one to talk to while it ebbed away from me. For the same reason, I would tend to attack the telephone as soon as I was inside that bedroom and fix a further series of interviews for myself, like a plain girl at a ball anxiously filling up her dance card before the opening waltz.

But it I did not first get someone to sketch in the background, that could prove a mistake. Priorities change, and the moment might soon come when — like the girl — I would curse myself for having committed myself on Monday to a string of encounters in the coming week that would be a waste of time by Wednesday. Selecting sources and timing meetings demanded strategy, and therefore advance intelligence, and that was where the friendly diplomat served a specific purpose. Watching from the stalls while others spouted on the stage, he could often produce a quick synopsis of the plot that made the correspondent who came in late feel that he could now follow the play without having to buttonhole all the actors in the first interval. And this could be true whether the diplomat was a committed American, whose merit was that everyone told him their side of the story, or an irrelevant voyeur from Switzerland or Swaziland, whose merit was that nobody bothered to mislead to him.

Correspondents are derided for pontificating like self-styled experts after three days in a country, and writing a book on it after two weeks. But sometimes they have no choice. For a long time, foreign journalists were virtually barred from Burma, but could wangle a one-day visa if in transit. Flying from London to Singapore in 1964, I won myself exactly twenty-four hours in Rangoon ('and don't be a minute late back here tomorrow', warned a nervous immigration officer at the airport). It was an exhilarating challenge, for it called for quick, crisp interviews interspersed with some canny first-hand observation if I was to get a story. In fact, I got three 1,000-word backgrounders out of the visit (written, of course, after I had left; I wasted no time at a typewriter), and that was thanks to the first person I saw, a kindergarten contact who taught me the ABC of the current situation, and then told me who best to see to learn more — the press officer of the British Embassy.

I had other sources of inspiration. For ten years after gaining independence from the British in 1948, Burma was governed by politicians, but in 1958 General Ne Win assumed power to bring order and discipline to the Union. The Burmese did not take to these soldierly virtues, however, and fewer than eighteen months later voted the civilians back into office. In 1962, accordingly, Ne Win took brusquer measures, mounting a military coup, locking up the president, arresting the prime minister, suspending parliament, and reorganising everything in sight. In consequence the lead for my first piece was the gift of a bus conductress who actually made all her passengers pay their fare (unheard of in the happy-go-lucky Rangoon of yesteryear). And the 'new broom under Ne Win' theme was reinforced by the nervous immigration officer at the airport, who had been so uptight about my reporting back to his desk within twenty-four hours that he had stamped a ten-day visa into my passport by mistake. I resisted the temptation to take it literally: he might have been shot. But it was good copy.

The synopsis of the plot provided by diplomats could only be a rough guide, of course, for everything is relative. They might seem convincingly close to the action compared with politicians in Washington, who sometimes sounded like a club of compulsive scriptwriters kicking the future of the planet around from a cislunar goldfish bowl across ten thousand miles of blank space. But they, too, were often at one remove from reality.

One had to be selective. Caged by privilege, bound by protocol, immunised from the everyday hazards of life outside, many diplomats gyrated endlessly within a closed cocktail circuit around which they passed the same gossip like a plate of limp but durable canapés. Unlike journalists, they could not go everywhere, talk freely to everyone, or ask undiplomatic questions. If they did, they were likely to get diplomatic answers — like the answers they habitually gave themselves. They were, moreover, paper-pushers, for ever in danger of twisting truth into appearance, and appearance into truth.

If they did not distort reality because they were insulated from it, they might distort it in order to keep their heads down — and sometimes well in the sand. In the 1950s, when Senator Joseph McCarthy was smoking out 'un-American activities' in a State Department that he had damned as a communist anthill, I heard American diplomats in Paris torturing facts and figures into gibbering nonsense in their anxiety to prove themselves patriots and evade the witch-hunt. And that included stonily dismissing every possible redeeming feature of life behind the Iron Curtain (which could anyway be counted on the fingers of one hand and still leave two free for typing).

Visiting Africa ten years later Premier Zhou Enlai, who usually picked his words as if they were a secret path through a malodorous swamp, perpetrated a diplomatic howler by declaring, 'Revolutionary prospects are excellent throughout the African continent'. At one stroke he antagonised every sensitive black leader between Cairo and the Cape to whom revolution had become a dirty word the moment he had taken over from his white predecessor. There was little doubt, however, that beneath this uncharacteristic gaffe lay several inches of despatches from Chinese ambassadors who had reported to Beijing what they thought their masters wanted to hear, rather than the distasteful truth.

It could also be objected that if the timid prevaricated, there was an equally compelling reason for diplomats of integrity to deceive — duty. 'An ambassador is an honest man sent to lie abroad for his country,' said Sir Henry Wotton in about 1612, and he should have known. An embassy was an extension of government, its staff the fingers of its foreign policy. An unknown correspondent coming into it cold could therefore expect to be fed the official line of the moment. If he interviewed a British diplomat about the Falklands and an Argentine diplomat about the Malvinas, he would get two sides of a story, but not the truth that separated them, and might wind up wondering whether they were talking about the same place.

In cases like that I would check with seemingly disinterested observers in other missions. But even neutrals could not be trusted with an objective truth (if it existed at all), for most were not neutral — only 'neutral against', as the Irish say. That was no reason for not talking to diplomats, however. Truth was not a standard measure in a vacuum, like the platinum-iridium 'metre' of all metres in Paris. There was rarely a single infallible source of it on hand, and the reporter usually found himself struggling towards it by reconciling opposites. Most of the time, therefore, his job was to balance accounts, correct the curves in the lines men shot him, and get his story straight by always allowing for bias.

A glass wall of discretion divided the inmates of an embassy from the reporter at large, but it was normally possible to break through the wall by going for the right men and gaining their confidence. The first principle was not to insist on dealing with principals only. An ambassador was not to be chased for an interview simply because he was the ambassador. He might also be new to the post and ignorant of the country, woolly-minded, close-mouthed, press-shy, brazenly partisan, playing politics, a smooth-tongued liar, or owe his promotion to other vices. By 1963 a thriftless President Sukarno had pawned his country to buy Russian arms and personal prestige, reducing it to a debt-ridden ruin. But Mr Howard Jones, the earnest American ambassador to Jakarta who believed that Washington should give the President more aid to stop him moving closer to the communists, could still vigorously protest to me 'Sukarno takes the economy very seriously'. The great thing at that moment was not to take Mr Howard Jones very seriously.

8 OFFICIALS AND 'UNOFFICIALS'

Two Wongs did not make a white — they made about six.

A GLANCE through my old notebooks nevertheless shows what valuable, even invaluable, sources diplomats and others sent to 'lie abroad' could prove. Arriving in Singapore on the tail of a bloody riot in October 1956, I found that nearly all the contacts whose names my predecessor had given me had been locked up forty-eight hours before. But my first notebook is completely filled by a comprehensive rundown on the political parties, the left-wing labour movement, the student union, the farmers' associations, and everything else caught up in the current struggle between the British colonialists, the nationalists, and the communists down to the 'Chinese Brass Gong Society', with lists of the names of all the leaders in each case.

And thirty years later this basic document, dictated by a British diplomat, remains a polished mirror of the past.

Among others, a notebook dated August 1957 gives the history of the Emergency in Malaya, with the entire organisation of the terrorist movement, an exhaustive breakdown of troops and casualties on both sides, and an analysis of the strategy and the cost as the interminable hit-and-miss jungle war which the outlawed communist party had declared against the British colonial power in 1948 struggled towards its tenth year. This came from a British army spokesman, and I could have put together a pamphlet based on it. A similar briefing from a forthcoming British military attaché in Cambodia in November 1964 left me competent to write out the order of battle of the Cambodian army, including the weapons of all its units, as Sihanouk fought to keep his country neutral in a Southeast Asian combat zone of 'pro-Soviet' communists and 'pro-American' anti-communists.

Another notebook reminds me of the lecture given by an American colonel to correspondents who were on their maiden visit to Saigon in 1968. It began as an almost insultingly elementary lesson with the words: 'Vietnam is 700 miles long and has 1,500 miles of coastline, 800 to 1,000 miles of border with Cambodia and Laos, and the South has a population of 14 million'. Not exactly the stuff for postgraduates. But although to my joy and sorrow I had been in and out of the country for the previous fourteen years by then, I tagged along. It was a refresher course, and brought me up to date amid the havoc left by the bloody communist bid to take over the towns of South Vietnam known as the Tet Offensive.

The silliest thing a reporter could do was to feel that this sort of thing was beneath his dignity. Humility paid, and to be a know-all was the surest way to know nothing, for knowledge could be almost as perishable as news, and rot away with the passing of time. Robert Stephens, the former diplomatic editor of *The Observer* and a travel-worn veteran with more than thirty years in the field, would book himself on a guided bus tour of any place he had not been to for some time, like any blue-rinsed matron from Minnesota or regimented tripper from Tokyo, just to pick up the scent again. It was always worth it.

Military briefings in particular were packed with facts, and when limited to the basic background, basically honest, the 'now-it-can-be-told' story (but not a word more) available to all comers with reasonable credentials. But they were not enough, of course. At their most mechanical they were little more than oral handouts, and their political equivalents could be far more equivocal. One still had to break through that glass wall and see the story from the inside, undistorted by refraction, and the problem of identifying the right contacts to cultivate remained.

One man to look for in an embassy, I often found, was an officer on the wrong rung of the ladder whose years and rank did not match. A middle-aged second or first secretary who should by now have been a counsellor might be one of two potentially useful sources.

He could be a contract officer, or locally employed, a professional who was not posted from country to country, but stayed in the same capital year after year to become the embassy's resident expert and adviser to the ambassador. He would sometimes be the 'Oriental Counsellor', a confident brown or yellow face amid the often bewildered pink; he would speak the language fluently and know everyone and everything that was to be known, a walking talking book worth his weight in encyclopaedias. (In Bangkok it seemed that appointments like this could almost become hereditary, when after long years of service to the British as an information officer, a Chinese gentleman named Henry Wong was succeeded by his equally perspicacious son, George Wong. In terms of local expertise, two Wongs did not make a white — they made about six).

Alternatively, the greying junior seemingly passed over for promotion could be the station head of the secret service — CIA, MI6, or their friends and enemies in other embassies. In the past CIA officers mixed openly with correspondents, even those that were not American, but since the late seventies they have become more exclusive. MI6 was always more secretive, and if this meant its officers were more difficult to identify, it also meant that the correspondent might tap a rich source of inside information without being accused of knowingly talking to an 'official' spy.

Protocol demanded that one arrange one's first meetings with other members of an embassy through the press attaché, but one then had to sort the quick from the dead, the warm-blooded one could chat with from the frigid one could only interview. Thereafter, I would see the stiff-necked from time to time after going through channels, but cultivate the warm-blooded direct for the less inhibited give-and-take that could prove profitable for both, whenever and wherever we met in the course of our careers.

The ideal working relationship between a reporter and a diplomat (or attaché) was based on an uneven game for two played across an invisible net. There would be a tacit understanding that while the diplomat might brief the reporter, the reporter did not brief the diplomat — he merely told him a thing or two. The thing or two would be all the more precious, not only because his free-and-easy ferreting gave him access to information the other did not have, but because his proper role was to ask questions, not answer them.

If the diplomat had to keep the net between them, so did the reporter, because if he crossed it to become an agent of government, he would no longer be a reporter. But meanwhile mutual cupboard love could take over, as trust was built up and each served his own master, until the diplomat would open up his classified files for the reporter, and the reporter would quote at length from his notebook when telling the diplomat of his latest encounter with the local despot. And I have known this to pay not only regular dividends, but unexpected bonuses.

In the 1950s the West became increasingly worried by signs that the anti-colonial President Sukarno of Indonesia was drawing closer to the Chinese communists, and might — as a roaring left-wing' non-aligned' demagogue — become their cat's-paw in a global operation to subvert the entire Third World. In 1959, however, a shadow fell across their courtship when the Indonesians banned all Chinese traders from operating in rural areas of the republic. Ears pricked, therefore, when Dr Subandrio, Sukarno's mentally sinuous foreign minister, flew to Beijing in order to dispel it. While the world still waited to hear the outcome of his visit, Subandrio returned to Jakarta, stopping only briefly at Singapore to change planes, and no one would normally have known what had taken place. But it so happened that a British official of rather un-British views who had earlier found favour with him was then stationed in Singapore, and as if by coincidence it was this man who went out to the airport to meet him, as diplomatic courtesy (it could be argued) required.

It proved easy to persuade Subandrio to talk before he flew on, for he was still furious at the punishment meted out to him in China, and for once had lost his flair for lissom evasion. After being treated with meticulous discourtesy by Zhou Enlai (who seemed to feel Sukarno should do what he was told) and then left to cool his heels, he had suddenly been summoned from his bed in the middle of the night to see Chairman Mao, who had dressed him down for Indonesia's discrimination against Overseas Chinese, and then sent him packing. And I was in luck. For I had made a friend of the British diplomat in question years before when we were both in Paris, and he gave me the story the same day.

When he saw Zhou Enlai in Beijing, said Subandrio, the Chinese Premier was 'not at all the same man who had made such a good impression at the Bandung Conference' (where he had peddled peaceful coexistence in 1955). In all his years as foreign minister of Indonesia he 'had never been treated in such a fashion'. It was now evident that the Chinese communists could be 'as aggressive, even more aggressive, than others when their interests and prestige seemed at stake', and could interfere in the internal affairs of independent countries 'just as capitalist states had done in the past'. Chen Yi, the Chinese Foreign Minister, had even threatened Subandrio, if obliquely, by saying: 'The Overseas Chinese have suggested we take military measures to protect them, but we do not plan to send warships into Indonesian waters.' Yet. The eyes of the Indonesians had been opened, it seemed, and fears of Sino-Indonesian reconciliation vanished (for the moment). Mao had turned the script upsidedown with the curt ruthlessness of a Hollywood film magnate, and I had the new scenario all to myself.

Greeting me with his quagmire of a smile as the 'chronicler of my humiliation' when I talked to him off the record in Jakarta three weeks later, Subandrio had more to add. 'China has been unmasked,' he said. While it did not appear 'possible to think in terms of a military solution to the problem of Chinese expansionism,' he went on, 'some means must be found.' China was 'a greater threat to Indonesia than any other country with the possible exception of Japan', and Indonesia had to be seen as a long-term Chinese communist target. The countries of Southeast Asia should try to establish closer links with each other to keep China out — 'and that would include defence considerations'. Sukarno agreed with him. He had been 'shocked by the behaviour of the Chinese, and his vanity hurt'. Strictly for background, you understand.

More delicate than my relations with diplomats, of course, were my exchanges with spooks — especially if I knew what they were. It seemed wise to treat these moths masquerading as butterflies as fellow predators, and I would make sure I interviewed them, not they me. On first meeting a CIA officer I would keep the dialogue open but watch my pockets. I might ask what angles he thought I should be following up for my paper, but if he responded by feeding me an intelligence questionnaire and trying to use me as a legman, I would on no account report back to him. My object would not have been to be recruited, but to learn who and what interested him, what questions required answers in London or Langley, even what axe his masters were grinding at that moment — in addition to what I should be chasing myself.

But when we next met, the dialogue might be resumed, and if I could answer his questions without breaking a confidence, I would answer — especially if my story was going to appear in *The Observer* the following Sunday anyway. The reporter who thinks he is the only one entitled to ask questions — and get replies — should give up journalism for religion, and address himself exclusively to the only contact in the universe who has all the answers and no queries of his own (as far as we know). The rest of us must be ready to deal with the devil, whether we see him as the CIA or the KGB.

If you shrink from contamination by the KGB, you cannot even talk to your Russian colleagues, for in a communist state the journalist is usually the servant of his government, and as his business is news, that means he is automatically the agent of its intelligence services. By that I do not imply that he is a dedicated spook with a microphone in his buttonhole and a concealed camera in his cigarette lighter. (Nothing sinister in that anyway: the Japanese used to sell them for about five US dollars; I still have mine somewhere, but I gave up smoking twenty-five years ago). He will doubtless be briefed and debriefed by the professionals behind him, and constantly fed the party line that he is to feed to others in turn, but the Iron Curtain is not a one-way mirror, and he assumes that the journalist on the other side is also exploited by his secret service. Nor is he always wrong — except that the Western reporter is not usually what the CIA calls 'witting'.

A correspondent who spends convivial evenings with his Soviet colleagues may have to fend off a clumsy pass from a KGB head-hunter in Tass. This does not pose a problem. If 'cultivated' with a gift of vodka, I would give something unwanted in return — sherry rather than scotch — to signify that there would be no profitable quid pro quo from me; I was not open to seduction. On the other hand one Russian journalist, back in the East from a stint in the Soviet Union, once drank himself maudlin in my house in Singapore while telling me how totally disillusioned he was with his homeland — he had had enough of the shortages, the queues, the corruption, the cynicism of youth, the stupidity of senile leaders, the betrayal of the revolution, etc. It was all good copy, even if his brief was to see if I would try to recruit him for MI6.

But such lapses into Le Carré were rare. One could make not only warm friends of Russian correspondents, but useful trading partners, provided one remembered that they were in business for profit, and carefully examined whatever it was they were out to sell — or steal. It they fobbed one off with the party line, it was at least useful to know what the line was that day — especially if there had been a sensational volte-face. But they were usually more subtle, and it was a congenial Tass correspondent called Sergei Svirin, waggling a well-manicured Muscovite finger, who first warned me to watch the clique of Chinese radical Maoists in Shanghai that would come to be known as the infamous Gang of Four. As a 'Russian revisionist' he had his reasons, but it was still excellent advice. If one recognised the motives, it was safe to take the tip.

The best propaganda contains a hard core of fact. A reporter could therefore use information even from a communist source and still write accurately, provided he aimed off for wind. But then he would do well to aim off for wind whatever the politics of a source. For he was not only the hunter, but the hunted: when someone wanted to feed the world a story, it was suddenly open season for reporters. He was the prime channel for disinformation, and his hunger for copy made him easy prey.

Did the Americans want to justify dropping 1.8 million tons of bombs on Laos — half a ton for every Lao, and no lower age limit? All they had to do was to feed correspondents, stuck in Vientiane and starved for something hair-raising to report, with tales of sinister sneaker-shod communist hosts closing in on the capital for the kill. The correspondents could be confidently counted on to raise the alarm worldwide, and the B-52s could then save the world for democracy by droning in from Thailand to carry out in peace their sacred mission of anticipatory retaliation. It was not as if the reporter had any choice. News agencies could not ignore an official announcement or press briefing, however dubious. And, whatever the country, no source could be more devious and deceptive than that self-styled arbiter of right and wrong, that ultimate repository of truth — the government.

9 THE PRESS AND THE POLITICIAN

The relationship between press and politician was always pragmatic.

'WE shall always put the interests of the nation and people above all...we will never shun any responsibility...guide the nation in these difficult times in the spirit of sacrifice...not afraid of the dangers...will do all to serve the country...' The string of empty clichés could have dribbled from the mouth of any politician from Taipei to Tegucigalpa. Only the succeeding platitudes narrow the field a little: '...fight the communist lackeys and also the colonialists, carry out the revolution, build the foundations of true democracy...'

But as General Nguyen Khanh, the latest strongman of South Vietnam, reels them off by rote in September 1964, more than a hundred correspondents in the Independence Palace must reverently scribble them down as if they are holy writ. No one can permit himself to laugh out loud at this tasteless joke.

It is not the first we have heard in Saigon (nor will it be the last). It is already ten years since the woodenly dogmatic Ngo Dinh Diem, armed with an impeccably anti-communist record and the darling of the Americans, began digging himself in with their help. It was not easy, for he had to outfox a motley of 'pro-French' enemies behind whom were the French themselves. These ranged from the Emperor Bao Dai and a clique of hostile Vietnamese generals and politicians to the private armies of not only the powerful Cao Dai and Hoa Hao religious sects, but the Binh Xuyen. And the Binh Xuyen was a super-Mafia which ran everything that stank in Saigon from the Sûreté Nationale to the biggest gambling casino (the Grand Monde) and the biggest brothel (the Bull Ring) in Southeast Asia. However, in 1955 Diem had broken the Binh Xuyen in a straight street-fight that sent much of the capital up in smoke, and he had banished or bought off the rest.

So far, so good. But having consolidated their claim in the South, Diem and the Americans rejected the terms of the Geneva Agreement whereby the two halves of Vietnam would hold joint general elections in 1956, and winner take all. Instead, Diem became president of a new 'Republic of Vietnam' with its capital at Saigon. By 1959 in consequence the Vietcong, the second generation of communist-led guerrillas and legitimate heirs of the Vietminh, were sending shivers through the South like a familiar, recurrent fever. The Americans then moved in with money and military advisers to defend 'democracy' in a police state whose rigged elections and rod of iron for all who gainsaid Ngo Dinh Diem had earned the reluctant admiration of experts in the business even among their communist enemies. But in

November 1963 Diem was assassinated, and a few weeks of political euphoria under a weak if willing government of bureaucrats ended in January 1964 when General Nguyen Khanh mounted a coup d'état and seized power.

After seven months of governing through a Cabinet that was little more than a screen for a military cabal, General Khanh proceeded to finesse the fragile freedoms of the Vietnamese people by promulgating a 'Charter' of democratic liberties which could be suspended if there was a state of emergency. Since he had taken care to declare a state of emergency just eight days before, this made him an ostensible champion of democracy constitutionally free to play the dictator. On the same day, therefore, he had himself elected president of the republic in his turn by a sanitised Military Revolutionary Council. But the trick was too transparent. By the end of the month the cheated mobs were rampaging through Saigon, and the haemophiliac government was bleeding to death as ministers resigned almost daily.

It was at that moment that Khanh, taking one step back to clear the next hurdle, called us to the Independence Palace to tell us he had submitted his resignation as president and prime minister, and to promise as a plain soldier to 'put the interests of the nation above all', etc, etc. But he had not finished with us. One week later he again appeared before the press, this time without his beard: He had shaved it off, he announced, to show that he 'had taken a final decision about the past' and was returning to his military duties. Confronted with this barefaced deceit, I suggested to him that since "military duties' meant that he remained chief of staff, all political power would stay in his hands (in anti-communist South Vietnam, as in Mao's China, it 'grew out of the barrel of the gun'). The point proved apposite.

True, a certain Pham Khac Suu was now appointed chief of state, and a Mr Tran Van Huong became prime minister. But by November, Khanh was commander-in-chief of an army that had capped every province and district in South Vietnam with a military boss, by December he had formed a new junta, and by the end of January 1965 he had engineered another coup that eliminated the obdurate Huong and left him master of the government again.

Not for long, however. Within six months Khanh would give way to Air Marshal Nguyen Cao Ky, who would give way to General Nguyen Van Thieu, who ten years later would swear that his government would 'never allow the communists to annex our beloved free South Vietnam'. This would be taken down and reported with the same reverence accorded to Khanh's protestations, whereupon the communists would overrun the country and seize Saigon within six weeks. It would then be their turn to insult the intelligence of the press. None better qualified.

Good politicians may talk good sense, but since nothing rings so well as a hollow promise, the temptation for the second-rate leader to shout suspicion down with trite doubletalk when things go wrong (as they usually do) can be irresistible. And the news reporter who must faithfully record this stuff but may not comment on it is doubly humiliated, for he must not only listen to the latest lie as if he took it seriously, but pass it on — often verbatim — to the public, a duty that may leave him with a strong urge to wash out not only his ears, but his mouth.

Conversely, a government may remain primly silent on a story that screams for the catharsis of confession, as the Russians remained silent (for as long as they could hold out) on both the shooting down of a South Korean airliner in 1983 and the Chernobyl nuclear disaster three years later. And between these extremes lies the deceitful ministerial statement or press release that blows up or deflates an issue, drops a couple of salient facts and throws in a couple of specious statistics to tidy the tale up, deploying verbal trick-lighting to put a pious slant on a scandal by illuminating a half truth while leaving the other half in shadow. 'To thine own self be true.' said Polonius, 'and it must follow as the night the day, thou canst not then be false to any man.' But the more a government is true to itself, the more certainly will it fool some of the people at least some of the time.

In most cases it is a matter of expediency; in others a fastidious refusal to face reality, or even a moral principle that the boss (and not the customer) is always right, may prompt self-righteous sleight-of-hand with the facts. For many Malays, for example, truth must be 'appropriate'. In consequence, responsibility for the Malaysian race riots that followed the general elections in May 1969 was officially pinned to a 'disloyal' Chinese opposition. Notionally funded by the communists, this opposition had provoked the violence in order to 'overthrow the government by force of arms'. The inappropriate truth was that the Chinese opposition had, in fact, defied a communist call to boycott the elections, but the Malays had been alarmed by their success at the polls, and at least six Chinese had been hideously murdered for every one Malay that was killed in revenge.

The official version was an idiosyncratic response peculiar to the Malay leaders of a multiracial society in which canny, hardworking immigrant Chinese and Indians formed nearly half the population, made most of the money, and now threatened to steal the remaining birthright of the less business-like natives — their political mastery of their own country. But similar defensive reflexes are common to all politicians, for truth is like the sun — a blessing at a distance, terrifying close to — and few men can bear to look at it with the naked eye. The moral squint may frustrate the reporter, but it is not as dangerous as the predilection of governments for selling journalists the dummy. This can range from the feudal despot's unless-the-West-gives-us-another-fifty-million-dollars-this-place-will-go-communist ploy (so threadbare that it is now soft porn) to some of the equally crude inventions of the communists themselves.

Caveat emptor. But the correspondent who turns his back on the state-run news market will not be a correspondent for long. On arriving in a country, his first chore must be to make his number with the government press office, apply for accreditation, and get his name down on the distribution list for press releases, press conferences, public documents, official invitations, and whatever else those in power want to thrust upon him. He has always to bear in mind, of course, that when the press office sends him a handout, or a minister gives him an hour of his time, it is because they have something to peddle. But then business is business, and the transaction may frequently be to their mutual profit. As I discovered during *Konfrontasi*.

Troubled above all by a lack of unity in the patchwork of islands now called the Republic of Indonesia, Sukarno nevertheless saw it as a minus that could be turned into a plus. For it enabled him to convince himself that he must give priority not to the tedious job of feeding his 100 million-odd charges, but to the glorious task of forging them into one nation, of giving them a sense of pride and a single identity in order to hold them together. And he was all the more convinced of it because it dovetailed so satisfyingly with the personal dreams of this strutting demagogue, who was bent on inflating himself and his country simultaneously until they were both larger than lite.

Self-styled champion of anti-colonialism, he would unite all Indonesians against a common enemy by first claiming West New Guinea from the Dutch, and in 1963 rouse their patriotic instincts further by launching a military *Konfrontasi* against the newly-created imperialist puppet of the British next door — Malaysia.

This was a military folly in which the Russians might meddle to advantage, and in June 1964 Anastas Mikoyan, the Soviet First Deputy Premier, told a mass rally in Jakarta that the USSR was now ready to send Sukarno very modern weapons — 'far better than the British possess in this area' — in order to help Sukarno 'crush Malaysia'. In consequence tension was rising, and there were fears of a low-level sneak attack by Russian-built Badger bombers on Singapore, which had become one of the fourteen states of the new federation the year before.

The British defending Malaysia therefore riposted with an invitation to me to have a quiet drink with Air Vice-Marshal Peter Wickham at his residence on the island. Why me? It was a Saturday, and I had a paper on Sunday. 'I've no idea why I'm to give you the story,' the Air Commander said, a little disapprovingly when we were alone, thus dissociating himself from what was obviously going to be a plant, 'but…' An hour later I rushed to my typewriter to mark up a minor scoop: 'Bloodhound Mark II ground-to-air missiles are being despatched to air bases in Singapore and North Malaya to meet the increasing military threat from Indonesia, the Commander-in-Chief Far East Air Force told me here today…' There may be nothing wrong with a plant: It is the weeds one must watch for.

It was not the first or last time that I had been slipped a story because the powers-that-be wished to sell it to the world on a Saturday. Singapore, which had shed its colonial status when the People's Action Party of Lee Kuan Yew formed a government in 1959, had achieved full independence from the British when it joined Malaysia four years later. But the federal government in Kuala Lumpur was predominantly Malay and conservative, the state government in Singapore predominantly Chinese and progressive, and the mixed marriage was to break up within two years on grounds of incompatibility. By 1964 the crockery was already beginning to fly, and it was then that Dr Goh Keng Swee, the Finance Minister of Singapore, invited me on a Saturday to publicise the latest act of perfidy in the federal capital: A Malay assistant minister had taken it upon himself to hijack for the Malaysian mainland most of their joint quota of textile exports to Britain.

Goh's lurid language seemed justified, for there was a mongrel in the manger. Four mills in Singapore had already been forced to close for lack of business, eight more had retrenched workers, and the unions were getting restless. No such problem existed across the Causeway, for the simple reason that mainland Malaysia had no textile industry, and would only now be starting to open new plants on the strength of the British market that Singapore would be denied. Goh Keng Swee was to fly to Kuala Lumpur to confront the Malaysians and later see the British High Commissioner, Sir Anthony Head. Head 'effectively twisted arms and KL soon called it off', he recalls. (Britain could not yet be dismissed as a 'toothless old lion'). But when we met, it still looked as if the Malaysians might get away with their 'piracy'.

'It's outrageous,' Goh exploded.

'Would you say a stab in the back?' I asked, riding on his fury.

He thought for a second. 'All right, yes, a stab in the back.'
(To extract a strong quote, strike while the ire is hot).

On the same spot on another Saturday in January 1968, Lee
Kuan Yew exploded even more violently in my face over the sudden
decision of the British to break their earlier promises to him and
close their military bases in Singapore by 1971. The island was
now a diminutive independent state nudged by none-too-friendly
Malaysian and Indonesian neighbours, and he had been counting on
his friends in Whitehall for protection. The quotes came quickly. The
treachery was going to cost the British all their business profits in the
republic and the withdrawal of all its sterling reserves; they would
not get a cent for their land, and as for the safety of their people in
the island…Although this time Goh censored the language instead of
sanctioning the quotes ('they'll think we are a bunch of gangsters'),
it was still an exclusive. But then I made an elementary mistake.

Having slipped into the usual state of careless rapture that
follows filing a good story, I told an enquiring BBC correspondent
in an unguarded moment that the Prime Minister would — with
exquisite irony — be playing an inaugural round of golf that
afternoon on a new course opened by the (departing) Royal Navy.
Irony? Feeling mellow, I explained. A newspaper reporter whose
copy will be read only tomorrow must remember that radio is instant
journalism today. The correspondent caught Lee at the 19th hole,
and my scoop dissolved into the ether on the seven o'clock news
from London that evening. If Lee and Goh had been hoist by their
own anger, I had been hoist by my own euphoria. Perfidious Albion.
I knew just how Lee felt.

The relationship between press and politician was always
pragmatic, and could therefore be symbiotic — as long as the first

wanted the story that the second wanted splashed. In 1955 I flew back to Hanoi from Saigon for the first time since I had watched the Vietminh march in and Delassus drive out with my doomed copy. But this time I was accorded very different treatment. In fact, I was invited to a dinner unique in my career. In a little box of a house with a pocket garden to which I was driven almost surreptitiously after dark by a Vietnamese interpreter, I found myself sitting down at a small table with four Cabinet ministers of communist North Vietnam, and nobody else in sight apart from two comrades to cook and serve.

It was a deceptively cosy affair, the conversation ambling around a curlicued course that touched on everything peripheral from liquor to soccer (the Prime Minister, Pham Van Dong, had played centre forward for his school, it seemed). But it was also the first leg of a round of meetings that would take me to Ho Chi Minh (who murmured platitudes but gave me the cachet of a personal interview), and to Pham Van Dong (who would talk endlessly at me over a single drink that he did not want). And these meetings had only one purpose.

In Saigon, Ngo Dinh Diem and the Americans were by now no longer keeping their voices down when they dismissed with righteous anger any suggestion that North and South must hold joint general elections in 1956 just because the Geneva Agreement said so. The elections could not possibly be fair, they argued; the communists would beguile and bully the voters into giving them the victory, and so become masters of a reunited Vietnam. And as the communists themselves entirely agreed with this forecast of the end, it not the means, they were anxious to find out from me the answer to one question. Would the British, as co-chairman with the Russians of the Geneva Agreement, insist that those elections be held — or block them on the instigation of the American imperialists?

They also wanted to warn me, strictly off the record (so that I could tell it to the world), that if the elections were blocked, the guns would come out again and there would be hell to pay (which there was). I had no idea what the British were going to do because they hardly knew themselves, but I had a good story because I was the only British correspondent from the south in Hanoi, and I would be returning to Saigon to pass on the message — perhaps at a cosy little dinner given by four anti-communist ministers of Ngo Dinh Diem.

When a table tennis team from the United States visited China in 1971 to open the ping pong diplomacy that was to reconcile the two arch-enemies, the Chinese provoked much malicious amusement by ignoring the light-weight left-wing Far East correspondents who were forever fawning over them in the hope of getting a visa, and who expected to cover the event. Instead, they invited veteran anti-communists from Associated Press, NBC and the *New York Times* whom they had been rigorously keeping out of the country since the founding of the People's Republic. Times had changed, and they regarded the switch from friend to foe as no more inconsistent than walking on two legs. They were not going to waste time converting the converted. Sentiment did not come into the matter. What they wanted was worldwide publicity for the new, smiling Chinese face that had replaced the fanatical grin of the Red Guards. And they knew where to get it.

IO MAN BITES WATCHDOG

Their idea of a watchdog was a beast that bit its owner's enemies, not his family and friends.

THE correspondent could not afford to be sentimental either, or to be fussy about being used if it was all in the cause of good copy. But if he passed on lies for publication, he would soon be censured for dropping bricks without straw. He had to know enough to spot a fake, and he had to avoid being so eager for a story that any political huckster could sell him one. One quote deserves another, and if he was a straight news reporter, he could balance the boast of a government with bile from the opposition. If he had a byline and could comment himself, he had a duty to tear the frills from any official claim and cold-bloodedly analyse the anatomy beneath it.

It was for these unpopular practices that governments began

to brand the press 'adversarial', conveniently forgetting that it took two to quarrel even over nothing, let alone the truth. Nor was the cantankerous love-hate relationship between them softened by the presence of journalists in both camps. The reporter who becomes a politician — or even a public relations officer — is like an airline pilot who flies as a passenger. Where others may be merely nervous, the pilot will be neurotic, for he knows all the hazards, from the guile of the elements and the age of the aircraft down to the favourite whisky of the captain and the hairline cracks in the flight control system. And when a journalist crosses the lines, he knows far better than his ministerial colleagues just what they are up against, just how much mischief that unruly array of sceptical, ill-shaven, pen-chewing faces below the dais at a press conference can make for them all. Not to mention the female of the species.

It takes one to know one. When first interviewed on television, I felt like a Gestapo interrogator who had fallen into the hands of the KGB, and hardly dared open my mouth — whereas an innocent housewife stopped in the street will calmly outface the camera and answer the most provocative questions without (often quite obviously) a moment's thought. When I gave a press conference myself in 1986 after spending thirty-five years on the right side of the rostrum, I was suddenly a delinquent facing cross examination by twenty public prosecutors, if not the firing squad itself. I could sympathise with my colleague, the warm, easy, let's-kick-it-around Bernard Kalb, as soluble as he was voluble when he worked for the *New York Times* and then CBS, who earned the reputation for saying 'no comment' more often than any of his predecessors once he had become spokesman for the State Department. By extension I can almost sympathise with political leaders like Lee Kuan Yew, who sometimes appears to look on the press much as others may look upon some primitive form of plumbing.

In 1972 Lee drew blood when he remarked cuttingly, 'I read reports of all the bright students going into engineering, the sciences, medicine, economics, and so on. The not-so-bright go to political science and sociology. When they cannot get a good job, they go on to journalism.' Ah, but where do they 'go on to' from journalism? In Singapore at that moment the Minister for Foreign Affairs, the Minister for Social Affairs, the Minister for Culture, the Minister of State for the Prime Minister's Office, and the Minister of State for Foreign Affairs were all former newspapermen who had gone into politics with Mr Lee. Burke had called the press, 'The Fourth Estate, more important far than they all.' It was surprising that Lee seemed to forget this disagreeable fact of life, given the sort of company he kept.

His government had always included a huddle of journalists, yet from the outset it displayed a studied ignorance of their craft. Ministers cried sabotage when their outpourings were not published in full down to the last wearisome word. Foreign correspondents were dismissed as layabouts who simply copied stories from local newspapers and cabled them to their editors overseas. If one of their number asked a question at a press conference that Lee had answered a week before, the Prime Minister would bark, 'Why don't you read my speeches? I'm not going to waste time repeating what I've already said.' Yet he must have known that they had not been despatched from London and New York and Los Angeles to the Far East just to cover his particular dot on the map, that they had a dozen other somewhat larger countries to nurse, and might well have been in Vietnam or Indonesia or Burma or Taiwan at the time he spoke. Moreover, none of the ex-editors and leader writers and political reporters on his team seem to have pointed out to him that in any case last week's speech was last week's news, and a new deadline sometimes required a new affirmation (or, with luck, a contradiction) of what he had said before.

The Western press in particular took a whipping in the East. For Lee, its correspondents treated presidents and prime ministers 'like clay pigeons' and what they reported was 'gleaned from the bars of hotels' haunted exclusively by malcontents. For President Marcos of the Philippines, 'If the world ultimately degenerates into a second Dark Age, the Western press will certainly have contributed its share.' The Malaysians and Indonesians were no less scathing. Foreign journalists ('who the hell do they think they are anyway?') scavenged for the bad news, rummaging through the capitals of Asia for malodorous copy about despotism, nepotism, bribery, profligacy, muddling and fiddling at the top, and breathlessly filed stories on coups and rebellions, famine and drought and the misery of the millions at the bottom, while ignoring 'positive achievements'.

Sinister construction was put on straight reports. In August 1964 I was publicly attacked in Kuala Lumpur for pointing out that only one minister in the federal government of Malaysia had been drawn from the newly-joined states of Singapore, Sarawak and Sabah (in which non-Malays were in a majority), and writing that in the army 'there can be no wholly Chinese or Indian infantry battalions, I am told, *for security reasons.'*

'Isn't this an attempt to belittle us before the eyes of the world?' fulminated the acting Minister for Information. 'Isn't this an attempt to split us?' Twelve years later, a backbencher out of office, he was to call plaintively for more press freedom to allow the mass media 'to report objectively, without fear or favour' (which, quoting the Malaysian Commander-in-Chief, was exactly what I had been trying to do).

Since foreign correspondents obstinately declined to file only what was considered seemly, Asian leaders often saw them as paid agents of a totally immoral conspiracy to undermine the society their governments were trying to build, and looked upon their opprobrious literary antics much as an audience of 17th century Quakers would have looked upon a high-kicking chorus line. And at times understandably so. Press tycoons like Rupert Murdoch threw out the concept that 'we must be colourless to be credible' and proceeded to give the world not only Page Three cheesecake but stories in 'the interests of the ordinary people'. It was this definition of news, apparently, that inspired headlines like 'Bizarre Cult Rituals Bared, Woman Put in Cement' and 'Uncle Tortures Pet with Hot Fork', while in Palm Beach zany tabloids fought for circulation behind two-inch banners reading 'Man Marries Cow' or 'Sex-change Nun Now TV Wrestler'. If these aroused ire in Texas and Florida, how comic was Kuala Lumpur supposed to find a London newspaper report slugged 'Egghead Cop Dogs' which began, 'Handsome and nosey, two Egyptian bred police dogs with a gift for languages have been awarded Bachelor of Arts degrees by the University of Malaysia'?

When the press made equally free with the facts — or lack of them — where matters of national moment were concerned, faces fell much further. By 1976 the communist guerrillas in Malaysia had long since been cut to a fraction of their former strength, and pushed back to the Thai border, but the London *Daily Mail* could still report that they had shot down twenty helicopters in six weeks, using Russian Sam-7 missiles. If that were true, said the Malaysian Minister for Home Affairs with excusable hyperbole, 'there would be no more air force in Malaysia', and he went on (predictably) to castigate the correspondent who had filed the story for gathering his facts from malcontents in 'bars and hotels'. The greater the offence to those in power, the more serious the political repercussions — especially when those in power could not believe that democratic niceties prevented Western governments from curbing their own press. Ten years later the gossamer thread of goodwill between Australia and Indonesia was snapped by an article in the *Sydney Morning Herald* on 'Suharto's Millions' which alleged that the President (who had succeeded Sukarno) and his wife and family were energetically on the make. Jakarta banned Australian journalists, cancelled free entry for Australian tourists, and threatened to freeze military cooperation between the two countries.

In the same month three Californian journalists received Pulitzer awards for their reporting on the massive graft so ably practised by Ferdinand Marcos and his friends and relations while he was president of the Philippines. But by that time Cory Aquino had supplanted him, Marcos was plain Marcos, an exile in Hawaii, and there was no international whiplash. Does that make a difference? It is immaterial, say Western editors who insist that the millions have a right to know if there are reports that the government they put into power pockets or squanders or juggles with their money or trust — and so do its allies, backers, and investors, whatever the repercussions.

The press is their watchdog, and its freedom is not to be feared, it is argued, for it imposes a duty to be responsible and even-handed, censorious yet objective. And there are safeguards. There are watchdogs for the watchdog, like FAIR (Fairness and Accuracy in Reporting) in New York and the Press Council in London. The media must also answer to the law on everything from obscenity to libel, and at times they are constrained by clamps applied for their own good and everyone else's, like wartime censorship. Furthermore, news may be whatever sticks out like a sore thumb, but it is not the journalist who wields the hammer. The West does not complain, although it, too, is the victim of biased and distorted stories in Third World newspapers in which countries like Britain and the United States are sanctimoniously decried as sociological disaster areas.

Serve Britain and America right, retorts the Third World. What authority have they for preaching smug, sectarian professional ethics they do not themselves practise? Who are they to impose on others a further set of holy commandments that the sinners among them promptly flout by stealing, fornicating, murdering, and dishonouring their betters, if only on paper this time? In the mid-sixties, tens of thousands of Indonesians were slaughtered, the communist party was outlawed, and a conspiring Sukarno stripped of power in favour of Suharto after an abortive left-wing coup in which six generals were barbarically mutilated and their bodies tossed down a well. But what kind of a code is it that allowed an American correspondent to celebrate President Reagan's visit to Indonesia twenty-one years later by branding his host 'a murderous right-winger who has killed half-a-million of his compatriots…as corrupt as Ferdinand Marcos, as repressive as General Pinochet and Pol Pot, the butcher of Cambodia'?

The smiling Suharto might be no seraph, but when 'Suharto's Millions' hit the breakfast table the neighbours looked askance at the morality of those on the *Sydney Morning Herald* who were so ready to damage the interests of Australia and Asean (the Association of Southeast Asian Nations) in order to exercise their right to 'publish and be damned'. Freedoms like that were luxuries that young, weak and struggling countries fighting their way through the dregs of a dangerous century could not afford. What they needed from newspapers were helpful articles and 'good news' that did not sow dissension and frighten off investors, but 'contributed to stability', as one minister put it. The press a watchdog? Their idea of a watchdog was a beast that bit its owner's enemies, not his family and friends. The media should be domesticated and house-trained to serve the nation, not soil it.

****

At this point the dark side of the revolving argument swings into view. The press has not been elected, and therefore its self-appointed role of national nit-picker is a piece of breathtaking impudence, say affronted leaders in Malaysia and Singapore. Its duty is to serve those to whom the people have given their sacred trust at the polls — the president, the parliament, the party, and the government that must guide the media as it guides the country. In 1978 the Indonesian government allowed seven banned newspapers to appear again only after their editors had pledged themselves to uphold the repute and authority of the leadership, and to give no coverage to student protests or the statements of prominent personalities who were critical of the regime. 'I don't think we can profit from an antagonistic, adversarial style,' said Lee Kuan Yew in 1987. A government could not achieve much if it had to spend all its time and energy just outwitting journalists'. Me for one had made sure that he did not have to do so.

Accused of putting the press in harness and cracking a whip, Asian politicians justified curtailing its freedom by claiming that there was no such thing. Newspapers (and the media in general) were always controlled and directed, whether by their owners, trade unions, political parties, or editors — and told what to print. This was the thesis of the Malaysian Premier, Dr Mahathir Mohamad, who in 1986 charged the foreign press with trying to destabilise Malaysia. 'Many famous international publications are controlled by Jews who are now citizens of many Western countries,' he added, by way of example. 'Clearly these foreign papers are more controlled by Zionist forces than are Malaysian papers controlled by the government.' Dr Goebbels might have concurred, but the whole argument fell flat on its face at once because it tried to stand truth on its head. The control of the media by warring tycoons, unions, parties and editors was in itself an expression of the democratic free-for-all, whereas control by the government was the exact opposite. But then ministers who complained that journalists talked sweepingly of 'the Third World', as if Paraguay and Papua New Guinea were all one, would in the next sentence talk sweepingly about this ragbag of rival publications from Los Angeles to Lagos as 'the press'.

In an attempt to liberate the Third World from the grip of the major news agencies, in whose stories even the selection of cold facts and figures reflected a Caucasian bias, many countries not only created their own, but proposed in 1976 to form a coordinated 'news pool'. It then became clear that in recoiling from what they saw as the sick and slanted wire services of the West, they were turning to what the American chairman of the World Press Freedom Committee saw as 'a worthless government propaganda machine' which would only push out 'positive' reports. One understood the urge of the Asians to have a service that said the things they wanted said, and said them their way. But if truth was already among the walking wounded, it seemed that it might now become a stretcher case.

Those who shook their heads over a press that was not 'elected' were often the first to question the validity of one-man-one-vote Western democracy when it produced inconvenient results, and the itch of a government to muzzle the media was often in direct ratio to the degree to which it had rigged its own election (when it had not simply seized power at the point of a gun). I had seen those 'elections' — in Vietnam, in Laos, in Cambodia, in the Philippines, and notably in South Korea, where in 1960 matters were so deftly arranged that the ageing Li Ki Poong, crony and running-mate of President Syngman Rhee, won a landslide victory over the outgoing vice-president, a popular leader of the opposition Democratic Party. That was a foregone conclusion. What was newsworthy was that he won it although he was paralysed in both legs and down one side of his body, he could not stand for more than thirty seconds, and his speech was so painfully impeded that his campaign addresses had to be laboriously tape-recorded, and the tapes then cut and spliced so that his sentences would have a semblance of continuity. Even the disabled, it seemed, could perform exercises in double-jointed democracy.

Despots bent on moulding the millions into a nation of yesmen are not troubled by their own dubious legitimacy, however. By the following year Lieutenant-General Chang Do Yun had hijacked political power in South Korea, and at once begun tossing off draconian decrees under which 3,000 suspected pro-communists and hoodlums were flung straight into jail during his first week in office, and innocent bystanders were threatened with arrest for crimes that included jaywalking, smoking American cigarettes, and picnicking on Sundays. He was by no means unique, nor was the I-beat-you-for-your-own-good brand of political sophistry confined to dictators. So what could a dissenting journalist expect?

Throughout the world the press was taking a hiding as governments exercised their power to censor, ban, and close down publications, imprison editors and throw out reporters when what appeared in print was not to their liking. 'Ethiopia has expelled all Western correspondents, apparently because it finds it easier to murder its people without them around,' wrote an *Observer* colleague in 1977. In that year journalists, too, were murdered in six countries; others were kidnapped, bombed or assaulted elsewhere, and 104 were either in jail or missing. States that enjoyed freedom of the press were a 'shrinking minority', according to the International Press Institute. Ten years later the minority was still shrinking. In 1987, twenty-six journalists were killed — most of them 'singled out and intentionally eliminated'— and 185 arrested or kidnapped.

The Far East correspondent of a British newspaper, sweating it out in the tropics and far from his little grey home in the West, was caught in the middle of a stormy *affaire* whose capricious, ill-matched partners — government and media — were forever either fighting or fornicating. He was also stretched on a rack between local and London lore. Local leaders demanded tact, London editors truth, and the twain did not always meet. Yet he could not, like mad dogs and other Englishmen, simply ignore the torrid climate in the tropics. 'In Singapore,' said Sinnathamby Rajaratnam, elder statesman and Lee Kuan Yew's closest lieutenant in June 1986, 'foreign pressmen must abide by our rules of the game, regardless of whether they consider them heathenish and sacrilegious.' The correspondent must conform with native practice, not the exotic principles of his masters on the other side of the world. Trapped in a no-man's-land between the two, the reporter could, in fact, expect to be fired on by both. But between fellow-journalists who sneered that Malaysians gave degrees to dogs, and Malaysians who sneered that freedom of the press was no more than a 'tool for conquest' manipulated by pernicious imperialists, he could still tell right from wrong. And there lay the answer to his dilemma.

Lickspittles don't last. Lee Kuan Yew, explaining his unlovable role as taskmaster of Singapore, has always said that he did not take the job to get himself liked. It did not occur to him, perhaps, that the same must be true of the journalist, whom governments love only when he writes what they want. But that is no reason for the reporter to be eternally digging up dirt about them. There are times when he feels strongly that the politicians are right and the press wrong, and must say so. In ambivalent situations (and most are) there is only one thing for him to do —judge each case on its merits, and write as conscience dictates. This may sometimes involve him in contradicting himself from one story to the next, praising on Tuesday where he blamed on Monday, whereupon bewildered partisans of this or that cause will ask indignantly, 'whose side are you on anyway?' None, preferably.

Objectivity does not absolve the correspondent from passing judgement, but it is not always easy. Faced with the atrocities of Pol Pot or the antics of the anthropophagous Emperor Bokassa, he can let his account of the facts speak for his anger and disgust. But the script is rarely as simple as that. How can he remain impartial when his innate sympathies lie with one of two legitimate sides to a story (and there are usually at least two)? By studying the motives of the other, and giving them the time and space they deserve, I suggest. An anti-communist reporter might look askance at a 'neutralist' Sihanouk for allowing supplies to flow through Cambodia to the Vietcong during the Vietnam War, but he had to acknowledge that the Prince was primarily a patriot who thought he was buying a greater good with a lesser evil: the security of his weak and imperilled country. If the might of America could not stop the Vietcong, how could the puny Cambodian army? (And my notebook was witness to just how puny it was).

If the correspondent played fair he might incur the wrath of the committed, but he would also win respect. After pricking holes in my sometimes critical copy until it looked like a pincushion, Sihanouk sent me a polite note in April 1965 saying that he was grateful for a letter in which I had told him why I wrote what I wrote, adding: 'Whatever reservations it may inspire, I don't see any point in replying anew, because I don't wish to envenom things — and for the rest, we would never finish, neither of us believing himself in the wrong. In memory of our cordial past relations, please accept the expression of my consideration…' Pax, and eight months later he would send me a telegram beginning, 'Allow me to thank you very sincerely for the objectivity you have manifested towards my country…'

II PUBLISH AND BE DAMNED — SOMETIMES

He did not know she had forgotten to take the lens cap off her camera.

THE reporter with a conscience may have to weigh his moral obligation to file a story against the mischief it may do. But while it may be relatively easy to resist the temptation to start World War III for the sake of a headline, it can be difficult to make the right decision when the stakes are lower, and — if one has a sensitive scoop — one cannot ask for a second opinion.

In July 1964 the backbiting between the governments of Malaysia and Singapore was leaving permanent scars, and Lee Kuan Yew was under heavy attack from 'ultra' extremists in Kuala Lumpur who accused him of persecuting the local Malay minority in the island. Syed Ja'afar Albar, secretary-general of the ruling party and ringleader of the mob in the federal capital, gave a virulently racist speech to a Muslim convention in Singapore headed by a 'Malay National Action Committee', but it was lukewarm when set beside an incandescent leaflet of the Action Committee itself that I picked up the same day. Addressed to 'Malay brothers and sisters' in the vernacular, this pulled a knife in an already ugly situation by urging, 'Before Malay blood flows in Singapore, it is better to flood the State with Chinese blood.' Race riots then broke out, in the course of which thirty-five were to die, many of them hideously. I hesitated. Should I publicise the leaflet (which no other journalist seemed to have) and risk responsibility for triggering more mayhem?

At this point the Malaysian Inspector-General of Police called a press conference in Singapore at which he shook his finger at the assembled foreign correspondents as if they were a gang of juvenile delinquents, and threatened to kick out of the country within twenty-four hours anyone who sharpened tempers further by trying to pin the blame for the whole sorry business on this or that group. The bullying tactics were a psychological mistake. The 'ultras' in Kuala Lumpur had blood on their hands, and I suspected the federal government was trying to cover up their guilt. I filed the story that night, and *The Observer* ran it under the banner headline 'Malaysia Premier's Party Extremists Inflame Killings'.

Albar circulated an unsigned letter accusing me of contaminating the world with lies, and Tun Abdul Razak, the owlish Deputy Premier of Malaysia, summoned me to Kuala Lumpur to dress me down and show me the yellow card. In September there was more bloodshed, but not of my provoking. While on leave a few months later, therefore, I went to see the Tunku, who was in London for medical treatment, and safeguarded my Malaysian visa by giving him my side of the story. I had taken a chance in leaving Malaysia at all, as I could easily be denied re-entry. But when in trouble go to the top, and I was comforted by the knowledge that while his deputy had read the Riot Act to me, the Tunku himself had read the Riot Act to Albar. That same year, Singapore was ejected from Malaysia — and Albar from his party post.

A correspondent would be a fool to invite expulsion unless the copy was worth the price, for his editor wants him on the spot, and if he gets thrown out of the country he is paid to cover for carrying a placard in a local protest march (and I have known it happen), he deserves to be thrown out of his job the same day. But he must always be ready to take a risk. He cannot pass up a story because some minister may not like it, or he may find in these days of competitive tourism that he cannot even criticise the weather without being accused by some paranoid politician of writing malicious 'negative' copy carefully calculated to hurt the national economy. When the *Economist* published an unfavourable report about Malaysian development in 1987, it was charged with 'sabotage, malicious propaganda and slander', no less. It could not possibly have been guileless in Malaysian eyes. But the reporter still holds strong cards. Intelligent government leaders know that no one believes a servile press, and the public will simply turn for their news to foreign publications — or rumour — if their own media are muzzled. The best publicity comes from a dispassionate reporter who maintains credibility by refusing to be bought or bemused and serves up a balanced diet of the stuff.

Bought? A bribe may not be recognised as such by the giver or the taker. I shied away from accepting personal favours from political leaders after my wife and I spent a weekend at Angkor at the expense of Sihanouk in 1960. Having interviewed the Prince on the Saturday morning, I cabled my story before lunch, and *The Observer* ran it on the front page the following day under the headline 'Cambodia Threatens The West'. 'Prince Norodom Sihanouk, Cambodia's young and dynamic Head of State, told me in an exclusive interview today…' He had said that if the Americans did not stop giving more and better weapons to his hostile neighbours than they gave to his country, just because it was a neutral enclave at the heart of their anti-communist defence system in Southeast Asia, he would turn to Moscow and Beijing for arms instead — 'Our pilots may be trained on MiGs in Russia, and our artillery may come from China."

The story was still on the stone in London when we reached our hotel near Angkor Wat on Saturday evening, to hear with mixed feelings that Sihanouk had meanwhile phoned the manager to say that he would pay our bill. But as I sipped his wine at dinner the following evening while listening to the news, Phnom Penh Radio — in the unmistakably florid style of the Prince at his most fretful — began flaying my article as scurrilous, full of tendentious inaccuracies, and totally false. It turned out later that Sihanouk was basing this bruising judgement on a misleading wire service extract (*The Observer* itself had not yet reached Phnom Penh, of course), but Nuits St. Georges has never tasted nastier.

By definition, political gasbags burst when pricked, but when 'scurrilous' stories that would make the soundest of leaders flinch do not appear in print, no credit goes to the journalists who gave them a decent burial instead of exposing them to the light. At Angkor my wife and I were followed everywhere by a military jeep packed with armed men. Why, I asked Michael Field, resident correspondent of the *Daily Telegraph*. Because on the eve of an official visit by Princess

Alexandra to Cambodia the previous summer, two Khmer thugs had ambushed and raped a member of the British Embassy as she toured the ruins. (One of them, caught with her camera on him, was shot without further ado on the orders of a furious Sihanouk). Neither Michael nor any other reporter wrote that story, for the embassy appealed for a self-imposed embargo 'for humanitarian reasons', and 'in those days journalists were prepared to comply with this kind of voluntary blackout' (as he remarked nearly thirty years afterwards). Some even connived at the cover-up by attending a farewell cocktail party for the victim designed to demonstrate that her immediate recall to London was routine.

Nor did I write it when I heard it half a year later, although our military escort at Angkor provided an obvious peg. But Sihanouk, sulking in Phnom Penh over what I had put into my piece that Saturday, would never consider what I might have left out. (There are exceptions to this rule. Estelle Holt once earned the gratitude of an American ambassador to Laos for not publishing compromising pictures she took while he climbed a wall to talk to Souvanna Phouma, who was under house arrest at the time. But then the gratitude was misplaced anyway. He did not know she had forgotten to take the lens cap off her camera).

Sins of omission? The correspondent on the spot must decide what news is fit to print for the delectation of that imaginary public who 'have a right to know' everything. Those who protest that 'my first duty is to my paper' might reflect that the best guide to professional conduct is the knowledge that one has to live with oneself. And charity begins at home.

Every day around the world a million tip-offs and tales true and false filter through the ears of journalists like plankton sieved through the maw of a baleen whale. But no more than a tenth of what the reporter learns reaches his typewriter, let alone print. And among the discards will be not only insubstantial whispers, but solid texts. Going through my Singapore cuttings files in 1986 before lending them to the Department of National Archives to be microfilmed, I found myself extracting a thick sheaf of documents I had never quoted. These ranged from the last letter of Andrew and David Chou, two brothers awaiting execution in Changi jail, to a confidential report by the chairman of *The Straits Times* on Lee Kuan Yew's almost ungovernable fury with the way the Singapore press had handled two of his trips abroad.

The first — written by two of six men about to be hanged for their part in the so-called Gold Bar Murders — was a long and terrible pilgrimage into repentance for three despicable, cold-blooded killings. It was addressed by a pair of frightened Christians to their pastor, and it seemed to me that to publish it would have been a violation not only of privacy, but (although they were not Catholics) of the sanctity of the confessional.

The second, written in January 1968 but acquired later, described Lee as beside himself with rage. Having summoned the editors of all local newspapers to his office in November, he had lashed out at them for their unhelpful coverage of his first visit to Washington, threatening to 'wring their necks' and close their papers down if they did not 'mend their ways'. The following month (the report continued) Lee was again incensed by the failure of *The Straits Times* to publish a press photo of him talking to Harold Wilson, the British Prime Minister, during a visit to Australia. This time he had the chairman himself on the carpet, and ordered him to sack his editor-in-chief; if he were not dismissed at once, the Trades Union Congress would take industrial action against the paper, whose shares on the stock exchange would become valueless, and that action might be extended to five other companies in which the majority shareholder of *The Straits Times* had important interests.

All for want of a picture with Wilson? The chairman's account might sound exaggerated (as Lee himself was later to comment mildly) but the story was still a gift; it would write itself. And there was more to come. 'He's surrounded by sycophants and bumsuckers,' one of Lee's ministers explained to me inelegantly just one week after the second explosion. 'So he gets arrogant, gets testy, goes through the roof, won't listen, shouts you down. He grinds people into the ground, and bores everyone on TV with it. The press should tell him. Singapore's a small place. It needs friends.'

But that was just the point. As I have said, what looks like lunacy to one profession is logic to another, whether the professional is an ambassador bent on dressing a journalist up (to dine with a Brazilian cardinal), or a prime minister bent on dressing one down (for some seemingly inexplicable sin). In the first instance, Lee's speeches in the United States were widely interpreted by the press as support for American policy on Vietnam. What goes down well in a belligerent Washington, however, can stick in the throat in neutral Singapore: the publicity left an unhappy impression which on his return to the island he was quick to correct by declaring on television that he 'was not going to be the monkey of the American organ-grinder'. Lee was worried about the security of the region as a whole and Singapore in particular. He wanted to urge the Americans to stay in Vietnam and 'slog it out' with the communists, fearing that if they lost that fight they might pull out of the mainland of Southeast Asia altogether (as they did). He had no intention of kowtowing to them and committing Singapore, as many readers of the local press seemed led to believe. But the trouble with trying to get the best of both worlds is that there is only one.

His concern was doubtless all the greater because the British were already looking over their shoulders. In the second instance, in consequence, he had seized the opportunity offered by a meeting in Australia to impress upon a reluctant Harold Wilson the vital need for British troops to stay in Singapore, and felt it imperative that he should be seen to be doing so — on the front page, with captions. Taking the Labour government at their word, he had announced publicly that the island would be safe from aggression 'with our British friends remaining until 1977'. The snag was that he had been a mug to trust them, said my candid friend at court, but it was 'the old school tie business', and the Cabinet could not shift him — 'if you argue, he shouts and never stops'. He might learn too late that the British were ready to ditch him in their own interests, that their troops would be gone by 1971. As for the Australians, they were 'cowardly and niggardly' and would do nothing to defend Singapore if it were attacked unless the Americans pushed them into it.

Was there any danger of an attack? Links with a hostile Malaysia were so taut and tenuous that in October the Tunku had felt it necessary to assure Lee that the federation would not violate the island's sovereignty. But while Lee had time for the Tunku, he had no reason to trust the Malaysians —'he hates the rest of them up there'. Within a few months, moreover, relations with Jakarta would dissolve in a cloudburst of irrational fury when two Indonesian marines would be hanged in Singapore for a bomb outrage committed during *Konfrontasi*, and their commander would announce that he was ready to lead an invasion of the republic. That was over the horizon, but if Lee Kuan Yew was on edge, so was the future of Singapore. It was two weeks after I saw the minister that Goh Keng Swee stopped Lee in mid-spate during his tirade against the British by protesting, 'They'll think we are a bunch of gangsters'. For the minister had been right, and the troops were to leave before 1971 was out.

However, no one is more contemptible than the voyeur watching from the safety of the terraces who barracks the bullfighter risking his life in the arena. As an onlooker whose only responsibility is to arrange a few hundred words on paper, the reporter must at least deal fairly with the harassed politician whose responsibility is to arrange the fate of millions of people on the ground. And I held a key to Lee's hair-trigger temper at that moment. I had returned to Singapore from Washington just before he took off to go there, and he had questioned me privately over a beer about what to expect. How had I found the Americans? It was to be his first visit, and it was clear that he was uneasy, like a man flying in blind. 'I see myself landing in a helicopter on the White House lawn, Johnson welcoming me…and what then?' He was frowning with uncertainty over how to proceed from there. There were so many points on which they could not agree, yet somehow he must avoid a quarrel if he was to influence the President. It could be important for Southeast Asia and Singapore…

That was still no reason for my failing to file the full inside story about his confrontation with *The Straits Times*, however, and although Lee's 'I'll-fix-you' threats to erring editors were no longer news, this one was different: For one thing, I do not remember any specific mention of castration before. No, it was a matter of discretion. I had been slipped both documents (the condemned men's letter and the report of the chairman) under the counter, and been asked to keep them to myself. They went straight into a steel cabinet. My talks with Lee and his candid minister had been strictly confidential, but even when an official deliberately leaks information so that it may appear in print, the reporter must still judge for himself whether 'the public has a right to know'. In this case I simply decided they had not. Not for the next twenty years, anyway. And perhaps not even then.

But if I could not expect Sihanouk (or Lee) to thank me for the copy I did not file, Sihanouk could not expect a free trip to Angkor to change the copy I did. By the same token, a reporter must always be ready to join an official press tour and then bite the hand that feeds him the official line that goes with it. If a government is trying to buy him with bus rides, it deserves what it gets. He must never feel he is in debt to those in power for the time and trouble they take over him. Paradoxically, nowhere more than in communist states does the solitary correspondent feel he is being treated like minor royalty. In Mao's China he might be given a ninety-minute press conference by the entire management staff of a farming commune, or taken around an electronics plant by an escort of fifteen assorted senior technicians, trade union secretaries and political commissars, all of whom apparently had nothing better to do for the rest of the day than answer his ignorant questions and ask for his "suggestions'. But it earned them no marks with me. On the other side of the fence. General Sayyud Kerdphol of the Communist Suppression Operations Command in Bangkok once treated me to a personalised two-hour briefing with sliding charts and oscillating maps as I sat in lonely state in the stalls of his lecture theatre. But he had no reason to like the story I wrote.

The more philosophical governments tend to accept it as

axiomatic that the journalist is an ungrateful wretch. The General Information Office in Seoul regularly handed out a pile of presents to every visiting correspondent, including long-playing records of classical Korean music, silver chopsticks (very suitable gifts: they turned black if the food was poisoned, so it was said), and a stack of fancy hardback doorstoppers on the glories of the Land of the Morning Calm under Syngman Rhee. 'Why do you keep on giving us all this when we write such terrible things about you?' Keyes Beech, then of the *Chicago Daily News*, once asked a ministerial official. 'Oh, well,' came the disarmingly frank reply, 'we always hope that one day it will pay off, and you will say something nice.'

The Koreans were so disarmingly frank that it was sometimes necessary to sacrifice a good quote to save them from their own indiscretions. But that was not true everywhere. Even Imelda Marcos accused the Filipino military of 'looking at members of the press as interlopers and spies', and an exasperated BBC correspondent earned the quarrel into the opposing camp when he told a business association lunch in Singapore that the local bureaucracy itself was responsible if a reporter did not get his story straight. 'Government leaders refuse to talk," he said. 'Every effort is made by officials to prevent him getting even the most innocuous facts and figures. People are afraid to speak.' Check. In 1987 an information officer at the Ministry of Defence told me I would have to get my publisher to submit a written application to her superiors if I wanted to know whether men who wore glasses could serve in the Singapore infantry (although, as I pointed out, the first soldier I saw would probably give me a straight answer — *and she agreed*).

I was never a head-hunter, but rather than break through the walls of silence, I found it best to aim over them, for the more senior the hierarch the reporter saw, the more would he dare to depart from his script. Even then, it was not good enough just to listen to press-drunk premiers playing their well-worn LP discs, reciting routine answers to routine questions already put to them by a hundred other journalists — sometimes before the questions were asked. Once in the groove, Ngo Dinh Diem could talk non-stop for two hours without changing a word of what he had said at his last interview, and the one before that, and the one before that…Once again, the correspondent had to look for the warm-blooded source who would give him the inside track and so keep him on the rails.

Sometimes the source would be a man at the top whom one had known in less exalted days. One of my brother officers in World War Two was to become the army commander in Singapore, and another — Denis Healey — the defence minister largely responsible for the British military withdrawal from the Far East. Sinnathamby Rajaratnam, a leader writer on *The Straits Times* and stringer for *The Observer* when I arrived in Singapore in 1956, was to be the island's foreign minister and then deputy prime minister. But it was important not to rush in and try to convert auld acquaintance into instant copy on these occasions, brazenly exploiting the old boy net. When Rajaratnam first became a minister I stayed away from him for several months, and at his first press conference in Singapore in 1967, I did not greet Denis Healey until he greeted me. Ghosts from the past are not always welcome and — given the nature of ghosts — those that materialise in the horrid guise of eager reporters claiming favours on the first trivial excuse may be quickly seen through, and thereafter looked through.

The correspondent who does not push the door too hard too often finds it open once he really needs the entrée. When Vietnamese anti-communists hijacked a commercial aircraft on a local flight out of Saigon and killed two of the crew before seeking asylum in Singapore, Rajaratnam held the key to the story. Hanoi was angrily demanding the men and the machine, Singapore was anxious to avoid a quarrel with the bellicose Vietnamese, and editors around the world were waiting to see what Lee Kuan Yew would do. But the bureaucracy had clammed up. I therefore telephoned Rajaratnam at his home, and he gave me the answer at once: Singapore would not bow to threats; the men would not be handed back to Hanoi, but tried for the killings in the local courts. I had my exclusive, because I had Rajaratnam's new unlisted number — possibly because I had not dialled the old one more than three times to ask a professional question. My gaffe in not calling the British Embassy in Saigon when the prime minister of South Vietnam disappeared within it had been made good.

One friend in the right place who will trust a reporter with the truth is worth a dozen official contacts who will cut it to fit the policy of the day. Riffling through old notebooks full of the sibylline clichés of politicians anxious to shelter the innocent correspondent from the ugly facts of life, I find odd interviews that are like windows flung open to reality.

Take the year 1968. Talking to me of the 'pacification' of the South during the Vietnam War, an American official back in Saigon from the sticks waves away the predigested purée of official fiction strained for domestic consumption in a queasy US, and gives me a few home truths not fit for the home market. It is more than ten years since the first Vietcong guerrillas materialised in the Mekong Delta, three since the first American marines 'stormed ashore' in South Vietnam to crush them. But — security? The army sweeps through the countryside like a passing ship, and the Vietcong return like water as soon as it has gone. Some districts have been completely abandoned to the enemy, and of the 219 fortified 'strategic hamlets' in one province, he would dare to sleep in only twelve.

Winning hearts and minds? Most Vietnamese officials are no more than corrupt time-servers who take their cut of rural aid — medicines, clothing, blankets, even newspapers — all down the line as it passes from Saigon to the village, so that the people themselves may get nothing. The peasants are apathetic, scared, sometimes resentful; half of them do not know the difference between their former French masters and their present American mentors — they simply see them as the foreign devils responsible for all their misery. It is sources like this that will earn correspondents the accolade of Richard Nixon, who will later describe the Vietnam War as the most 'misreported' event in American history.

An adviser to the anti-communist Southeast Asia Treaty Organisation, back in Bangkok from the hills, strips the gilt from official propaganda about 'counter-insurgency' in Thailand. It is four years since Thai guerrillas, their cadres trained by Hanoi and supported by infiltrators from Laos and Vietnam, began shooting it out with the police in the northeast and haranguing the hill peoples at the point of a gun on the sins of government and the wonders of communism. But now the government is giving them a hand by treating local inhabitants who refuse to be resettled elsewhere as Reds, bombing their villages, sometimes sending in troops to kill them. The Meo minority are outraged, and the communists are luring their young men over the border into Laos for training as terrorists; local intelligence is therefore poor, and the army wastes its time on useless sweeps…

In the same month a senior minister in Laos gloomily dissects the quarrels that are tearing apart the latest anti-communist government in Vientiane; one general is making a fortune out of opium, another is making a fortune out of the Customs, the minister for finance is being blamed for relying on gold smuggling to balance his budget and threatens to resign, the prime minister is a sick man — he has hard patches on the stomach…A mile down the dirt road a self-effacing emissary of the communist Pathet Lao sits cross-legged on a low platform wearing nothing but an old sarong, and tells me his side of the same story. These are the Cassandras of Southeast Asia, and I do well to heed them, for in 1975 all Indochina will fall to the communists, as Troy fell to the Greeks.

If a correspondent is to make his mark, he must have confidants who will give his copy the truth behind the truth, a particular perception beyond the universal stereotype. And these will often be men and women on the dark side of reality as it is presented by governments: during the anti-Tito campaign in the communist bloc one of my most illuminating sources in Beijing was a Yugoslav contact from Paris days, and during the Sino-Soviet quarrel that followed it, a Russian contact from Singapore. It is a question of balance, not bias: any reporter can get the government's story without lifting a typing finger. But he will share it with all his rivals unless (once again) he can establish himself as an individual. For to presidents, premiers, ministers, bureaucrats, army commanders, police chiefs, and all the other registered actors who make or mar the news, the press is essentially a mob, and to be subjected to mob control.

12 COVERING CONFERENCES

I remember his once picking his nose outrageously to stop a inquisitive diner from staring at us over his escargots.

THE reporter has two public images, and both are faithfully distorted on screens of all sizes. When he is the hero of a television series, he is depicted as a lone champion of truth and justice, fearlessly challenging shyster lawyers and cops on the take to the strains of noble background music up to the last sequence ('OK, Commissioner, this is the end of the line). When he plays a bit part, he is just one of a snapping pack of paper hyenas barking questions at the weeping heroine as she stumbles blindly through her mascara from courtroom to car ('Is it true on the night your husband was murdered you were shacked up with…?'). In real life, however, the correspondent is at his most secure and relaxed when he is out there on his own, boldly confronting the world and its five billion illusionists single-handed; it is when he is one of the yapping mob that he has more problems than the heroine and is to be found at his most neurotic. For there is no safety in numbers.

My most agreeable memories include rattling across some remote part of China alone by train in 1958, while loudspeakers hoarse with fury threatened all British imperialists with bloody annihilation for their latest outrage in the Middle East. (I had already rattled across Beijing itself in a pedicab to thread my way through the word-perfect mob that was yelling precisely the same imprecations outside the British Embassy). I might be in the middle of half a billion mock-maddened Chinese, but there was not another British newspaperman in sight, and for a few blissful days I had the story to myself. But when I was one of three hundred copy-starved rivals baying after the same half-exhausted story before we tore it to pieces between us in some otherwise peaceable city like Paris or Geneva, I might chew my pencil down to the quick, for it was then that the competition became so stift that stimulus tightened into stress.

Of all assignments, international conferences were the most trying, particularly those convened in a great cause to pluck harmony from discord, even peace out of war. Television viewers might applaud as brandished fists finally dissolved into boneless handshakes and frowns into wary smirks for the camera's uncritical eye after a night spent squabbling over the last word in the joint communiqué. But my memory of those auspicious occasions dissolves into a chaotic pastiche of crammed hotels, nose-to-tail press conferences, an *Observer* press box stuffed daily with mounds of indigestible bumph, tight knots of impatient colleagues clamouring to get at the telephones and telex machines, and a conference building on which a swarm of journalists converged every morning to interview the same handful of newsworthy delegates, only to find yet again that forty into one did not go — not before the next deadline, anyway.

The secret was not to strive against the mob, but to use it. I would take part in crowd scenes I could not afford to miss — a crucial press conference by a star performer, or a secretariat briefing on the next day's play — but otherwise branch out on my own. I could not compete with the agencies, and it was pointless to try to duplicate their work by covering all routine proceedings elbow to elbow with the man from Reuters, when I could ride on his back by reading his copy on the ticker within the hour. And I could not compete with television teams, even if I worked for a daily, for their output would be on the box long before the first morning paper appeared. My advantage was that while the agencies had to cover non-events like the official opening of the conference or the platitudinous speeches of minor actors for which we already had texts, I did not. And meanwhile they drew off most of the pack in hot pursuit, fearful of missing something, for a mob is always a mob.

Led by the agencies, the routine reporters would go for the big names, ultimately producing a hundred variations of the same interviews granted by a small bunch of key participants to the conference who had long since run out of new clichés, let alone new ideas. But this meant that lesser men from lesser countries would be neglected, readily available, even flattered when approached. Nor were these delegates to be despised as sources, for they were often being lobbied for their vote by several major powers simultaneously, and sometimes knew what was in everyone else's mind better than they knew themselves.

One modest inside source can be worth a galaxy of diplomatic dissemblers, as I learned very early in my career as a correspondent when the United Nations General Assembly convened in the shadow of the Eiffel Tower in 1951. At the top of the agenda was the crisis in the Anglo-Egyptian quarrel over the continued presence of British troops in the Suez Canal Zone and the refusal of London to allow Egypt to absorb the Sudan, which had led to a fire fight followed by rioting and terrorism in Cairo. The main question mark was pencilled against the readiness of the Arab League, then a cabal of seven countries, to gang up behind Egypt against the British. The main targets for the corps of correspondents were therefore the leading delegates from these Middle East states, and above all Nahas Pasha, the Egyptian Prime Minister, whose answers to their earnest enquiries were frankly ambiguous when on the record and distinctly shifty when off it.

And, by mere chance, I knew why. I had talked to none of these potentates and plenipotentiaries, but I had been given an introduction by a mutual friend — 'he is my elder brother' (hand on heart) — to a Syrian who sat in as a mere observer with his own delegation when the Arab League went into a huddle at the end of each day to hammer out their next move. This invaluable source was shy of being seen with me in public — I remember his once picking his nose outrageously in a small sidestreet restaurant to stop an inquisitive diner from staring at us over his escargots. But he was keen to talk to someone and pleased by my interest, and I became his 'younger brother'. He introduced me to a comely wife heavily hung with gold, and confessed to an illicit affair with cognac. And every evening in his offbeat hotel he would brief me in rasping French and exquisite detail on the secret deals and interminable wrangles of the Arab partners that were slowly driving Nahas Pasha crazy, as he strove forlornly to talk them into a serviceable anti-British alliance while each steadfastly pursued his own labyrinthine interests. That was the inside story, step by step, of their road to nowhere, and worth a score of interviews with the mighty pitched for the Anglo-Saxon ear. But that is not to downgrade the press conference, which is so often the centrepiece of a reporter's copy and must be handled with care. I liked to arrive at these functions early, choose a good seat in the front stalls, and have my questions listed in my notebook in advance. I would then let the mob work for me again. It was often absurdly easy. There were nearly always pushy rivals with eager shining faces ready to fall over each other in their anxiety to hog the floor and hear themselves speak, and these would ask all the obvious questions on behalf of the rest of us. (They reminded one irresistibly of those odious know-alls at school who were forever sticking up their hands and shouting 'Sir! Sir!' in agonised voices when they thought they knew the answers).

The correct procedure, it seemed to me, was to let these performers get on with their act for half an hour, scribbling the replies they were given in one's own notebook while they (if the speaker was a prime minister or some similar dignitary) would be too busy nodding at him politely as he held their eye and answered their queries to be able to write down anything intelligible themselves. The moment would come when the pacemakers had energetically extracted all the basic responses one wanted (with luck getting themselves blacklisted for putting the 'adversarial' questions one would otherwise have had to put oneself), and exhausted their right to ask anything more. It would then be time to leave them contemplating their blank notebooks, assess what had been said and left unsaid, and take one's turn to cross examine the witness from one's new point of vantage.

Ideally — but it did not always work. I found Asian reporters were either very crafty at this game, or too shy to open the bidding, and I have more than once been shamed into asking the first question — sometimes the first two or three — simply in order to end an aching silence at the beginning of a press conference. It is a temptation to be resisted. (On the other hand waiting until the conference breaks up and waylaying the speaker as he walks out in the hope of getting the exclusive that could give you the front page lead has its own perils. He may wax indiscreet, but he may equally accuse you of cheating and turn on his heel — as Duncan Sandys once did to me when British Commonwealth Secretary).

There are nevertheless risks in letting the prima donnas of the press conference take the stage in the first place. They may so harass the man on the dais to show how adversarial they can be that he loses his temper and clams up. This can leave one nursing the question one has been carefully saving to the end precisely because it might otherwise lead to a premature explosion or a fit of sulks. In these circumstances, the solution is to ask it before it is too late. Even a question that is obviously going to earn a stony snub can still be worth putting for what they both reveal: 'Pressed for further news of the fate of sixteen workers rumoured to have been asphyxiated in a chemical warfare plant disaster at Pinsk, the Soviet spokesman said he had no comment.' (But no comment means no denial).

Compulsive interrogators may also ask questions that should never be asked after the speaker has — warily or unwarily — opened his mouth too wide. A reporter must be constantly on the lookout amid all the rhetorical mush he has to endure for the Freudian slip, the tell-tale verbal twitch, the missing word that aches like an amputated leg and may be the story beyond the story. Speaking in Jogjakarta as the guest of President Sukarno in 1960, for example, Nikita Khrushchev predictably praised the Indonesians in strip language correspondents already limp with long speeches could have written for themselves: '...heroic struggle for independence...thrown off the yoke of colonialism...the need for peace and coexistence...' But as eyelids drooped the Soviet Prime Minister added, 'Many socialist and other nations in Asia practise peace and coexistence, like India and Indonesia...'

We jerked awake. What about China? In fact, he would mention China only once, pairing her off with India in a somewhat sly reference to the importance of both — given that India was China's current enemy-of-the-month. Later that year I would be writing: 'October 1. Moscow sent no official delegation to attend the celebrations of the eleventh anniversary of the Chinese People's Republic in Peking today...in the immense Square of Heavenly Peace there was this year no portrait of the Soviet Premier...' The Sino-Soviet split — a split essentially over Khrushchev's policy of peaceful coexistence with the imperialists, which was anathema to the blood-and-thunder revolutionary Mao — was about to hit the front pages.

In 1963 Sihanouk ('If I talk like a madman, the press is also mad...') gave us a seemingly endless hour on why he hated the predatory Americans, who were forever trying to turn his country into an imperialist puppet, and loved his loyal friends the Chinese, who did not even want a communist Cambodia. But then he made it all worthwhile by adding four words: '*at least for now*'. In 1965 General Maxwell Taylor carefully unrolled the reasoning behind the American decision to bomb North Vietnam, which was everyone's story of the day. But while explaining that it was all the more necessary to curb Hanoi's support for the Vietcong because South Vietnam was incurably racked by political convulsions, he added that Washington was 'resigned to coups' in a shaky Saigon, for 'stability is too much to hope for'. Check. It had become a cockpit of rival generals. *But then what had happened to 'saving Vietnam and the world for democracy'*, which was what it was all supposed to be about? Why were the Americans there at all?

Such pearls call for a reverent silence while the conference holds its breath. For it requires only one fool to ask the wrong follow-up question, giving the speaker a second chance to backtrack or qualify or relegate to 'background' what he has — or has not — said, and that momentary glimpse of truth on the record will be gone. Unfortunately, there are ten fools for every Freudian slip.

In the sixties the reporter found himself fighting frustration in all its forms if, like mine, his targets on the rostrum ranged from LBJ to LKY. Two years after Maxwell Taylor's memorable quote, there was talk of a possible pause in the American bombing of North Vietnam, and President Lyndon Johnson called one of his (at that time) relatively rare White House press conferences. Lucky enough to be in Washington, and on the edge of my chair as he came on-stage to face his inquisitors, I was chagrined to find that I was to be a mere spectator at a set performance governed by stultifying conventions.

Under the House rules, no foreign correspondent was allowed to ask questions, the first of which — a dolly drop lobbed gently to the President by a prompter from the White House press corps — was nothing more than a prearranged cue to enable him to start saying what he had come to say ('Bombing pause? ...glad of a proposal that could lead to productive discussions or negotiations...United States anxious to meet representatives of the North Vietnamese government at any time to agree on some plan to settle their differences… would welcome any indication from North Vietnam for cease-fire negotiations or a pledge not to take advantage of the pause to kill more men…') The bombing intensified.

Where LBJ was tantalisingly canny, Lee Kuan Yew was tantalisingly candid after the race riots in Singapore in July 1964. Reviewing the tempestuous ten-month-old marriage between Malaya and Singapore which was already heading for a divorce, he said that he, too, would be glad of a proposal that could lead to productive discussions or negotiations, to meet representatives of the other side at any time to agree on some plan to settle their differences, etc. Of course. But 'they must decide if they want Malaysia or not', he went on. The riots were the work of Malay 'ultras' in the federal capital bent on discrediting him, destroying the (predominantly Chinese) government in Singapore, and imposing Malay supremacy over all other races in Malaysia. The extremist Syed Ja'afar Albar and the 'Malay National Action Committee' were behind the mischief, and had security been in the hands of Lee Kuan Yew, 'they would have been behind bars and smacked down in twenty-four hours'. But the federal government had done nothing, although were such people to be responsible for future racial harmony, there would be 'an arsonist in the fire brigade'.

If there was no change in the attitude of Kuala Lumpur, therefore, 'then Malaysia dies…What we are going to bring up (with them) is not just the security of Singapore, but whether Malaysia is to survive. We could secede at any time; there is no need for a constitutional basis.' But having proposed to throw into jail the secretary-general of the ruling party in Kuala Lumpur and postulated the break-up of the federation only ten months after its formation, Lee jerked the story from under us by putting all the best bits off the record. We were left with the threat of the Inspector-General of Police — at another press conference — to kick us out of the country if we had the temerity to echo Lee and tell it as it was.

I3 FOLLOW-MY-LEADER

A friendly voice said, 'Hello, Dennis, Miss Han is waiting for you outside with a car.'

THE prudent correspondent starts as a member of the mob and strikes out on his own only when he knows he can float — or flounder — unaided, and this is never more true than when he is one of a pack of reporters trailing after a peripatetic VIP on a visit to another country. The most sensible thing for him to do is to join the group at the point of departure, when his name will go down firmly on the manifest, he will be given a programme, and his visas and passes and accommodation and all the other potential hazards in this kind of obstacle race will be handled by the organisers of the package tour. All he then has to do is to turn up at the airport on time.

I was rarely to be found among the wise virgins myself because (apart from the two more obvious reasons) few VIP tours began in Singapore, and *The Observer* seemed to think it good for my soul if I was thrown into the fray only at the last moment, or even half way through the trip. Editors whom I took care to warn well ahead that one of these junkets was coming my way would preserve a thoughtful silence until two days before take-off, and then cable (as one did in 1960) something like

COULDST JOIN KRUSHCHEV INDONESIA
TOUR SOONEST FILING BACKGROUND FRIDAY
SPOTNEWS SATURDAY LUV NEWSED.

The consequence in that particular case was an exercise in split-second timing, with the timing in everyone's hands but my own. It was too late even to alert my tame bus driver in Jakarta to meet me at the airport, and I had to move fast, for Khrushchev would be out of the Indonesian capital within forty-eight hours of his arrival and off on a swing that would take him as far as Bali.

Armed with an Indonesian visa, I frightened a seat out of Garuda Airways in Singapore by taking the names of Sukarno and Khrushchev in vain, and after spending an uneasy night in James Wilde's pavilion in Jakarta, went straight to the official in charge of the press (a sympathetic woman whose favourite gesture was a sad shake of the head) to apply for accreditation to follow the Soviet Prime Minister around Indonesia. I was then told that I would have to pay all expenses in advance, depositing 250 pounds in rupiahs with the Presidential Cabinet Office before I started. I would also have to obtain two different press cards from two widely separated bureaux, and acquire a lapel badge, a brassard, three different ribbons, two official invitations, a press sticker for a car and a special cabling card, in exchange for all of which I must hand over fourteen passport photographs. It was precisely twenty-four hours to touchdown.

Suppressing otiose comment in the interests of good international relations, I first took a trishaw to the Chartered Bank, meandering through motionless traffic constipated by nervous police and troops who were already busy blocking off the route for the Khrushchev motorcade. At the bank I threw myself on the mercy of a compassionate manager, and crawled back to the Cabinet Office with the cash. I then set off again to fight my way around the town and through the forms that had to be filled out everywhere I went (Grandfather's date of birth? I kept a note of this purely fictitious detail in my diary in order to be consistent) on a day that alternated between blinding sunshine and blinding rain. But with the last piece of bureaucratic miscellanea stuffed safely into my damp pocket by the following morning. I staggered sweating on to the tarmac at the airport in time to watch an immaculate Khrushchev amble down the gangway of his Ilyushin turbo-prop, greet Sukarno like a long-lost debtor, and fire the Soviet Ambassador to Jakarta on the spot for mismanaging the arrangements. I could only applaud.

Some people never learn. Twenty years later a belated nod from London would send me off to catch up with the press group accompanying Big Jim Callaghan, the former British prime minister, who was already in Beijing and would be leaving two days later for a swing around China. This meant that within the next forty-eight hours I had to fly to Hong Kong, wheedle a visa out of the China Travel Service, take a train to Canton, and then try to catch a plane to the Chinese capital 1,000 miles to the north.

It was not, of course, as simple as that. The China Travel Service in Hong Kong had to refer my application to the authorities in Canton before they could give me a visa, and that normally took twenty-four hours. Furthermore: 'We can't book you on tomorrow's flight to Beijing,' said the bespectacled young woman behind the counter, shuffling papers and avoiding my eye, 'so we suggest you

go to Canton, pick up your visa there, and see if you can get on...'
'Don't do it!' hissed a small, agitated American standing behind me,
strangely moved by this helpful advice. 'Whatever you do, *don't do
it*! I've been had that way myself — spent nearly a week kicking my
heels in Canton.' He shook his head for a moment, remembering.
'*Boyoboyoboy*!' Alarmed, I raised my voice to make myself better
understood and began dropping names...British Prime Minister...
personal meeting with Chairman Hua Guofeng...absolutely
imperative...The China Travel Service promised to telephone Canton
about a seat on the plane, but...

But often when Nemesis stares you in the face, it is only to
remember you better next time. On the last occasion that I had —
to my astonishment — flown safely to Beijing (via Nanking), I had
found myself wedged immovably into a window seat of a palsied
Russian-built Antonov 24 workhorse. This fellow-hack looked as if it
belonged in a knacker's yard, roared and juddered like a pneumatic
drill even when stationery, and enveloped the passengers in an
inexplicable cloud of steam when it finally took off. Having risked
the train to Canton this time, however, I was not only handed my
passport on my arrival, duly stamped with a visa, but given a ticket
for the one direct flight of the week to Beijing on China's only
Boeing 747, which left on Mondays. And it was Monday.

Seated comfortably beside the octogenarian manager of a
Manchurian shoe factory, and munching my complimentary apple
as the People's Republic rolled smoothly beneath us, I was able to
confront my next question mark. What would happen when we
arrived? It would be about midnight, no one knew I was coming
on that flight, there would be no one to meet me, no transport into
the city, and no bed even if I got there. The scenario grew on me as I

stood beside the baggage carousel in Beijing airport waiting to see if my suitcase had been loaded at Canton: I would be alone in the dark, deserted streets of a dead communist capital with my solitary bag (if I was lucky) in a puddle beside me…But my number came up, the roulette wheel delivered my luggage, and a friendly voice said, 'Hello, Dennis, Miss Han is waiting for you outside with a car.'

The voice belonged to a third secretary of the British Embassy, and Miss Han, who specialised in foreign correspondents, was a delightful government cadre with whom I had quarrelled violently over a hotel bill on my last visit the year before. 'You will never get another visa to China,' she had barked at me, her eyes narrowing — yes — to slits.

'Please get in,' she said now, smiling and shaking hands and nodding towards a handsome limousine with a uniformed driver. 'You are booked into a room at the Min Zu, next to David Bonavia. He is waiting up for you.' David Bonavia of *The Times* was of Callaghan's press party, and he was standing in the doorway of his room with a bottle of whisky in his hand as I walked down the corridor to mine. I was home and suddenly very dry.

All may be well that ends well, but I had missed the first two days of Callaghan's visit to Beijing and there was only one to go. I had paid with news and nerves for being the maverick that had not moved with the herd. But the time to leave the herd does come. During the visit of Khrushchev to Indonesia twenty years before it had come after we had conscientiously trailed the Russian Prime Minister to three of Sukarno's palaces, driving past ragged lines of regimented schoolchildren waving paper Soviet and Indonesian flags, and Javanese peasants who clapped with circumspection, as if afraid to damage their calloused hands. We had seen Khrushchev bored in

Bogor, and had been bored by him in Bandung ('famous city of the Afro-Asian Conference…ideals in common…time of colonialists is past…their turn to be buried…'), and when he took off for Jogjakarta by air, two American correspondents and I decided to take off by road.

Journalists covering a VIP on a tour of a foreign land too easily fall into the trap of treating it as a visit to a vacuum. Like cops chasing a robber through the Louvre, they are too intent on their quarry to see what drew him there in the first instance. The story is not just the personality; it is the personality plus the place. But a reporter clinging to the coat-tails of a VIP will see only what his host wants the VIP to see — 'the best bits', as Prince Charles once put it half-ruefully. What Sukarno gave the often listless, perspiring, and short-tempered Khrushchev was a round of cultural rubbernecking that took in palaces and temples, botanical gardens and Balinese dancing, and became ever more mystifying and meaningless — especially to the dutifully enchanted populace, many of whom had no idea who he was.

Instead of flying direct to Jogjakarta to be there when the Russian arrived, therefore, we hired an ageing Chevrolet with an incontinent radiator that could have been a stand-in for the Last Car To Goa. Coughing self-deprecatingly, it took us to Semarang and Surabaya over 250 miles of decomposing road, through glum villages whose impoverished peasants moonlit as muggers when occasion offered, and past fields listlessly cropped by a few gaunt, tired beasts. This, as I wrote before we drove on to Jogjakarta, was the Indonesia Sukarno would not be showing to Khrushchev, any more than he would show a visitor the squalid shacktowns of Jakarta, and the rest of the republic's wretched reward for a decade of corruption, inefficiency, extravagance, and presidential megalomania. Here was a corner of the jigsaw that was the answer to the question every reporter must ask himself when tracking a VIP on the move. Why had he come? — *asked to come*, so the Indonesians said. Why Indonesia? And why now?

The fraternal quarrel between Beijing and Moscow, kept within the family for the past two years, was about to burst into the open. The revolutionary Maoists in China were outraged by the 'revisionist' Khrushchev, who had denounced Stalin himself, peddled the heresy that war with the capitalist world was not inevitable, and hobnobbed with the arch-imperialist Eisenhower on his home ground. On his side, it seems. Nikita Khrushchev was angrily derisive of Chairman Mao's rash attempts to take short cuts to the ultimate socialist paradise through his catastrophic Great Leap Forward and the formation of people's communes. He was also vexed by the ugly image of international communism created by the sectarian masters of the People's Republic in Beijing, whose follies at home and fire-breathing abroad could fatally discredit it, particularly in China's sphere of influence — Asia.

Accordingly, Khrushchev was visiting India and Indonesia and making a stop-over in Burma to show Asians the acceptable face of communism. He posed as the champion of peaceful coexistence between nations of all political creeds, a godfather bearing gifts of industrial aid and economic assistance whose concern was not war but the wealth of the people. His object was to carry Russian influence into a continent dominated by the Americans and the Chinese, and Indonesia offered a natural opening. Relations between Jakarta and Beijing were already strained over the status of local Chinese: it was only a few months since Subandrio had made the humiliating pilgrimage to China that had given me a minor scoop. President Eisenhower was touring the region, but had cancelled his call on Jakarta. Khrushchev stepped into his shoes, bent on winning

Asian support for his side at the forthcoming summit conference of the big powers. But those were not the only reasons he was in the right place at the right time.

Sukarno was not content to play the swelling bullfrog in his own pond, even after he had renamed the pond 'the Indonesian Ocean'. He was, he believed, destined to lead the 'new emerging forces' of the underdog continents against the 'old established forces' of the West, and within five years would plan to set up his own rival United Nations with a grandiose headquarters in Jakarta. This would be the latest of the prestige projects which the peasants could not eat, but on which he had already squandered hundreds of millions of unearned dollars.

As Khrushchev must have seen it in 1960, Sukarno was broke, he needed money and guns and know-how to realise his dreams, and he was showing signs of angling for the role of charismatic messiah of the Third World. It could prove a winning combination — for Khrushchev. Sukarno could be the stalking horse that brought the underdeveloped countries into line with the socialist camp in 'peaceful competition' with the capitalists, whose industries depended on their natural resources. He was up for sale, and if he showed unwonted reluctance to put himself in hock to Moscow, the PKI — the biggest communist party outside the Soviet bloc — was on hand in Jakarta to whisper (or shout) in his left ear.

Given this script, Khrushchev's speeches fell into place as he flew east across Indonesia: 'The Soviet people respect the struggle for independence of other nations, for the Soviets have themselves struggled against the imperialists; because of this the USSR is openheartedly prepared to extend to the countries in the East not only moral or political support, but material support which will grow every year…' Nor were these empty promises. Within five years Jakarta would owe Moscow more than a billion dollars, much of it thrown away on the purchase of second-hand MiG fighters and a clutch of obsolescent Soviet warships, and there would be even less money in the till than before. We had been in at the beginning. But we had had to drive through Java, past the rural slums and the wasted cattle, to see the roots of the tragedy.

I caught up with Eisenhower in June, when at the last moment *The Observer* sent me skittering across the Far East to cover his weekend visit to Taipei, and I saw coat-tail reporters at their most myopic. Most of the White House corps of correspondents accompanying him behaved exactly as if they were still in the White House, dividing their time between the President, his entourage, and his spokesman. They were interested only in Taiwan on paper, and their questions about 'ChiNats' and 'ChiComs' at the main briefing reduced 600,000,000-odd Chinese to the stature of opposing pawns on a chessboard. They would have had to go no further than the National Historical Museum to see revealed in the cultural artifacts of a civilisation 4,000 years old the tremendous human phenomenon they were talking about so casually. But that was not on Ike's schedule.

For this was an age of ignorance, in which the West reduced the subtle, sometimes obscene political arabesques of the East to a rough and misleading shorthand. 'Pro-American' autocrats ruled in Asian countries that were naively called 'free' — Syngman Rhee in South Korea, Ngo Dinh Diem in South Vietnam, Sarit Thanarat in Thailand, Chiang Kai-shek in Taiwan itself. Upper case 'Nationalists' fighting to keep despots in power were 'anti-communist', lower case 'nationalists' fighting for freedom or democracy were 'pro-communist', and 'SEATO', the great Southeast Asia Treaty Organisation, had yet to be exposed as a cliffhanging nest of evanescent paper hawks. The hostility of the Taiwanese towards the ageing rump of a Chinese government that had parked itself on their island when Mao chased Chiang from the mainland in 1949, and the brutalities of the police state designed to keep them cowed, were simply ignored by the visitors. So was the heterogeneous opposition group that had prepared a petition for the American President, but got nowhere near him. He was far too fleeting a target.

Keeping up with Khrushchev and Eisenhower was nevertheless a stroll compared with keeping up with Prince Philip when he toured North Borneo the year before, for the Queen's Consort personally piloted his Heron aircraft from point to point in his own time on a tight schedule of town-hopping that took him from Kuching at one end of the island to Sandakan at the other. For the press gang, this meant a series of scrambled departures starting at five each morning to get to the next stop ahead of the Duke, and then a dash for cars to follow him in the motorcade from the airport to the next ceremony or reception when he arrived.

One was tempted to stay close to Philip in the hope that he would drop one of his more memorable bricks, or at least treat the press to the tart side of his tongue. (Off form, he only managed to fall asleep between the two Dyak chiefs who were his hosts during a performance of native dancing, after yelling with laughter when an erratic 'buzz bomb' beetle for which he could not claim responsibility threw the assembled journalists into disarray). Wherever he went, moreover, he was in the thick of the people — not only the Malays and the Chinese, but the native Dyaks, Ibans, Dusuns. Muruts, and Bajaus dressed in their best, a jangling mass of bangles and beads and silver medallions, hornbill plumes and dusky tits and intricately tattooed bottoms that were good copy in themselves. But when I and a French correspondent decided at two in the morning in a stifling bungalow in Sarawak that we would take to the road on our own instead of flying the next leg to neighbouring Brunei, we discovered there was still a story behind the story.

As our hired American jalopy lurched down the laterite track through a night shrill with cicadas, the screen of jungle trees on either side suddenly gave way to a dead forest of silent oil rigs, their silhouettes like mourners in a graveyard. But the moment we crossed the border from Sarawak into Brunei, the track became a smooth highway and the flares of the bonanza oilfield at Seria lit the skyline. Nature had played a cruel prank on Sarawak, for it had been a British official from the crown colony, walking along the beach just over the boundary in the run-down and shrunken Sultanate of Brunei some forty years before, who had sniffed the air and said, "I smell oil.' Since then output in Sarawak itself had dwindled towards zero, while by 1959 Brunei was already producing more than three million barrels a month. Sarawak had remained primitive and poor, its dirt roads matching its derelict rigs, while in Brunei the Sultan had just built a marble mosque and covered the dome with gold leaf. The oilfield stopped at the border, and it must have seemed to him like poetic justice. His powerful forebears had ruled the entire territory from coast to coast, before their domain had been whittled down progressively until it was no more than a tiny protectorate jammed between the two sprawling colonies of Sarawak and British North Borneo. But the tiny protectorate was precisely where the oil was, and now he had the last laugh.

And he was to continue to laugh. The oil at Seria would be exhausted in turn in thirty years, it was calculated, and as the free-spending Sultan seemed to regard it as an inexhaustible pot of black gold, his British protectors became fidgety. 'I keep warning him that it will run out and he must diversify his economy,' the exasperated Deputy High Commissioner to Brunei told me some four years later. 'But all he says is, "Don't worry, Angus, Allah will provide".' And, of course, Allah did. Thanks to off-shore drilling, Brunei produced 130,000 barrels a day and 900 million cubic feet of natural gas in 1985, and exports were worth more than three billion US dollars. This was the key to the future of North Borneo, where the two great British colonies — economically puny on their own — were obliged to join the Federation of Malaysia, but diminutive Brunei would become an independent member of ASEAN, and its Sultan would be named by *Fortune* magazine the richest man in the world.

14 BREAKING RANKS

We plunged into a tumultous ocean of eager, friendly Chinese youth.

THE argument for sticking close to a blue-blooded VIP was equally strong when the Duke of Kent flew to Beijing in 1979 to open an energy exhibition, for the almost dreamlike incongruity of this first encounter between British royalty and Chinese revolution was going to be good copy in itself. Not immediately, however. We did not toil up from Canton in a sweating proletarian Antonov 24, but took off from Hong Kong in an RAF VC-10 of the Queen's Flight to slide serenely over China on a diet of smoked salmon sandwiches and dry white wine. But once on the ground the impact was immediate. The long black Chinese limousine that was to carry the Duke behind closed curtains from Beijing to the city was called a Red Flag, but now a banner with a strange device was dangling improbably from its mast — the Royal Standard.

The sense of illusion deepened when the Duke exchanged phrase-book banalities with a burly Chairman Hua Guofeng dressed in a buttoned-up Mao suit in the Great Mall of the People ('Is this your first visit to China?' — pause for thought — 'Yes'); when he inspected the Dragon Throne in the Forbidden City with the expert eye of the insider; when his VC-10 taxied grandly down the tarmac at Hangzhou and past a smart line-up of Chinese air force MiGs as if reviewing a guard of honour. 'Tell me,' one fascinated cadre asked. 'How many years are your dukes appointed for?' A good question — and a reminder that the Duke's visit was a pretext not for covering the Duke, but for covering China, a country whose exotic politics were not only the ninth wonder of the world, but for many years had made it difficult for foreign correspondents to get into it at all.

Chairman Mao had set out in 1958 to 'overtake Britain in fifteen years' with a Great Leap Forward in agriculture and industry that overheated both until they seized up, and to that end had compelled hundreds of millions of people — peasants, soldiers, doctors, factory hands — to drop whatever they were doing in order to forge 'back yard steel' (which for the most part came out as poor quality pig iron). He had also set out to overtake the Soviet Union ideologically and in far less time by converting his gigantic fief into the first true communist state — a selfless, classless society organised as a patchwork of people's communes within which, ideally, the individual would own nothing, and all men would labour in disciplined production brigades for the good of the collective.

This crash course in regimented egalitarianism led to three years of near-famine and, one way or another, killed off more than sixteen million starving, sick or seditious Chinese (the figures were constantly being revised upwards). But the Chairman was not without his detractors. A distinguished marshal named Peng Dehuai was pitched into political limbo in 1959 after delivering a scathing commentary on Mao's policies, and mounting opposition among other leading revolutionaries finally goaded him into launching the Great Proletarian Cultural Revolution against his own Communist Party. That Chinese holocaust reduced the republic to a state of confusion approaching anarchy, as rival factions of young Red Guards and Maoist 'revolutionary rebel' workers rampaged through the land on an iconoclastic spree of unprecedented magnitude to 'smash the old world' and destroy the existing structure of party and state. Meanwhile, in the sacred name of Mao, the left-wing Gang of Four wreaked vengeance on the sane for their sanity in a gigantic witch-hunt that killed or ruined millions more.

In 1976 the senile Chairman died, and four years later his heir and successor, the ambivalent Hua Guofeng, was eclipsed by the thrusting arch-reformer, Deng Xiaoping. The madness abated. Mao's hardheaded critics began picking over the rubble of the recent past, and putting together another kind of China by fitting capitalist patterns into the communist framework. The days of full employment and the 'iron rice bowl' (whereby each was rewarded not 'according to his labour' but irrespective of it) were numbered. The communes were abolished, peasants worked the fields for profit, making money was no longer a vice but a virtue, private enterprise was respectable. Men could start their own businesses, even employ their own staff, and factory managers could sign their own contracts and share the take with the workers. As the Mosaic law of the market place took over, China moved inexorably towards becoming a consumer society under a system euphemistically described as 'socialism with Chinese characteristics' (among which, of course, is a quick eye for a quick buck). Chinese Marxists might be squaring the ideological circle, but the result was that Chinese communism began to burst at the seams.

Much of the change was still to come, but the Duke of Kent's visit gave me my first view of the brave new China of the pragmatists, and no rigid programme designed for royalty could be allowed to obscure it. While he covered the Great Wall, the Forbidden City, and the rest of the tourist traps in Beijing and other cities, I escaped on foot to the 'Democracy Wall', to streets where money changed hands fast, a family-owned mobile canteen might be doing a brisk trade in doughnuts, one-man 'cooperatives' were busy working for cash — a sidewalk tailor cutting out a suit, a carpenter knocking up a wardrobe — and rival hawkers peddled songbirds in elaborate cages.

Political diatribes had been banished from the Democracy Wall, but the heady sense of a new freedom — even if it was only a lengthening of the leash — had bred a healthy discontent: the wall was now thick with posters pasted up by soldiers complaining that they were not given plum jobs when demobilised, ana resentful families transplanted from their traditional *hutung* courtyard homes to high-rise blocks in the suburbs. In the big department stores Chinese crowded around displays of the latest necessities of life — Swiss watches, Japanese calculators, transistor radios and television sets. In the bookshops the shelves filled with predictably uniform ranks of Mao's *Selected Works* were ignored, while the young jostled each other at the counters where Chinese translations of everything from Jane Austen to a home course in electronics was being sold.

On a Sunday night in Shanghai we abandoned our press bus on the Bund, and were at once plunged into a tumultuous ocean of eager, friendly Chinese youth that isolated and then engulfed each one of us — smiling, questioning, sometimes airing astonishingly idiomatic English painstakingly learned from the BBC or the Voice of America ('You flatter me,' said a young artisan as to the manner born when I complimented him on his). There was an unmistakable plea for contact, a thirst for information from the West —'we want to learn from you'. We were drowning in a human sea, but it was they who were calling for help.

Most Chinese appeared to be turning from Mao to Mammon with a sigh of relief. Girls were sporting perms and paint and powder, wearing coloured blouses or jackets, well-fitting pants or the odd flowered skirt. There was colour TV in my hotel, and black-and-white in many homes, and in the cinemas *Limelight* and *Jane Eyre* were playing to packed houses. People elbowed each other around a shop window displaying fancy bras and bags, while a fat middle-aged man in dark glasses leaned against the wall, sucking a lemon lollipop. The mood was tangible. Across Nanking Road, billboards advertised Hennessy brandy, Marlboro cigarettes, and a popular 'Recovery of Youth' tablet for those limp with years. It seemed to symbolise the cultural counter-revolution. When a casual stroller fell into conversation, and went on to tell me he was 'fed up with Mao and his *Thoughts*', it was I who glanced around to see if anyone was listening.

But China — the China the Duke was not to see any more than Khrushchev had seen the real Indonesia — was still painfully poor. The Chinese might gaze hungrily at displays of the good things of life, but for the most part they were still a nation of window-shoppers. One person in ten did not have enough to eat. Dysentery was common, and there were rows of latrines in back streets where the plumbing in old houses had broken down. At least ten million young people were joining the queue for jobs every year. In Beijing the market stallholders were selling only apples, peanuts, and a few wilting vegetables. In Shanghai old men defiantly set up tables under the street lamps to play a late late hand with decks of dog-eared cards because their homes were too ill-lit.

The Duke was not to be shunned as a decoy from reality, however. He visited factories and farms at which a reporter with his eye on the people and not the prince could learn much in a situation where he had much to learn. Quick takes flash through the mind. Outside the Shanghai Machine Tool Plant an elderly worker is arc-welding without a mask, and the safety standards inside would make Sheffield blench. At the docks loads of scrap iron, swinging high from antique cranes in nets of frayed, rusty steel cable, drop with a crash into buckled hoppers. In the Shanghai Carpet Factory I ask a nimble-fingered weaver how much she earns: she would have to save her entire salary for four years to buy the rug she is making.

The Chinese were nevertheless on the road to tomorrow, and not too particular how they got there. They had been told to 'make use of the latest technologies from abroad' — but with the aim of 'improving our ability to do things by ourselves; we don't want new foreign machines, but new foreign blueprints so that we can make our own', a managerial cadre told me. And we could see this copycat principle in action at the British Energy Exhibition, which began to look more like a mass operation in brain-picking than buying as the first waves of 200,000 'interested' cadres besieged the 700-odd stands, and whipped away every scrap of printed matter they found because it might yield technical information (including an invoice one unwary exhibitor had left on his counter). We were, as they say, witnessing the beginning of an era.

****

I found it more difficult to know how to divide my time between visitor and visited when I toured China ten months later with Jim Callaghan. The Duke was bland and affable but intrinsically a non-story, whereas sticking to Callaghan — big, genial, quick-witted and quicker-tempered — yielded copy of its own. The rewards came fast. While Chairman Hua Guofeng kept the former British prime minister waiting in the Great Hall of the People in Beijing, we could see the temperature rising to flashpoint in the round red face as he paced to and fro, and when Hua finally appeared, Callaghan greeted him with an explosive 'At last!' — which he converted from insult to compliment just in time by adding nimbly, 'At last we meet!' (or words to that effect).

But Hua impressed him. The Chairman had exuded the confidence of a man who had things under control, he told us in the anteroom after they had talked. What did we think? I said I believed the pragmatists in the Politburo put up with this relative newcomer, whose dubious reference was that a dying Mao had appointed him his heir, mainly because they had him cornered anyway; but he would not last long. 'Something like my position, you mean?' shot back Callaghan, who was even then being eased out of the Labour Party leadership. He had a nice sense of humour, at least in the old-fashioned meaning of the adjective. A few days later we were snaking through the Yangtse Gorges on a ferry whose short flagstaff at the bow acted like the foresight of a rifle, enabling the pilot to guide her through the (then) treacherous narrows. Up on deck with Callaghan, I pointed to the sheer face of rock hundreds of feet above us and said, 'How would you feel if you were clinging to that with your fingers and toes, and no help in sight?'

'Well,' he replied, 'I'd say that I'd had a good run for my money, and mustn't complain if this was the end of it all.' 'Can I quote you out of context?' I asked swiftly, thinking of his coming political fade-out — and he laughed as if he meant it.

He could be the victim of his own trigger-happy tongue, but then so could others. Just a few minutes later he asked me if Lee Kuan Yew had mellowed as he grew older. I said I thought so, but I had hardly seen him since I attended a banquet he had given for Harold Wilson, who had been Callaghan's predecessor as Labour prime minister.

'Lee gave Harold a *banquet*?"

'Well, a formal dinner; he felt indebted to him.' (A warning from Wilson to the Tunku had reputedly saved Lee from arrest when Singapore was cut out of Malaysia in 1965).

'Sounds to me,' said Callaghan, 'as if he was not only mellow, but *senile.*'

But if Callaghan was good human copy at that moment, so was China. The ferry was alive with cadres and soldiers and a mixed mass of other comrades, leaning over the rails to spit, chatting idly, playing cards, arguing and laughing and eating their way through the incessant blare of the loudspeakers. Outwardly, all seemed normal. But their inattention was a story in itself. The loudspeakers were relaying a special radio broadcast from Beijing of a solemn memorial service being held for that great party hero, the late President Liu Shaoqi, who had been done to death by the infamous Gang of Four in 1969, but was now being honoured by the new masters of China. And no one — so it seemed — gave a damn.

Certainly not Callaghan. Callaghan could afford to go through China without knowing the significance of what he was looking at, and even crack the wrong jokes — 'Pity you weren't all Christians; it would have saved a lot of trouble,' he remarked to his dumbfounded hosts while staring blankly at an ancient Confucian stele in Xian. But the more the correspondent has the feel of the place and the people, the better his copy. Without it he, too, would miss the inner meaning of the very ordinariness of the scene on the ferry, just as he would miss the inner meaning of Xian itself. He might be told that this dusty provincial town was once the magnificent capital of China at the beginning of the Silk Road, that it had played Byzantium to Beijing's Ankara. But if he did not have the background info which to absorb names and dates and facts as a guide reeled them off, they would be as incomprehensible as the isolated pieces of any jigsaw puzzle. And so, if the reporter was an ignoramus, would all China.

In an art institute in Shanghai, Audrey Callaghan glanced for a moment at an indifferent oil painting of a soldier pointing sadly at what looked like a grounded missile. 'The work of a student,' the curator explained. 'We have had it for some time, but could only hang it recently.' She nodded politely and passed on. She was not to know that the failed 'satellite' symbolised the unnerving revolutionary schemes of Mao Zedong which had so futilely defied the laws of gravity, and that the contemplative soldier was Marshal Peng Dehuai, who had fallen into disgrace for criticising the Chairman twenty-one years before. Now — so the painting told me — the 'renegade' marshal was being rehabilitated and his criticisms upheld, as Mao and Maoism sank slowly into discredit in their turn. The ideological seesaw that had been mesmerising Chinawatchers for thirty years was still in motion.

I visited the institute that afternoon because almost no one else wanted to. On a VIP tour the press is sometimes offered a choice of programmes, and if that happened I would wait to see where the main pack was going, and then opt for the alternative. When the group accompanying the British Foreign Secretary, Sir Alec Douglas-Home, chose a Shanghai shipyard one afternoon in 1972, for example, I went off to an electrical machine plant with one other journalist. As he was the industrial editor of a Birmingham newspaper, and I could wrap my ignorance in a few rags of knowledge picked up in my Peckham workshop days, we were able actually to see what we were looking at for once. In consequence, we winkled out of the slightly surprised cadres a sharp story of obsolete machinery (twenty years behind the times and turning out more of the same), export rejects, rigged bonus schemes, and take-it-or-leave-it safety measures (no guard even on a guillotine, until someone shouted a warning that we were coming).

And we had it to ourselves — almost. To cover the programme we had missed, I had promised to swap notes with a colleague I was not competing with. He would give me the shipyard; I would give him the electrical works. For if the reporter must enjoy the confidence of diplomats, soldiers, bureaucrats and statesmen to get one jump ahead of the mob, he must above all win the trust of the mob itself, of which he is a paid-up card-carrying member.

I5 LADIES AND GENTLEMAN

I made the mistake of scorning a hired launch that I would have had to share with a dozen other members of the mob.

AS IVANSONG said, the reporter in the field has nothing faintly resembling the pillow-breasted nanny of an organisation that every soldier can count on. Paradoxically, therefore, he must rely heavily on his own rivals for help if he is to be a successful loner. Journalists who respect one another normally work as a fraternity in which each watches the other out of the corner of his eye to see not only that he does not get ahead, but often that he does not fall behind either. Theirs is an unwritten do-as-you-would-be-done-by contract, and if I used the mob, I made sure I let the mob use me.

The perennial problem of the foreign correspondent is that he cannot turn his ears and eyes in all directions simultaneously twenty-four hours of the day. Before I flew off anywhere I would cover my back by arranging with Reuters that, wherever I went, their local bureau would let me see their daily files and (if they had the means) transmit my copy to London. That removed the itch between my shoulder blades. I would also book myself into a hotel favoured by the foreign press to make sure that if I was asleep, or ignorant of a sudden newsbreak, someone would bang on my door — as I would bang on theirs.

There was the odd thief who would not bang, of course; who would fail to pass on the news of a press conference, refuse to wait and share his taxi, or decline to translate for a colleague who did not speak the vernacular, on the grounds that he did not have time; who would hug his notes to himself, yet take sneak previews at the copy of rivals as they bashed it out in hotel lobbies or crowded press rooms, and then bribe a post office cable clerk to put his takes on top of the pile awaiting transmission. Challenged, he would plead that in the race for the story his first loyalty was to his paper (or editor, or readers). But this was empty hypocrisy, for when angry colleagues cut the delinquent out of the club and left him to slumber through the next coup d'état, his paper would be the first not to know. The same held true for the snob on the broadsheet who wrinkled his nose at the slave on the tabloid, as if he stank of semi-literate libel and split infinitives. Some of the best and most dedicated reporters write for the popular press, whereas I have known a cheat working for a British 'heavy' in Southeast Asia whose copy I would trust no further than I could spit his baseless insinuations.

Yes, 'he'. There is an evil theory that women reporters are more prone to cut corners to keep up with the men. But while some can be ruthless, and many pushy, most are simply more energetic. They also tend to display the fierce maternal instinct towards the story they have just acquired (or the copy to which they have just given birth) that prompted Kipling to claim that the female of the species was more deadly than the male. It was nevertheless a woman correspondent of *The Observer*, Flora Lewis, who gave me my first break in Paris by passing the Indochina coverage over to me, and a second, Nora Beloff, who widened the scope of my work enough for me to be offered the paper's Middle East slot by 1952. And as a mere male in the field I could feel nothing but a slightly apprehensive respect for the professional acumen of these unstoppable ladies, for the accurate yet vivid writing of reporters like Ann Leslie of the *Daily Mail*, and the unrivalled courage and expertise of Clare Hollingworth of the London *Daily Telegraph*, for long the only woman defence correspondent in Fleet Street.

At the height of confused and bloody fighting over the birth of Bangladesh, the diminutive Ms Hollingworth confronted the frightened members of an entire Japanese television team who were on the point of fleeing Dacca and stopped them dead with a magisterial, 'Where do you think *you're* going? The story's *here*.' After the Pakistani headquarters had been heavily bombed and abandoned, she coolly climbed the half-wrecked staircase that led to the deserted office of Major-General Farman Ali Khan, noted with disappointment the clean blotter on his otherwise empty desk-top, but pocketed as a souvenir a routine paper which he had evidently discarded as unimportant. Neither could know how important to him it might later prove. When the advancing Indians occupied Dacca, vengeful Bengalis claimed they had found a damning list of locals to be summarily executed lying on the general's desk. But this miserable attempt to frame him collapsed when Clare declared emphatically that there had been nothing of consequence on it when he left his office, and produced the document she herself had taken to prove she had been there.

One has heard lurid talcs of rapacious sirens in the business, but I have to admit that no dedicated red-nailed reporter, ready to make the supreme sacrifice in the service of her paper, has got at me to get at my copy (though whether I should feel slighted or flattered depends on how you read that). The best journalists are simultaneously tough and tender, like certain crabs, and the cynical carapace of some women correspondents has often been acquired to protect the sensitive tissue beneath. At times the hard and soft may complement each other. Estelle Holt was for long obliged to live in a Laotian hotel of shame, but acted as fond auntie and adviser to all the girls, who in turn told her hilarious stories about the bed manners of their customers, including political and diplomatic figures then downstage in Vientiane. This neatly satisfied her feminine instincts for both compassion and copy — even copy she could not write.

But I have seen them jar. In 1955 Lois Mitchison, then correspondent of the *Manchester Guardian* in Saigon, was eager to acquire local colour by visiting the Bull Ring, the vast bordello run by the Binh Xuyen mafia which took the form of a hutted camp and was said to boast a thousand whores recruited from all over the Far East. Solicitous for her safety in Saigon's most notorious cathouse, three of us quickly volunteered to escort her. But the experience might have proved less harrowing had she gone alone.

While we sat drinking and eyeing the girls, one of our number succumbed to his masculine frailty (despite his professional carapace) and decided to explore the amenities further. Borrowing 150 piastres and leaving us to our glasses, he snapped his fingers at a smallish

Cambodian miss he had selected from the array of talent around us, and disappeared into a cubicle for a while before rejoining us at our table a beer or two later. Lois was shocked into silence until we were back in the Hotel Continental, when she burst into tears. 'She couldn't have been more than sixteen,' she explained, between sobs. 'And he was away twenty minutes. *Twenty minutes!*' She had counted them, like a good pro. But — twenty minutes? I never discovered whether she thought that a distressingly long time, or a deplorably short one.

Women have also been accused of poaching on the beats of other reporters from their own paper, but all the poachers I have known have been men — like the Indian correspondent of *The Observer* who slipped into Singapore in 1976, wrote a censorious piece about the tough 'cold turkey' treatment given to drug addicts in the republic, and then slipped out again to leave me to live with it. (When taxed, he endeared himself further to me by saying 'he didn't know I actually worked for the paper': I had by then been its chief Far East correspondent — based on Singapore — for exactly twenty years).

On the other hand, the only journalist who came close to accusing me of poaching was a woman correspondent of *The Observer* in New York, whom I failed to warn that I was going to interview the Secretary-General of the United Nations while there. It was 1967. A week later President Johnson would be saying in Washington. 'Bombing pause? …glad of a proposal that could lead to productive discussions or negotiations…' But Hanoi had already inverted this order of events by telling Secretary-General U Thant (who then told me),'We are ready to negotiate, once there is a pause in the bombing.' Our talk was thus about Vietnam, not the UN, and the UN was not New York. However, I should have told our resident correspondent as a matter of courtesy, and when she asked for a transcript of my notes, I sent her a copy.

The canny do not cheat, whatever their sex. The correspondent who will brief a newcomer, warn him of the local hazards, and tell him who is worth seeing and who not, will soon know the form, the hazards, and whom best to see when he himself comes back after a long absence, or is a newcomer in his turn somewhere else. If he will act as pigeon and carry copy for others when leaving Laos, give them a lift when they are waving futilely at taxis in mid-Jakarta, tip them off to a coup in Bangkok, read them his notes on an interview in Taipei, share the BBC News on his transistor radio in Phnom Penh, and swap ideas and whisky and commiseration over the iniquities of sub-editors everywhere in the world, he will be repaid in kind and serve his paper better.

There are, of course, limits to this insider trading. A reporter keeps a legitimate scoop to himself, and he is a fool twice over if he even hints at it to a colleague in the fast lane — as I did the day I pointed a BBC correspondent at a Lee Kuan Yew exploding over the perfidy of the British. For a quarter of a century my immediate rival in the Far East was Richard Hughes, the expandable Australian correspondent of the London *Sunday Times* whose only euphemism was to call vodka 'Russian water'. He was like a lot of heavy men, nimble and cunning on his feet in his earlier days, but he always played straight, so much so that I once told him I felt guilty because I had scooped him on his home ground and not tipped him off (it could have happened only once). He was aghast. What was I talking about? All was fair in love, war, and scribbling, wasn't it, Your Grace? He was the professional, straightening out the fatuous amateur.

Dick Hughes was a chivalrous adversary, and more often an ally than an opponent. If we were both filing on a Saturday from Hong Kong to our respective London Sunday newspapers, we would go out and check the news together until late at night, however much our deadlines clashed. If I was caught by a typhoon in the wrong place or had simply succumbed to flu, moreover, I would telephone Dick and he would file for me — on at least one occasion he wrote the story himself and wired it to *The Observer* when he sent his own copy to London.

Wherever we ran into each other, as we inevitably did — in Indochina or Malaysia or Thailand or Taiwan — my fear of this formidable competitor who suddenly darkened the skyline, bellowing imprecations against conniving Poms, was swamped by the pleasure of seeing the familiar figure in the sand-coloured or blue safari suit. His professionalism never obscured his generosity of spirit, his innate sense of decency and the done thing. He had a very cold eye for meanness in any form, and would speak up loudly and at once whenever his feeling for truth or justice was affronted. But he was also blessed with a sharp, sly sense of humour, and was a master of impish asides craftily compounded of warm human understanding and detached malice. No one looked the other way when Hughes needed a lift, or left his name off the list when correspondents were clubbing together to hire a bus or a plane to reach a difficult target, or to pay a pigeon to carry out their combined copy.

And however much one wanted to cut one's own groove, it did not always pay to dodge that kind of group operation in the hope of outflanking the competition, as I learned in January 1974. When the faint, female, slightly asthmatic and embarrassingly distant Voice of America in Washington asked me to cover the terrorist attack on the

Shell oil refinery in Singapore, my first problem was transport. Having bungled the sabotage and done only a paltry ten thousand pounds' worth of damage, the four guerrillas — two Japanese and two Arabs — had hijacked a ferry boat called the *Laju* with five hostages aboard (two of whom promptly escaped), and were threatening to blow it up in the middle of the crowded sea camp of Singapore harbour if their terms for a flight to freedom were not met. Somehow I had to get to that square, squat box of a ferry, which lay like a time-bomb among more than a hundred cargo vessels but was cordoned off at a respectful distance by a dozen police launches and patrol boats. And it was then that I made the mistake of scorning a hired launch that I would have had to share with a dozen other members of the mob.

Instead, I telephoned Peter Simms, then of *Time* magazine and a seasoned sailor, and he in his warm and impulsive way at once offered to take me with him to the *Laju* in his outboard. He also proposed, however, to take a case of booze and a boxer bitch called Diggey to cover the story, and with a sinking heart I began to suspect that I was drifting into a sequel to *Three men in a boat* (less one of the crew). I consoled myself with the thought that as I knew nothing about outboards, I would perforce be left to drape myself negligently against the gunwale while Simms did the driving. But as we set off, he thrust me unceremoniously behind the wheel, making some trivial excuse about having to fill the petrol tank, and laughing away my urgent protests of ignorance ('very simple; just this button here for starting and that gear lever'). And as I gingerly fingered the inadequate controls (*no brakes?*), the boxer made things no easier for me by taking up a stance on the small foredeck with her head pointing eagerly forward and her naked bottom (a bitch with a discreet brush instead of a short and unattractive stump of tail would have been less disconcerting) fewer than five inches from my nose.

Not to lose face altogether, I slammed the lever out of neutral and we set off with an intimidating roar, whereupon Simms thrust an ice-cold glass at me from behind, and before I knew just what was involved in going to sea with one man and a dog, I found myself skimming over the ocean clutching the wheel in one hand and a gin and tonic in the other while peering around the backside of the bitch to see where I was going. In no time at all we were hemmed in by coral and the outboard had sheered a pin. And when we at last spotted the *Laju*, wallowing in choppy water and ignominiously dwarfed by the great merchantmen around it, a police launched scuttled out from under the lee of a Soviet freighter and intercepted us. 'No nearer, or you may get shot at,' yelled an officer. He did not say which side would do the shooting — presumably both — so we peered at the hijackers through binoculars, took a few pictures, and discreetly withdrew. The following day a group of reporters in a hired boat were able to get within shouting distance of the ferry, and so run their own impromptu 'press conference' before the four terrorists were whisked ashore and out of Singapore on a plane to Kuwait. But I was not among them.

Nevertheless, Simms had been ready to share his boat with me when he might have landed a scoop, just as ten years earlier his predecessor Alex Josey had given me the spare seat in a Beechcraft that took us up the Straits of Malacca at about one thousand feet and then flew back over Batam Island. It was 1965. Indonesia's *Konfrontasi* with Malaysia was approaching its whimpering climax. The Straits were threaded with a chain of British warships patrolling the Malaysian coast to forestall any seaborne invasion, while on Batam the enemy was training guerrillas to infiltrate the federation.

The Indonesian islands were so near that the Beechcraft could hardly gain height without violating hostile airspace, but the danger did not come from that quarter. The flying club pilot, finding Alex a slightly nervous passenger, set out to amuse us with a few tricks, which included doing a couple of victory rolls and then deliberately stalling the engine when we were almost over Batam and climbing steeply, so that a klaxon suddenly jerked out a warning screech not a yard from my ear. But thanks to Josey I came to realise just how close the enemy was, and took exclusive pictures that sold as far away as Stockholm.

Hughes, Simms, Josey, Robinson — scores of colleagues must have held my arm as I stumbled through the years, but it should be a source of pride and not shame to a reporter that he is indebted to his fellows. Robinson? Learning at Kaitak airport that a colleague with terminal cancer was flying back to America from Hong Kong economy class, an outraged Jim Robinson, then of NBC, pulled out his wallet and upgraded the ticket to first class on the spot. I first met him in November 1954 when he patiently briefed me — a lost newcomer — in a Hanoi that was holding its breath before the arrival of the Vietminh. Six years later he was to give me a scoop during President Eisenhower's visit to Taipei.

Aboard the aircraft carrier that brought him from Manila, Ike was apparently in a confiding mood and poured out his feelings to those who happened to be around him, including his private opinion of the conniving British who were trying to push him into a summit conference with Khrushchev. The obloquy ended abruptly, however, when a horrified press officer interrupted the flow to tell the President that he had been letting down what hair he had left in the hearing of a bunch of American newspapermen. The chummy mood changed at once. The press officer told the correspondents to forget every word they had heard. They could use nothing. And that was an order. Journalists are a mutinous crew, and do not take kindly to orders. On arrival in Taipei, therefore, Jim Robinson took me aside and spoke those golden words that are so often transmuted into lead: 'I've got a story for you.'

'I can't use it,' he went on, 'but you can', and gave it to me, together with much more.

'But how can I source all this?' I asked a little stupidly when he had finished, the usual evasions sidling through my head ('well-informed quarters…circles close to the President…it was learned here today…') only to be discarded.

'Don't,' said Jim simply. 'Don't mention sources. Just say what happened.' He had given me not only a good story but a good lesson in straight reporting. After talking to other American correspondents, I filed the news to *The Observer* that night as a flat statement of incontrovertible fact, and it made the front page. Who cared what Ike said to Chiang and Chiang said to Ike solely for the record and the reader? Just for once we had the truth wriggling on a hook.

I6 THE SPECIAL RELATIONSHIP

Burchett became more expansive as I matched him, cognac for cognac.

A CORRESPONDENT does well to team up with one or two reliable colleagues who are not his rivals (though rivals can be as close as jealous lovers that do not trust each other out of their sight), for the synergy is such that six eyes and ears add up to far more than three pairs of two. But he does even better if he chooses partners from another country with their own angle and access to the story. When a British reporter pooled resources with an American reporter in the Far East, the benefit to both was not doubled, but squared.

In consequence, I had good reason to be happy that I had fallen into an unspoken understanding with men like Keyes Beech (of the old *Chicago Daily News*), Robert Pepper Martin (then of *US News and World Report*) and Stanley Karnow (then of *Time*), especially during the pivotal years of 1964 and 1965 in Saigon. For Washington was co-sponsor of the political soap opera in Vietnam and held half of the keys to the plot — keys to which respected American correspondents might sometimes have access, but not a perfidious Brit. What Eisenhower had felt about our reluctance to tangle with the communists over China, Johnson felt about our reluctance to tangle with the communists in Vietnam.

'The British can bellyache…' It was March 1964. According to my notes, the friendly American who — twenty-three years later — would have no recollection of doing so, was reading me his account of an off-the-record talk he had just had with the American ambassador, Cabot Lodge, as we sat in his hotel bedroom in Saigon over a late continental breakfast. The British could bellyache? That quote alone told me I was listening to something no British reporter could possibly get at first hand. And it was a time for listening. Robert S. McNamara, the US Defence Secretary, was about to visit Vietnam to assess the situation in the struggle between communist North and 'democratic' South. And the situation in March 1964 was that General Khanh was for the moment master in a volatile Saigon, but the Vietcong were seeping ominously across the provinces of the South like blood on blotting paper, they had started launching attacks in battalion and even regimental strength, and they had become dangerously unmanageable.

Cabot Lodge and General Harkins, the commander of about 17,000 American military advisers in South Vietnam, had therefore agreed to tell McNamara that they favoured 'an intensification of operations in North and South', read my colleague. So far, so good. But according to the rest of my notes this 'intensification' could include 'knocking out some areas of the north with air attack — Haiphong, not Hanoi — using small nuclear weapons if necessary… China will realise she can be hit harder than she can hit…The Soviet Union will hesitate to take direct action against the USA, but might hit Saigon, Singapore, with H-bombs…the Chinese for the moment 'don't have the atom bomb…the Afro-Asians don't matter; the British can bellyache…'

The trouble was that in the midst of all the madness the Americans were right in that one respect — and so were my notes. As I scribbled for dear life (and perhaps not only mine) a pain began to sharpen in my abdomen as inexorably as the scream of a falling shell. With sweat pouring from my face in the chilly air-conditioning, fighting an almost irresistible urge to eat the carpet instead of the croissants, I waited for whatever it was to explode inside me, while forcing myself to write. But the moment soon came when I was ready to throw away the rest of this blockbuster of a background briefing, and beg for mercy. My benefactor phoned for a doctor while I dug my fingernails deeper into my palms ('he does not seem to be feeling too good'), and supported me back to my room across the square.'Rhenal colic,' said the doctor laconically.'You don't drink enough.'When the stones passed, the pain miraculously disappeared. But I now knew that for Vietnam the real agony might just be beginning.

Five months later, increasingly fearful of attack, the North Vietnamese fired on two American destroyers in the Gulf of Tongking, and the Americans retorted by bombing their naval installations. 'Small nuclear weapons' had not been used, but the war had moved another rung up the ladder to nowhere. And might move much higher. Bombing the North was supposed to offset the military and political frailty of the South, but in August 1964, ironically, it shook

Saigon more than it shook Hanoi. For it prompted General Khanh to declare a state of emergency under which he made himself president, only to be forced by popular fury to resign within ten days. Would more political turmoil in the South be answered with more military mayhem against the North?

It was vital at this point to know how the Americans were reacting in order to read the future, for they were going to write the script. In the week between Khanh resigning and Khanh shaving off his beard (as I have described), General Maxwell Taylor seemed unworried. 'Khanh does not intend to abdicate power.' he told Keyes Beech. 'It is still Khanh's government, and the US will be behind Khanh as long as he shows a reasonable chance of success…' He understood that Khanh might not survive, but it was a risk worth taking: 'I never bet on anything that's not 50-50.' Khanh went, but only to inspire another army coup against the civilian premier Tran Van Huong in January 1965, and it was then that Taylor told a small group of trusted American correspondents (including Stanley Karnow) that Washington was 'resigned to coups' in South Vietnam —'stability is too much to hope for'. He was right. Although abortive, yet another coup just one week later would lead indirectly to the downfall of Khanh in turn, this time for good.

The instability of South Vietnam now took the Americans two ways: some claimed it was an argument for escalating the war; others that it was an argument for pulling out of the whole malodorous mess. In February 1965 McGeorge Bundy, Johnson's special adviser on national security, told a press conference in Saigon that he in turn had come to review the situation on behalf of the President. The United States was nevertheless 'deeply committed to the common effort against the terrorist aggression of the communists, and has every intention of maintaining its commitment in full partnership with the people and government of South Vietnam…have found no significant desire to make peace, and the United States is not involved in any such initiative…We are constantly seeking ways of making our part of the effort more effective.'

That was the sort of stuff I was allowed to hear. But just twenty-four hours before, Bundy had told Pepper Martin (who had told me) that his brief from the President was in fact to determine *'whether we should go on with the war'*, what peace terms the Vietnamese wanted, and, 'if there was a sell-out', whether the Catholics in the South could be regrouped to continue the fight. The State Department, the Pentagon, and the CIA had all submitted their assessments. The question was, which was right?

In the event, the hesitations were to be eclipsed by history. The generals had their way (almost always a bad omen). Bundy went back to Washington, and one week later Maxwell Taylor told Stanley Karnow that the communists had 'handed to us' a justification for reprisal bombing of the North, and 'we will hit back harder and harder'. The US was fighting a war, despite promises of 'never again'. Within a month two battalions of US Marines would 'storm ashore', the first of half a million American troops to be thrown into the lost struggle for Vietnam. Two years after that President Johnson in Washington and U Thant in New York would make it clear to me (among others) that those responsible for the Vietnam scenario were still far from writing a truce into it.

That lay in the future, but I meanwhile had further cause to be thankful for my American connection. Three months before Bundy spoke in Saigon — one way in public and another in private — Keyes Beech and I had been given some of the answers to his questions in Phnom Penh, where we had sat up drinking one night with the affable Australian communist writer, Wilfred Burchett. For Burchett's friends in high places in Hanoi were the other sponsors of the Vietnam soap opera, and (it was reasonable to assume) had sold him the other half of the plot. Suitably plied, he started off by outlining their plausible terms for ending the war, which would ensure that Hanoi could take all. These included a cease-fire, a neutralist government in Saigon with which the Liberation Front could form a coalition and establish a 'democratic' Vietnam, and, of course, the withdrawal of all American advisers. But that baited trap was only the beginning: we were off to a long evening.

We were sitting in the dim-lit bar lounge of the Hotel le Royal, a solitary Cambodian waiter yawning in the background. Burchett became more expansive as I matched him, cognac for cognac, while eagerly soaking up what I hoped were his boozy indiscretions with the liquor. But by the small hours of the morning the drink had me yawning too, and I committed the inexcusable error of flopping into bed and falling asleep without making any notes. I awoke at eight, appalled. I could not remember a thing Burchett had said. When I ran to Keyes in a panic, however, he just pulled a notebook from his hip pocket. 'You did your job,' he said simply, 'and I — er — I did mine. You acted pacemaker, and I stayed sober to pick up the bits.' I had forgotten in my misery that Keyes was a teetotaller. He had drunk nothing stronger than *citron pressé* the whole night. He had got it all down, to Burchett's last, slurred word, and he now read it out to me at dictation speed. We had — quite unwittingly — set Burchett up as neatly as if we had planned the whole dubious exercise.

Stinging Burchett almost by mistake was symbolical of our relationship, for we were natural partners. Keyes and Pepper were better placed to get the inside story of the American dream in Vietnam, but as a neutral whose country was co-chairman of the Geneva Agreement, I was better placed to get the inside story of the Vietcong and their backers in Hanoi. My contacts ranged from anti-American Vietnamese nationalists undercover in Saigon to communist cadres who slipped into the city from guerrilla bases out in the Mekong Delta. But they were still talking to me as a journalist, and I could pass on what they told me to Keyes and Pepper— strictly for background — with a clear conscience. It was never misused.

Then in February 1965 Colonel Thao, a conspiratorial man-in-the-middle who had a live line to the Vietcong while ostensibly serving Saigon, gave me a letter to pass on to McGeorge Bundy. The letter urged the Americans to sponsor an honest, democratic government in South Vietnam that could end the war by bringing the true nationalists on both sides together and cutting the two odious extremes — the communists and the Khanhs — out of the script. Hanoi's beguiling 'neutralist' government as described by Burchett? Or the reverse side of the coin? It depended how you held the idea up to the light, but it was another piece of the puzzle, and the letter was unsealed. One good turn deserved another,' and I gave it to Keyes to copy before sending it on to Bundy through channels.

We shared tips and transport and hotel rooms, pigeoned each other's copy and picked each other's brains — in Vietnam, Laos, Cambodia, Indonesia, Thailand, Singapore, Hong Kong. We bussed our way through the Colonels' Rebellion in Sumatra together in 1958, took an infirm American sedan across Java when Khrushchev visited Sukarno, but flew into a firefight in Vientiane in the belly of a lumbering British cargo plane carrying medical relief. In the mid-sixties the Americans had the inside story on the struggle against communist aggression at one end of Southeast Asia, while the British had the inside story on the struggle against Indonesian *Konfrontasi* at the other. The Americans had the edge in Saigon, but a Briton could get a visa for Hanoi. We swapped notes, but we betrayed no trusts, for a confidence safe with one was safe with the others, whether off the record, unattributable, or for background only.

I was furious, therefore, when in January 1965 I appeared to have cheated my way into a scoop over the bloodless military coup that had disposed of Premier Tran Van Huong. As front page news, it brought out the blasé in Saigon veterans. Huong was an unprofessional politician who had aroused the ire of almost all factions by misguidedly telling them the blunt truth about themselves, and warning soldiers, students, and Buddhist monks to stay out of politics. He had not been expected to last, and anyway military coups were at a discount — there would be another within a month. Dog had bitten man again. But there was a twist to the hackneyed story that might be worth a headline: Huong had disappeared. Liquidated? Like other correspondents. I rummaged through Saigon for him, and having picked up what seemed to be a good tip, self-importantly told about fifty other reporters attending the five o'clock daily briefing given by the Americans that he was no longer in town.

'Who were you trying to fool over Huong?' an American correspondent called out to me in the street the next day.

'What do you mean?'

'Ah, come on. AP finally got the story he was holed out in the British Embassy all the time. Don't tell me you didn't know.' It was obvious the Americans thought I had been 'lying abroad' for my country. I rang up the British Embassy and asked why the hell, as almost the only British special in Saigon, I had not been given the news the day before when I had called. 'It was embargoed until nine this morning; H.E. decided that the first journalist to phone us after that wanting to know where Mr Huong was would be told the truth,' said the press officer. 'You did not phone. AP did.' I caught *The Observer* by the heel of the third edition, but the memory is burned into my ears. It is one thing to hug an exclusive to oneself; quite another to mislead an entire press corps in order to protect it.

But a journalist cannot always be one of the gang, and must therefore be ready to risk their wrath in a just cause. In 1977 the Singapore government called a televised press conference for two political detainees, who had confessed under interrogation to their part in an improbable conspiracy to wreck the patched-up relations between the republic and neighbouring Malaysia. Correspondents regarded the conference as a stage-managed 'production', a form of show trial, and passed the word among themselves suggesting that while all might attend it, no one should actually participate by asking a question. The set would then be reduced to silence. But I broke the boycott.

One of the detainees, a voluble lawyer talking his way to freedom, implicated a man named James Puthucheary in the plot. I had known Puthucheary and felt sure he was innocent, at least of this. I therefore challenged his accuser to deny on camera that he had not a shred of first-hand evidence to support his statement, and that it was based entirely on hearsay. He admitted that I was right, and afterwards no bona fide reporter damned me for a scab. Puthucheary did not return the compliment by challenging a local hack stringing for the London *Times* in Kuala Lumpur, however, when the man cited him in support of a defamatory falsehood he published about me in the Malaysian *Sunday Star*. But that is precisely the sort of experience that makes real journalists watch each other's backs.

17 KNOWING THE FORM

The journalist seeking an interview must not offend.

KNOCKING the newspaperman is such a popular pastime that it is a wonder the Japanese have not developed it into a computer game. Nor is it uncommon for other journalists to do the knocking, especially when the chairborne turn on the airborne. In 1985 an untamed Australian television reporter named Neil Davis was shot dead at point blank range in the streets of Bangkok while covering an abortive military coup. At once, one domesticated columnist writing from his air-conditioned ivory tower in Singapore implied with some disdain that Davis was not only wasting his time finding out what was actually happening on the ground: he was the passive victim ('sacrificial lamb') of the box-watcher's demand for sensational pictures — or of a boss who had told him to get in there and bring back the bloodshed on film, or else.

The idea that a correspondent runs towards danger of his own will, his blue funk losing out to his blind instinct to get the story (which brought him into the profession in the first place) is alien, even obnoxious, to the more sedentary members of the species, it would seem. Yet it must be so, for journalism can be the most hazardous profession in the world. In the Korean War the casualty rate in the press corps was higher than among the soldiery, and seventy-five more correspondents and photographers were to be listed killed or missing in Vietnam and Cambodia — twenty of them between March and December 1970 alone. It was noteworthy, moreover, that not one of them was propping up a bar when last seen on his feet. But one should not make too much of that, should one? After all, more people die on the roads, let alone in their beds, even reporters. As for live Western correspondents…'What type of copy can one expect from men who rush to the topical hot-spots and with the subtlety of an elephant demand: "Anyone here been raped and speaks English?"' asks another tame Singapore columnist with a holier-than-thou shake of the head.

What indeed? But then what sort of copy can one expect from a columnist who implies that the question is typical of her Western colleagues? It was precisely because it was singularly outrageous that another correspondent, Edward Behr, made it the title of a book which he dedicated to (among others) seven journalists killed on the job. But it makes a point. One does blush for reporters who blunder around Asia banging the table and demanding hamburgers and democracy American style in a loud voice, who assume the local currency is the US dollar, who will gatecrash a prime minister's office and expect an immediate interview as a God-given right, and who will interrupt an elder statesmen in full flood to shout impatiently 'Yeah, yeah, I've heard all that stuff, but what I wanna know is...' Yeah. But if the culprits are often American, it is because they are the spoiled brats of the profession for reasons that do them credit. Americans are self-made 'haves' in a predominantly have-not world — 'haves' in terms not only of cash in the bank or bonds, the biggest and (sometimes) the best of everything from Disneyland to deficits, but freedom of speech and the prerogatives of the press. What is more, these were guaranteed by the First Amendment to the Bill of Rights not in an age of political strength and affluence, but 200 years ago when America was weak, disunited, and crawling away from the wreckage of colonialism. And those are precisely the conditions that Asian governments with a siege mentality arc quick to make a pretext for beating newspapers back into pulp if they fail to play Echo to the leadership of the moment. (Echo, it will be recalled, faded away until she was nothing but someone else's voice).

America can be a busman's holiday for a British reporter resigned to the bureaucratic prissiness of Whitehall, let alone his browbeaten brothers elsewhere. Finding myself in New York in 1967 to promote a book, I slyly suggested to my foreign news editor that I might slip down to Washington and try to see one or two people about Vietnam (not to mention the sights of the city and a couple of old friends in Bethesda who owed me a drink or so). Equally slyly he agreed, and our resident correspondent picked up the phone in Washington to make appointments on my behalf.

My dream of a little leisurely rubbernecking between beers with some token Vietnam veteran in the Press Club dissolved on arrival. I saw the Vietnam veterans all right — but only in between scuttling through the furnace of July from one interview with Secretary of State Dean Rusk at the State Department to another with Secretary of Defence Robert McNamara at the Pentagon, from National Security Adviser Walt Rostow two floors down in the White House to his brother Eugene, Assistant Secretary for Far Eastern Affairs back at the State Department, from Averell Harnman to William Bundy to President Johnson's press conference at the White House, from senators to congressmen…'And you mean to say you were there a whole week and didn't see Vice-President Humphrey?' one American colleague asked me in wonderment. 'What were you doing all that time, Chrissakes?' I pleaded the heat.

I could not plead the heat the last time around, but Washington could plead the cold. It was February 1978, and the District of Columbia would be hibernating, the public affairs officer of CINC-PAC (the C-in-C Pacific) warned me when I was still 5,000 miles to the west in sunny Hawaii. People tended to go to ground when it hit 20 below — who did I hope to see there? I said I just wanted to talk to one or two Chinawatchers about the latest political puzzle in Beijing. He said he would telex someone anyway, just to let them know I was coming.

When I reached Washington it was buried in snow and as silent as he had said. I could not raise any of my contacts on the phone for two days, and it was just as I was getting frilly with the fear familiar to the correspondent when a deadline is looming but every line is dead that I finally got through to somebody on my list. 'Thank God,' I said, 'I haven't been able to reach anyone since I arrived, and I've only got a couple of days here. Is there some chance that I might be able to see you?'

'What the hell are you talking about?' he asked (one of these people who trump one question with another). 'I'm seeing you tomorrow at two, aren't I?' 'You're what?' 'It says right here I'm seeing you tomorrow at fourteen hundred hours. You mean you don't have your own schedule? You *don't*? Well, I'll read it out to you.' Stapleton Roy and Stanley Bedlington at State, Oksenberg at the White House, Horowitz at INR, Doak Barnett at the Brookings Institution, M (of the Defence Intelligence Agency) at the Pentagon, W (informally) of the CIA at his home…The PR man in Hawaii had fired his telex across the Union, and my dance card had been filled in at the other end before I even arrived at the ball.

The sheer accessibility of American men of affairs softens the muscles while stiffening the ego. If the snow had persisted and the city frozen up, I could still have gone through much of that programme without moving from my room. Security permitting (and sometimes not), senators and congressmen and bureaucrats and all the other denizens of the political pond that is Washington rarely seem too busy with affairs of state to put their feet on the desk and talk down the phone for the space of two or three cups of coffee to the enquiring reporter. But if the enquiring reporter takes his American telephone tactics to Tokyo, Japanese officials who can recoil from two minutes of prying over the wire as if their modesty had been outraged are likely to reject him as an alien transplant.

The odd thing is that no one is more conscientious than an American about studying foreign mores: the very word is essentially American, not British, Latin. Americans record and analyse the habits and customs of those they find themselves among, lecture to one another on the natives, and write books about culture shock (even if the natives are always at the bottom end of the microscope). But it is not enough for a journalist to know that he must take his shoes off when entering most Asian houses, that he should not sit crosslegged with the sole of one foot in his host's face, that in Palembang he must wait before sipping the coffee placed before him (however casually he might have grabbed it in Pittsburg), that he can slap local backs in Manila and Seoul with impunity but with uneven results in Makassar and Semarang, and that on meeting a Malay miss he should touch his own heart rather than her hand.

Beyond this, he must learn the local by-laws of his own game. Some professional rules are universal, of course: A reporter must be polite to pert secretaries, and patient with sentries who speak no known language (meaning English) and read his passes upsidedown; he must respect the siesta hour and understand that he cannot rush through it in sixty minutes (in French Indochina it lasted from twelve to three); and he must not burst into flames when bureaucrats working an eight-to-two day in Jakarta are not in their offices at nine. Time can be flexible, even fluid, and he must be tolerant when his programme springs a leak and dribbles away towards his deadline. If an Indonesian says *belum* — which may mean everything from 'later' to 'never' — it is probably to avoid saying 'no' outright, and he must be ready to smile at the rebuff.

He must know that he can dive into the deep end of an issue when interviewing a Filipino, but must wade into it from the shallows when interviewing a Japanese; that whereas he should only call on a Japanese after making an appointment, there are times when he should drop in on a Korean without one (so that if the secret police enquire, his contact can say: 'He just arrived; I didn't ask him to come'). But gatecrashing is like making love — necessary, even desirable, from time to time, but to be approached as a privilege, not a prerogative. Only when the intrusion is welcome are the best results obtained; to jam a foot in the door (metaphorically speaking) is often to ask someone to stamp on it. And even the quietest knock can earn a snub in some circles.

It was accepted in Laos in the sixties that since the telephones did not transmit speech (only the engaged signal) and everyone lived around the corner, the easiest way to see a minister was to go over to his office and ask for him. Wishing for some reason to interview the Governor of Luang Prabang (who was also the brother of the King), therefore, I once took a *cyclo* to his residence and simply walked up the drive to its massive front door. The door was closed, and there was no one in sight. I knocked cautiously a few times, but there was no response. I then tried the handle, and it opened. The great lobby of the mansion was empty. I called softly. Silence. But a reporter must go on until he is stopped. I knocked on a door to my left. No reply. I knocked again. Same answer. I then pushed it gently and walked into what I thought must be an anteroom of some sort, suitably equipped with flunkeys. Instead, I found myself facing thirty feet of empty space, at the far end of which an elderly Lao entrenched behind a desk like a miniature Arc de Triomphe slowly looked up at me from whatever he was writing.

The Laos are by repute a quiet, smiling people dozing through one long siesta on their way to the next life. I was about to learn better. His Royal Highness was neither quiet nor smiling, and before I could open my mouth raked me fore and aft (for the tirade continued when I turned to flee) with the lofty rhetoric of affronted royalty. *'Est-ce que vous avez l'habitude dans votre lamentable pays de…*Do you usually burst into people's private houses without so much as knocking?' he barked as I dithered in the doorway. 'Are you under the impression that because you are in Laos you can conduct yourself like a barbarian? Possibly you believe that since you have a white face you are absolved from any obligation to behave with ordinary courtesy. Allow me, then, to disabuse you — *Kindly stand where you are and do not interrupt.'* We all have our exits, and that was mine.

I had mistimed my approach shot. Had he wanted to air his views to the foreign press at that moment, he might have refrained from matching bad manners with bad manners. But he had no interest in me, and a circumspect entry that might otherwise have been tolerated as seduction (enjoyed, even, in a laid-back kind of way) was therefore treated as rape.

****

The journalist seeking an interview must not offend. He must not only be punctual and properly dressed, but know his man. And that knowledge begins with the name. An English reporter who knocked on the door of my hotel room in Hong Kong and said he had an interview arranged with a Dennis — what was it? Brodziewitz? — was told he could B...witz off and find him, then. If he did not even know my name, he certainly knew nothing else about me, and I would be wasting my time talking to him. That was an example of counter-productive cheek. But in a strange continent it is easy to make an innocent mistake. Is Dr Mahathir Mohamad to be called Dr Mohamad or Dr Mahathir? Is the orthopaedic surgeon Balakrishnan Ramasamy to be addressed as Dr Balakrishnan or Dr Ramasamy? (not Doctor, please; Mister — he qualified in London). Is Mr U Nu...? (not Mister, please; the U means Uncle). Well then, is President Ho Chi Minh of North Vietnam President Ho or President Minh? (President Ho). So President Ngo Dinh Diem of South Vietnam is President Ngo? (No, gotcha, he is normally referred to as President Diem).

But the reporter needs to do more homework than that, for the more he knows, the more he will be told. He should have not only his subject's name and rank, but his number — he should know something of his career and character (as well as the crisis that has focused upon him the swivelling antennae of editors). If possible he should dig up some private interest of the interviewee, so that mutual trust can be quite illogically established by the casual mention of golf or birdwatching or Chinese scent bottles, though these may have little to do with the murder or bankruptcy or political scandal that has brought them together. This can lead one into exotic byways. Asked to write a profile of the Abbé Breuil, the famous French expert on prehistoric cave paintings, I found myself plunged into a study of his current passion, and in 1954 this was a conviction that the lost civilisation of Knossos (which had disappeared in suspicious circumstances in 1,400 BC) had been transported to Africa. To talk to the good Abbé about the caves of Altamira in Spain, therefore, it paid to have a working knowledge of the dress and dances of pre-Mycenaean Crete. But sometimes the right metaphor is enough to soften a hard heart ('par for the course', 'the inside track').

Thus armed, the correspondent can frame his questions more effectively in advance — and he should have them lined up in his mind beforehand, particularly when he is gatecrashing. I myself favoured the Bruno Furst method of using 'hooks' to memorise the list of points I wanted to raise. At the outset this involved my learning the sequence of words that is the basis of the system — Tea, Noah, May, Ray, Law, Jaw, etc — and then, whenever the need arose, hooking onto each of them a picture of whatever I wanted to recall. If, for example, my first question was to be about the breakdown of talks on the return of Hong Kong to China, the picture in my mind might be of Deng Xiaoping and Mrs Thatcher drinking *tea* (the first hook) out of two halves of a broken cup. And since the more ridiculous the mental cartoon the easier it was to remember, the system was admirably suited to politics.

If banging on the door met with a rebuff, the correct response was to ask for an appointment, of course. That might be countered with a demand that the correspondent first submit his questions in writing. Repellent though that might be to a freestyle journalist, it would be no time for him to play the prima donna and flounce out. His best tactic would be to hand in, not a page of controversial corkers (for corkers do not uncork), but a short list of anodyne headings for discussion that the subject could seize upon to put across his own cherished version (authorised or revised) of the truth. This bait would be calculated to net the reporter a personal interview, at which — once inside the door — he could cross-examine his man on more obnoxious issues, raised in the form of supplementary queries that would seem to emerge quite naturally from their talk. Communist leaders often blocked this ploy by supplying written answers to written questions and leaving the correspondent on the doorstep. But he was no worse off. At least he had the party line which, if he was lucky, might even have changed since the last pronunciamento.

For a pre-arranged interview I would — as an aide-mémoire — list the main questions I proposed to ask on the first left-hand page of my notebook before going in, especially if it was to be on the record. I favoured an ordinary lined notebook with semi-stiff covers that fitted into the pocket, not the bigger flip-over reporter's pad that women journalists are always riffling through in bad movies while everyone waits patiently for them to find what they are looking for — 'But, Counsellor, you said earlier, er (flip, flip) — you said — er (back flip, back flip, mumble, mumble) — ah, yeah, here it is; you said…' The secret of quick reference, of not losing anything along the way, of retaining command of the field, is to write what the man actually says on the right-hand page of a notebook only. The left-hand pages are left blank for annotating and indexing the interview as it unfolds, and have a variety of other uses, some straightforward, some a trifle devious.

There must be no doodling. On these facing pages I would jot down, as they cropped up, further questions that I proposed to ask at the end of the interview; I would add random observations ('avoided my eye here', 'contradicts Mao Zedong', 'hasn't shaved'), and turns of phrase that would enliven my piece as they came to mind ('sawn-off shotgun of a man', 'mind like a cheese-cutter'). If on-the-record answers I was being dictated were political clichés, I might pointedly lay down my pen and fold my hands until the waffle had rolled past me, while nodding politely if a little somnolently. If the occasion demanded a simulated interest to keep the subject coming, however, I might scribble away dutifully as he spoke, but in reality be seizing the chance to write on a left-hand page something quite different that I was eager to commit to paper before I forgot it. This could be a description of the room, or some revealing pokerwork text on the wall with dogmatic capital letters designed to shout down sceptics: 'This Above All, To Thine Own Self Be True…' Or, even more brazenly, 'Honesty Is The Best Policy').

As Chiang Kai-shek answered some question in Taipei through an interpreter in his almost incomprehensible Zhejiang Chinese in 1962, I was able to get down: 'Ushers and guards in doorways, vast office, blue pile carpet, big desk, three flags. Smaller, gentler, less skull-like than in pictures. Plain uniform, no markings, khaki, buttoned at neck, close-trimmed white moustache hardly visible, nut-brown man, nearly bald, wisp white hair. Reminds of quiet retired colonel of gentle kind. Black strapover shoes, well kept hands, false teeth (?), steady gaze.'

That was not all. An interview could be split up and indexed on the left-hand pages as we went along by my drawing a horizontal line whenever the interviewee changed the subject, and writing against each section the code for it — EC (economic), AS (Ascan), HR (human rights), ELEX (coming elections), SOV (relations with the USSR). A glance through these pages would tell me at once where different subjects were dealt with, and enable me to join up instantly all references to the same theme, no matter where they had occurred during our talk.

A notebook is nevertheless like a gun — the owner should draw it only if he is prepared to use it. And that may depend on whether the interview is going to be on or off the record, attributable or unattributable, for background only, or not for publication in any form — the reporter must obviously make sure at the outset that he knows which it is to be. The textbooks say 'put it down; never rely on your memory' (along with 'check all facts, figures, names, titles, ranks, dates, places' and get to the church on time). But unless an interview was on the record, I would start by leaving my notebook in my pocket, for when confronted with a journalist, homo sapiens can be a nervous creature, and should not be startled by any sudden movement of the pen. If at some point I was obviously expected to make notes during an off-the-record talk — to take down a list of official statistics, or a self-conscious quote — I would dutifully pull out my notebook, whether I genuinely cared or just wanted to be polite. But (making sure my respondent was looking) I would put it away as soon as we went private again, he reverted to plain speaking, and I to asking indelicate questions.

The only time I reversed this procedure was during an interview with a vice-minister in Beijing. The vice-minister first upbraided me sorely for my inexcusably malicious and wildly inaccurate reporting on the Chinese scene, and after some minutes of this went on to reply to the written questions I had earlier submitted to him with a string of detailed trade statistics, the figures broken down to meaningless rubble. I faithfully took down all the recriminations, but when the statistics began, put my notebook back in my pocket and my hands in an attitude of prayer. At the end of the interview, the vice-minister patted me on the back and said with a friendly smile that he was sure I was going to write admirably 'objective' articles about China and he looked forward to reading them. I felt like a man who had won the heart of the belle of the ball simply by being the only person to ignore her. Dale Carnegie himself would have got it wrong.

Dale Carnegie would usually have got it right, however, for a reporter must establish a friendly rapport with his hostage (without actually inducing the Helsinki syndrome), and if he must use a tape recorder, the less obtrusive it is the better, for many interviewees will regard it with misgivings. But (as with a notebook) it is possible to turn these misgivings to advantage by switching it on to record a quote, but switching it off again with a loud click when angling for further confidences. For (as any yogi will confirm) the greater the tension, the greater the relaxation that follows, and the more inhibited the speaker may feel when the machine is on, the more happily he is likely to chatter once it is off— perhaps even forgetting that the man opposite him is still listening, even if his gadget is not.

The best thing about drawing a gun is the power it gives the drawer to win even greater psychological ascendancy by putting it away again. And the same is true of the notebook and the tape recorder.

If on the other hand the subject himself insists on taping what he says in an on-the-record interview (as Lee Kuan Yew usually did), the reporter must suppress his misgivings, even if he is not allowed to make his own simultaneous recording (the obvious countermove) and has to wait for a laundered transcript of the other's tape. He gains nothing by protesting, and the system can score points both above and below the line. When Lee edited the transcripts of what he had said, he left no room for the slip between ear and lip that can lead to those time-hallowed charges that the politician has once again been misquoted. But he also drew a revealing line between his public position (the printable stuff he left intact), and his private opinion (the unprintable stuff he amended or cut out).

I rarely asked for set question-and-answer interviews, for they tended to put my vis-à-vis — minister, general, tycoon, secret society boss (or all four at once) — on his worst behaviour, and leave me listening to prim platitudes that *The Observer* was then supposed to publish if I did not want to be turned away with oaths the next time I rang or knocked. Instead, I would put in for an off-the-record meeting, give my subject his head, and ask him only at the end of it whether I might quote him on specific points he had made. In that way we could have an informal dialogue during which he might loosen his collar and I might loosen his tongue, and with luck I could then put him on the record — after he had felt comfortable enough to be candid, even let a cat or two out of the bag. There was nothing to lose, for if he refused to go public on something he had revealed in private, he would not have said it in a formal interview anyway.

I8 FACE TO FACE

If he cannot get to a typewriter at once, he must seize the first seat he can find and scribble into his notebook.

THERE was, of course, more to lose if one made the fatuous mistake of thinking that the man one was interviewing did not want to be quoted when he did. After General Nguyen Khanh shaved off his beard at the end of 1964 and announced he would take orders from someone else in future, all eyes turned expectantly — but blindly — towards the elderly Buddhist civilian who then took up quarters in the presidential palace in Saigon. For Pham Khac Suu was an equivocal choice. He had been arrested as a pro-communist subversive by the secret police of President Diem, brutally tortured, and beaten about the head so badly that 'after two weeks he was mad', a fellow-prisoner had told me. He now indicated that he wanted a new provisional National

Assembly that could throw up a truly nationalist government capable of confronting Hanoi. This sounded singularly like the Janus-faced formula for victory put forward by Thao (for the South) and Burchett (for the North), but he said little and saw no journalists, and no one knew precisely what he meant to do.

When a left-wing intellectual in touch with both the Buddhists and the Vietcong offered to get me an interview with the new chief of state, therefore, I found myself metaphorically bowing and scraping like a top at the French court in my eagerness to see him. Suu was old and sick, I was told sternly, and he did not want to talk to the press. Just so, just so, entirely understandable, I babbled. I would be allowed only fifteen minutes with him. Of course, precisely, not a minute more. And the conversation would be strictly off the record — I could not even say that I had *seen* him. Not even say…? But naturally (gulp), whatever he wished. Just one week after he took office Suu, frail and scarcely audible, duly gave me fifteen minutes during which he spoke with almost childlike candour, and I left the palace biting my lips with frustration. How was I to handle this bomb of a story, when the mere fact of our meeting was not only confidential, but secret?

For Fortune to be fickle, she must sometimes be kind. Hardly had I reached the Hotel Continental and scribbled a few notes when I was summoned to its coffin of a call box in the foyer. The caller was the presidential press officer. He apologised for disturbing me, but he had a question: the Chief of State was a little worried; he wanted to know how I intended to use our interview, and in particular what I proposed to *quote* him as having said.

It sank in slowly, delicious as the first guilty drink after Lent. The President himself had said nothing about classifying our interview, for the simple reason that he knew nothing of such things. I took a deep breath, heaved my notebook out of my pocket, and spelled out what I would like to quote. The quote came back to me within twenty-four hours in a note headed 'Message for M. Denis Block Worth' (I still have it). I had played safe, but Suu had amended my cautious draft to read more boldly, and although the words *we think* had been added (his italics), they paradoxically strengthened my copy.

I was then free to cable *The Observer*: 'The Americans, who were the last to know who had become (the) latest leader a week ago, now face a "conspiracy of peace"…Behind his democratic demand for early elections to a new National Assembly lies one outstanding purpose: to arm the future Government with a popular mandate so that it can negotiate peace with the Communists without its authority being challenged.' But 'the soft-voiced Head of State told me earlier this week that he *thought* the elections for a democratic assembly must be held in the towns…"Then the question of ending hostilities will be decided…"'

The rest wrote itself. As a programme for peace, Pham Khac Suu's plan was a declaration of war on the anti-communist Khanh and his fellow-generals, and on the Americans who were already sinking three-quarters of a million dollars a day into the Vietnamese quicksand. But the doubt in that guarded yet italicised '*we think* the elections must be held in the towns' had been prompted by an even more grisly prospect. For the neutralists who had overthrown Ngo Dinh Diem were putting pressure on the new president to hold elections not only in the towns, but in the countryside. And since most villages had already been 'won over or bullied into obedience by the Vietcong' (as I put it) the logical outcome would be that their candidates would dominate the National Assembly, and 'the communists would have suddenly won the "constitutional struggle" after years of armed conflict in the jungle and swamps'. Predictably, the army staged a bloodless coup within three months, and Suu's dream disappeared, in turn, into the quicksand. But like so many other false alarms, my story was the truth of the day on the day, and I still flinch from the fact that I had to be coaxed into filing a spoon-fed scoop.

It is wrong to assume that when a politician explodes, he wants the blast to be muffled. In 1966 G. Kandasamy, a loyal member of the ruling party in Singapore and leader of a trade union movement tightly geared to government, told me he had sent Lee Kuan Yew a stiff letter crackling with half angry, half sarcastic reproof. His targets had been the government's two favourite occupations: prosperity could not be achieved simply by passing laws, he had written, nor by making fine speeches exhorting everyone to work harder while cutting their benefits. The government accused workers of 'malingering', he went on, but it had itself ratted on its earlier promises to improve working conditions as well as raise output, and the second must stem from the first.

There was much more besides, but Kandasamy had not received the courtesy of a reply. 'Lee has no idea how to treat people,' he said bitterly. 'At a recent meeting of Indian workers he told them they were lucky to be earning $4.55 a day. Their reaction? "He thinks we are all street-cleaners."' The government had lost touch with the masses — 'Who would have dreamed in 1959 that these champions of the underdog would be driving about in Jaguars in 1966?' The workers were fed up, the Malay and Indian minorities disgruntled. If Lee 'dropped the trappings of democracy, started running the labour movement as if this were Eastern Europe, and established a totalitarian Chinese government in Singapore' in order to crush the left-wing unions, the immediate effect would be that 'thousands of workers would cross over and join them'.

Lee had his own side of the story — which included his objections to a profitable caper whereby daily-rated Indian workers scrimshanked on weekdays and collected triple overtime on holidays. It was nevertheless sad, I reflected as I rose to go, that what the hot-tempered Kandasamy had said was strictly for background, for he was supposedly a close lieutenant of the Prime Minister, and this kind of talk was dynamite. But there was no point in asking if I could quote him. He had been running down the Lee who 'goes through the roof...grinds people into the ground', and, besides, the story had racial overtones. He would be lucky to lose no more than his job were we to syndicate it and send it around the world. But the next time I saw him it was my turn to get the cutting edge of his tongue: 'What the hell do you do with all that stuff I tell you? — I never see it in print. Do you think I talk to you just for the sake of talking?'

Interviewing is like everything else in life: it is asking for trouble to stick stubbornly to the rules. In principle, questions should be precise and simple in order to keep prattle to a minimum. But while a sharp one may impress the subject, it can also make him wary, whereas a naive and voluminous catch-all may — like the psychiatrist's ambiguous word test ('Blue?' 'Sea'; 'Green?' 'Jimmy Carter') — draw an illuminating choice of answer that will indicate what is really on his mind.

A colleague visiting China for the first time as the Cultural Revolution was beginning to falter asked a hard-shell cadre we were trying gently to decorticate, 'What has been the greatest achievement of the Communist Party since the Liberation in 1949?' I looked at him in horror. As the ideal cue for half an hour of hot air on whatever line the fellow wanted to sell us, it could have been devised by the cadre himself. But its sheer scope proved to be a stroke of genius, for he snapped out his reply as if he had been waiting for it, and it was as unexpected as it was trivial: 'Exposing the renegade and traitor Lin Biao.'

It was like saying that Napoleon's greatest achievement was the shooting of the duc d'Enghien, or Stalin's the murder of Trotsky, but it was the first time that any correspondent had heard a communist official confirm in so many words that the revered Chinese marshal and chosen heir of Chairman Mao Zedong had been cast into outer darkness. Asked directly if Lin Biao was in disgrace, cadres had until then turned the question with a giggle and a brazen non sequitur about the weather (which, unlike the political climate, was normal for the time of year). But our man now took off and told the tale as the tale was to be told many times thereafter.

Lin Biao had tried to sabotage the revolution by socialising everything before China was ready for it. He had served the nefarious ends of the unspeakable Russian revisionists, with whom he was in cahoots. He had tried to assassinate Chairman Mao himself, and when he failed, to flee in a hijacked Trident jet to the Soviet Union without a navigator. (It crashed). Calmly ignoring all the sickening adulation that had been poured upon China's foremost military hero for years past, the cadre unblinkingly declared that Lin Biao had always been a devious trickster swollen with secret ambition, and Mao had never trusted him for a moment — 'but I can assure you that Lin Biao is quite definitely dead'.

A silly question does not necessarily get a silly answer. 'So how did you feel about it at the time?' was the most moronic of all put to the captain of the *Mayaguez*, the American freighter that had just undergone the ordeal of being seized by the Khmer Rouge in 1974.

But it elicited the quote of the day: 'Mister, I would have promised the Khmer Rouge the moon between two slices of bread if I could have released myself.' I made it my lead, and the lead made the front page.

****

Riffling through a mental book of mugshots, I suddenly remember how different they all were. There were the idols whose names alone made their clichés worth the paper they were about to be printed on: President Ngo Dinh Diem, his white sharkskin suit vying with his black patent leather hair, droning through his automatic responses like the pious Catholic he was; President Ho Chi Minh in his khaki bush jacket and sandals cut from old motor tyres, his still, luminous eyes fixed in a kind of shining death as he pronounced his stock maxim ('The Vietnamese people are determined to carry on the struggle for unification by peaceful means on the basis of the Geneva Agreement'); President Chiang Kai-shek, the nut-brown colonel in his monumental Victorian palace, paradoxically ducking a receding issue ('I cannot give you a date when it will be possible to go back to the mainland; only when it has been established that there is widespread active disaffection against the communists will we send in our troops').

There is little one can do to bend these wooden nickels of well-worn prose one way or the other; one must be satisfied that one is in the presence of living history. But even history can become a bore if it repeats itself too often. I was elated to have been given a personal interview by the Generalissimo in 1962, and foolish enough to boast of it to Stanley Karnow the same evening. Everything is a matter of perspective, however. Karnow was accompanying Henry Luce, the owner of *Time* magazine, on a visit to Taipei, and — unknown to me — Henry Luce had been seeing his old friend the 'Gimo' several times every day. 'Jesus,' said Karnow with an appropriate glance towards the ceiling of the Snake Pit bar after I had been pontificating for some time. 'You mean you've only been stuck with him once? Some guys have all the breaks. If I have to see that man just one more time. I think I'll go round the bend.' That was not just cutting the Gimo down to size. Rarely have I been so ruthlessly *miniaturised* myself.

Right-hand men can be more rewarding when their masters behave like animated dummies. In Hanoi, Premier Pham Van Dong would talk for two hours about North Vietnam, shaking his head gloomily over the wasteland that he had inherited after eight years of war against the French, so that every now and then he could stick in a question to me about the South with the almost furtive skill of the acupuncturist. In a villa outside Taipei Vice-President Chen Cheng talked for another two hours, offering me tea and sympathy for the Americans: with all the problems they faced around the globe, no wonder they were ready to compromise with the Soviet bloc here and there ('neat, red-faced, small watery eyes, grey moustache, gold-tipped cigarettes, sick'). 'But whatever anyone else thinks,' he concluded with a sudden gust of anger, 'we are not going to give up the offshore islands in any circumstances.'

'*But whatever anyone else thinks…*' The denial came like a defensive clout from a mailed fist, and it was what I had been working towards for the previous half hour. For I had picked up a sensitive story that the neutralisation of the offshore islands (the Nationalist strongholds of Quemoy and Matsu just opposite mainland China) was part of a secret deal for an eventual compromise with Mao Zedong. And the deal had been worked out by intermediaries of the communists with someone even closer to Chiang Kai-shek than his Vice-President. Chen Cheng — furious at this treachery in high places — had made his contribution to it.

I remember the suede voices of Dr Subandrio in Jakarta and Premier U Nu in Rangoon, whose most casual asides had to be unstitched to see what was concealed in the seams; and the sharp, agonised bark of the unstoppable Sihanouk, arguing with Irish logic that if the skinflint Americans went on supplying him with obsolete arms salvaged from the scrap heap, he would be driven willy-nilly into the hands of the Russians in order to defend his neutrality (sic). *'Ce n'est pas du chantage*! It is not blackmail,' he cried. If I did not believe him I should go and ask General Lon Nol about the disintegrating helicopters Washington was sending him to kill off his own pilots, instead of the enemy: 'Lon Nol is absolutely honest. I have every confidence in him. He can be relied upon to tell the truth.' (In the course of time the honest Lon Nol could also be relied upon to seize power from Sihanouk behind his back when the Prince was away in France).

Questions could be spaced out methodically for Sihanouk, like the trail in a paperchase, for he was ever ready to pick up another and would always stay the course; and the same was true of men like Raul Manglapus and the urbane Vice-President Emmanuel Pelaez in the Philippines. But (as far as possible) they had to be force-fed to Lee Kuan Yew, for he would flag as soon as he lost interest in the questioner, and his track record was uneven. If he wanted to push his side of a story, or give his ideas an airing, or interview the reporter instead of the other way around, he might turn the tables on him and keep the dialogue going until it was the journalist (with another appointment looming) who began to fidget first. But if he saw no profit in an interview, he would treat it like a formal call and cut it short with an analgesic grin. I remember Richard Hughes pacing my patio and thinking up things to ask Lee, only to find himself dismissed after ten minutes of political small talk; one veteran of the *New York Times*, for long the doyen of Far East correspondents, was more than miffed to find himself on the way out after lasting only six.

I see again the suffused faces of quick-tempered politicians who automatically cast themselves as hostile witnesses. They included Denis Healey, Labour Minister for Defence, who took me for a hawk, and Conservative Prime Minister Edward Heath, who took me for a dove when I asked them the same questions about the withdrawal of British forces from Singapore; Dean Rusk, American Secretary of State, who took me for a Limey quitter when I questioned American policy in Vietnam — 'We know who our real friends are,' snarled the Rhodes scholar; and Toh Chin Chye, ex-vice-premier of Singapore, who took me for an agent-provocateur with the bedside manner of a KGB shrink when I tried to pin down responsibility for a wave of political arrests in the island. Each case called for different treatment — challenging Healey, provoking Rusk, abandoning Toh. You could always protest your objectivity, but once you were branded guilty it was usually too late to plead innocent.

There were the determined talkers with a line to plug like Dr Mahathir, who in 1969 accused the Tunku of betraying the Malays and was excommunicated for his pains (rule one: Don't interrupt); the taciturn like Robert McNamara, who gave short answers to long questions and then waited in silence to be asked more (keep the questions even shorter — don't be trapped into babbling yourself): and the unintentionally provocative like Averell Harriman, who told me confidently that World War II had been forgotten, bygones were bygones, and the Japanese were now back in everyone's good books in Southeast Asia (never argue just for the sake of argument; you may win the skirmish, but lose the source).

There were those, like Walt Rostow, who wanted to trade ideas, one for one, and tap the correspondent for what others had told him (exchange is no robbery, but a confidence is a confidence); or like Dr Lee Siew Choh, chairman of the left-wing Barisan Sosialis in Singapore, who in common with comrades the world over spoke through a visor of communist jargon (go for the man behind the Marx). There were those who had to be protected from their own engaging candour — the neutralist Prince Souvanna Phouma, to whom neutralism meant growling like a trapped bear at the mention of all the foreigners from the Russians to the Americans who were so touchingly anxious to play fairy godfather to Laos; the Tunku, who once remarked, 'Where there are Chinese there are communists; where there is shit, there are flies'; the defence minister in Singapore who sighed: 'God knows why I've been given this job; I don't know a platoon from a battalion'; and the necessarily anonymous elder statesman known for his keen interest in country matters who, when asked how he had enjoyed his last pleasure trip to Japan, replied with an eloquent droop of his index finger, 'Alas, the little fellow isn't as agile as he used to be.' (Play fair).

The mood and the tempo are all-important, and the reporter must play each encounter by ear, deciding quickly whether he and his subject see eye to eye or eyeball to eyeball, whether it would be more tactful to talk to him man-to-man or hack-to-hierarch. Tactics must necessarily vary. A display of ignorance — pretended or real — will delight the discursive (and inspire the indiscreet) but may infuriate the busy who do not want to waste time on needless explanations, whereas a display of knowledge will please the busy but may scare off the insecure.

If a hardworked whiz-kid is squeezing him in between an international telephone conference and the happy hour, the correspondent must obviously ask his key questions early in case their tête-à-tête is cut short before he has a chance to frame them. And when interviewing a friendly source it makes sense to waste no time but to open with the burning question of the moment, however incandescent. With strangers of dubious temper, on the other hand, I found it paid to reverse the order of events traditionally respected by secret police interrogators, and to produce the coffee first, the cosh later. My reasoning was simple. The object of the operation was to get straight answers, but the method was to win the confidence of the subject, and the reporter who forgot the method in his eagerness to achieve the object risked walking out of the door with an empty notebook.

At the outset, therefore, the journalist must be ready to listen with endless patience to whatever the interviewee chooses to say, giving him free rein and only pulling him up if his hobbyhorse threatens to become a runaway. No matter how absurd or revolting the ideas expressed, he should show he is listening carefully by nodding from time to time, and accompany the nod with a slight frown to indicate that he is not nodding with agreement or fatigue, but with understanding, perhaps even a modicum of judicious sympathy. He should say as little as possible himself, and at this stage never open his mouth to query, contradict, ridicule, humiliate, disconcert, enrage, or, worst of all, silence his vis-à-vis.

He must not disdain any figures he is given, however trifling — told by an indignant Cambodian officer that the unmentionable

Vietnamese had bombed a Khmer village and wiped out a house, a barn, a bicycle, four oxen and four pigs, I wrote it all down as if it were the Brazilian foreign debt. If he catches his man out in an error or a lie, he must keep it to himself until later. He must know what they are talking about, but never show that he knows more than the other unless they are trading tips. In short, he must be clever enough to resist the temptation to be clever.

It is when the harmless queries have been answered at length, and his subject is visibly losing momentum, that the continent reporter who can hold on until then may with profit relieve himself of his pent-up doubts, broach more controversial matters, reveal his unpalatable knowledge of something the other has dodged speaking about ('Oh, you know about that, do you?'), tell him that what he has said has been flatly contradicted by his friends (as well as his enemies), and ask his most objectionable questions. By that time he may have established the rapport he needs to get away with tapping the man on a nerve. And if not, he has less to lose than he would have had when they started talking an hour before. Faced with a somewhat laconic Robert McNamara at the Pentagon, I left it until I was ready to go through the door anyway before asking him whether — as I had heard — the Americans were contemplating dropping a string of atom bombs across the 17th Parallel to act as a chastity belt between North and South Vietnam.

Premature ejection is not the only hazard, however. The biggest mistake a correspondent can make is to assume that the interview he has just concluded is safely tucked away in his memory and can be left there to sleep it off while he relaxes at the nearest bar. If he has not taken down or taped what he has just been told, he must rush back to his hotel room to type it all out — not necessarily in chronological order, but as it tumbles from his memory. If he cannot get to a typewriter at once, he must seize the first seat he can find, whether it means lolling in an overstuffed fauteuil in a ministerial lobby or crouching on a plastic circle in the men's loo, and scribble it into his notebook. If possible, he must always arrange that there is enough time between appointments for him to record what the last man said.

If there is not, he must settle for the back seat of the taxi that takes him to the next, and put down — however illegibly — at least a list of headings on which his memory can enlarge later.

The meaning may fade with the years — my hasty notes on the Singapore race riots of 1964, wildly scrawled between police stations, read enigmatically: 'gongs and drums sound alarm, talismans, holy water, 14 RFU of 60 each, pull in gangsters ruthlessly, KL — nothing yet, 451 wounded, few shots, teargas, both mins SK shelter in police stas. LKY, Khir together 30 areas' — but they could be decoded at the time. On the other hand if a reporter waits until after his second interview before recording the first, he may lose both in a mental omelette.

Even that calamity can be overcome, however, as long as he does not slam the door on someone he has seen because he thinks he will never need him again. Wherever possible, he must be able to go back to his subject to verify his facts, to clarify his statements, to talk to him once more a week or a year later. He may have to turn aside a tiresome request that he show the man his copy before he publishes it, but to retain his goodwill he must agree to confirm any quotes (if asked) and to put them in their correct context, not cut and splice the interview so that they look like isolated gaffes.

Above all he must keep his confidence by keeping his confidences. The left-hand pages of my notebooks are disfigured by reluctant reminders like 'not to be quoted', 'don't mention', 'not usable', and (somewhat mysteriously) 'don't say they were wearing new clothing". The last referred to Indonesian infiltrators into Malaysia during *Konfrontasi* who had been easily identified and arrested because they had all been fitted out in new — and identical — civilian clothes. The enemy must not be told he had blundered, but left free to blunder again. Had I blundered by publishing the mistake, however, my source would never have given me a second chance.

I9 NOW IT CAN BE TOLD

Even the most closely guarded skeletons of World War II are being brought out into the open.

THE secrets of yesterday are like all the bones of the past: time buries some but exposes others. The story of the infiltrator's new clothes could not be told during *Konfrontasi*, but can be written with impunity today, while in Britain even the most closely guarded skeletons of World War II are being brought out into the open as cupboards are unlocked and files declassified with the passage of the years.

By 1970 I could reveal that six years before Goh Keng Swee, then Finance Minister of Singapore, had told me almost casually over a lunch of roast pork and apple sauce in the Adelphi Grill that he was planning to bring the Indonesians to their knees by cornering all the rice in the region, since they needed at least 1.2 million tons to survive the year. The rice would be resold cheaply elsewhere so that the loss incurred would not be more than five million pounds in all — 'a small price to pay for ending *Konfrontasi*, hm?' (The Americans were unscrupulous enough to supply Indonesia, of course, but they would not dispose of more than 200,000 tons).

If my mouth was watering, it was not strictly from hunger; but I could not write a word of that story until history had taken care of *Konfrontasi*, and Goh's exuberant adventure in economic warfare been abandoned. It was not just that it was strategic information that had to wait until it came of age before it could be allowed out. To publish it at the time would have been more than a breach of security: it would have been a breach of confidence. My notebooks and files are full of unused copy that, like time bombs which could have wreaked havoc then, can be harmlessly exploded now.

In September 1963, for example, General William Walker, the British commander-in-chief in Borneo, told me he would 'almost like *Konfrontasi* to continue for ever' if it meant the British government would change its mind about cutting the strength of the Gurkhas from 15,000 to 10,000. Meanwhile, he could do with all the troops he could lay hands on, and would welcome even the Australian diggers who were sitting on their broad backsides in West Malaysia. But there was little chance of his getting them, because the Australians were 'more concerned with staying friends with the Indonesian enemy than standing by their Malaysian allies'. He had Malaysians, of course, but 'the Malays are a pretentious lot; up in the border area they treat the native Ibans as if they were aborigines'.

"They're no good — they need more training,' said one tough, ascetic British brigade commander. 'They knock off for food.' (He himself chewed Oxo on the move so that war and aerobics need not stop for meals). According to Goh Keng Swee, the debacle at Sebatik in North Borneo in late 1963, in which Malay troops complained that they had been unfairly 'surprised at prayers' by Indonesian intruders who shot them to bits in their own camp, had prompted Walker to 'write a scathing report to Kuala Lumpur accusing the Malay Regiment of gross inefficiency, not to say cowardice. The Tunku was much upset by this, and retorted that he was fed up with the Borneo territories, which had brought endless trouble and would always be a drain on Malaysia's slender resources. Let the British take them back…'

The Malays of Brunei, said the British Deputy High Commissioner to that vest-pocket sultanate, hated and feared their Malaysian cousins, whom they also regarded as bumptious and ignorant. But then Brunei, where an armed revolt in 1962 had first triggered *Konfrontasi*, was going down a slope greased with its own oil. With a personal income of 120 million dollars a year, the Sultan was a feudalist who seemed to see money as a substitute for movement. A deeply religious Muslim with time only for poetry and the Koran, this excellent man did not leave his palace except to go to the mosque — the mosque he had built to the greater glory of the merciful Allah who had provided the riches to pay for it.

That made him the natural prey of venal advisers, and he appeared to have been persuaded that to squander his sacred inheritance on more schools or hospitals or pensions for the people, on roads, fertiliser and electricity for Malay farmers and similar temporal frivolities, would (for the most part) be a sacrilegious waste of God-given wealth. He could cite the Koran to prove it. As for the pig-eating Chinese who formed more than a quarter of the population of Brunei, they were treated as second-class citizens, and if they had the gall to qualify for an administrative job, they could always be rejected on the grounds that they could not speak 'perfect' Malay. 'The Sultan has learned nothing from the last revolt,' added Walker tersely, 'and the government is inefficient and corrupt.'

But Brunei was to change dramatically, and meanwhile a newly-formed Malaysia was fighting for survival against the megalomania of Sukarno. Although all the frank off-the-record backbiting indicated that it had been constructed on a midden of mutual distrust, therefore, no one could be quoted out of turn on the subject of race or religion — at least, not until Singapore snapped off from the federation, and the Straits of Johore became a narrow no-man's-land in a war of words. But there was even a moment when Lee Kuan Yew talked of going underground if the 'ultras' came out on top in Kuala Lumpur.

The Malaysians had treated Singapore not as a partner, but as personal property over which they could claim *droit du seigneur*. The ruling People's Action Party in Singapore, which had no intention of taking this lying down, had made tentative moves to improve its vulnerable position, one of which was to contest the general elections in peninsula Malaysia in 1964. That bid for political leverage on the mainland was a miserable failure, however, and only served to confirm the Malaysians in their suspicion of Lee Kuan Yew's 'inappropriate' ambition to be the federation's first Chinese prime minister.

Goh Keng Swee, who had kept out of this exercise, told me bluntly over a beer at the Istana in Singapore that it had been a fiasco. But he was not sorry the PAP had goofed. Had they not done so, they might have made a far bigger blunder later. The other party leaders had rushed off to the Malaysian hustings to produce this 'silly washout', leaving him to run Singapore with three ministers. In consequence, they had 'faced their moment of truth, and their reputation for infallibility had been cut down to size'. It was no bad thing. The irony of it was that where the PAP had won support, it had been at the expense of the opposition Socialist Front, not the Tunku's government coalition. So 'if they had any sense' the ruling Alliance in Kuala Lumpur would 'offer the PAP free accommodation so that they could continue to split the left-wing vote'.

The *schadenfreude* stuck out like a sore head, but two years later, with Singapore out of Malaysia again, Goh's sardonic joke was inverted. Rajaratnam confided to me in February 1966 that he 'had been discussing with some of his colleagues the advisability of not discouraging the emergence of a militant left in Malaysia in order to shake the complacency of the Alliance, and bring about a better state of equilibrium in which Malaysia might develop a more rational policy towards Singapore'. Drastic, if a little circumlocutory? But only one year before Kuala Lumpur had given solid backing to a notorious pro-communist and pro-Indonesian candidate in a Singapore by-election in the hope that he would wipe out the PAP nominee. (He lost).

Tempers were shortening. By October Lee Kuan Yew was telling me that he feared there was 'nothing to be done' with his abrasive neighbours for the next two or three years, and that he must take steps to ensure the survival not only of the state, but of his own person. He could not travel to the mainland, and he had to be careful where he went even in Singapore. Rajaratnam meanwhile accused the Malaysians of 'wanting to occupy Singapore militarily'. Why else would they be keeping a battalion of troops on the island in defiance of the wishes of its elected government? Although the Malaysians had said they were ready to sign a tripartite defence treaty with Singapore and Britain, Singapore would agree to it only on condition that it guaranteed the territorial integrity of the one-year-old republic against not only an outside aggressor *but the signators themselves.*

Rarely have allies been put so firmly in their place, but then there is nothing like interdependence for straining bilateral relations.

To give their side of the story of the split with Malaysia, a delegation from Singapore visited seventeen countries in 1965. 'Only in Uganda were its members treated with real reserve,' Rajaratnam told me afterwards. Otherwise the reception had been 'almost universally cordial', and many leaders had congratulated the Singaporeans on 'winning independence' from Malaysia. The strongest disapproval of Kuala Lumpur had been voiced in two Muslim capitals — Algiers and Cairo. In Cairo, in fact, the delegates had been told that President Nasser 'had no sympathy with Muslim states of this type, and had remarked that Malaysia seemed to be the one country in which sultans are not completely outdated'; whatever the circumstances, Singapore was 'well shot' of Kuala Lumpur.

****

Ironically, it sometimes becomes the reporter to maintain discretion when spiralling hatred prompts all others to throw it out — at least until the story dies. To write this chapter, I pulled out my notebooks of the sixties and turned these private confidences over as it they had been old love letters that I had locked away in a drawer for more than twenty years in order to keep faith with their authors. But there are correspondents who cannot keep faith for two consecutive press days.

Jostled by hostile, mainly Muslim countries, the Singaporeans had turned for help to those in a similar jam to their west, and Israeli military instructors were flown to the republic to train its embryonic army. But since their advent was likely to infuriate the neighbours if it was made official, a face-saving fiction was invented whereby they were always referred to as 'Mexicans', so that all concerned could quietly ignore them. As a veil over the ugly truth, it was sheer gossamer, but it held — until in April 1967 Andrew Wilson, then defence correspondent of *The Observer*, casually blew it away by breaking the story after a brief visit to Singapore. Freed by his indiscretion, Reuters picked up on his copy and gave it to the world, and within twenty-four hours I was on the spot because I was on the spot. Andrew Wilson, of course, was by then 7,000 reassuring miles away in London.

As foreign minister of Singapore, Rajaratnam was first on the phone, having automatically assumed that I had given the story to Wilson as 'one for the road' — that is, to be used once he had left the republic. After telling me what he thought about that, he asked me to even the score (and so placate the Muslims next door) by sending *The Observer* a piece about a proposal for instructors from Singapore to train the Egyptian navy, and see that it made the paper. I complied. I had no choice anyway. As I pointed out to London, the 'Mexicans' were protected information or they would not be called 'Mexicans'. Consequently, whatever one thought of the prose, the Republic of Singapore's Control of Publications and Safeguarding of Information Regulations (1966) clearly made me liable to serve a prison sentence of three years or pay a fine of ten thousand dollars or both. Had it not occurred to anybody to wonder why I had not written the story months before myself?

There is a time if not a place for all copy. Three years later I could legitimately lead a syndicated backgrounder with a deliberately cryptic 'They're thinning out the Mexicans in Singapore' — and go on to explain what I meant. Every now and then the correspondent must nevertheless choose between the story and the source, if filing the first means riling the second. When a senior American general in Saigon pinned behind his desk a series of two articles I had written headed 'The Vietcong Have Their Problems Too', I felt I had been justified in taking the risk that I would annoy my Vietcong contacts by writing them (I had). But I had broken no confidences, and — even more important — named no names. For information may be secret, but sources are sacred; in Hong Kong 800 journalists pledged themselves never to reveal their sources if they were charged under a new law passed in 1987 that would make the publication of 'false news' a crime, and in England others have gone to jail rather than divulge them.

Even without that hazard, it is not always easy to keep silent. In December 1966 I cabled: 'Communist China has sold several thousand tons of steel to the Americans in South Vietnam for use in the construction of new air and army bases needed in the escalating war against the Vietcong...The leakage closely follows accusations published in *Izvestia* last month that the Chinese communists were trading with their arch-enemies in the US on a grand scale through (Hong Kong).' Senators began asking questions in Washington, where this sort of irony has long since entered into the soul, but I also drew a burst of baseless insinuations from professional anti-communists in Hong Kong and a columnist named Nestor Mata in Manila. These implied that I had been the dupe of Sergei Svirin, the Tass correspondent in Singapore, who had sold me a tatty piece of shop-soiled Soviet propaganda.

Svirin then wrote to me complaining bitterly that I had been instrumental in losing him his first, infinitely precious visa to the Philippines. I wrote back saying that it was obvious he knew nothing of the story for otherwise he would have filed it to Moscow himself (though in truth the Russians must have been far happier that it appeared in a Western capitalist newspaper, and that since it already existed, it did not have to be invented). However, I could not refute the editorial rubbish that was being heaped on both of us by disclosing my source to Svirin or anyone else. The source was, in fact, my bank manager. The Chinese steel was sold through intermediaries in Singapore who dealt with a local American purchasing agent; the intermediaries shipped the steel from Singapore to Saigon, and the agent paid for it through his office in Hong Kong. This was in-house intelligence from the Chartered Bank, and about as far from Soviet disinformation as Wall Street is from Dzerzhinsky Square. But I could not say so.

A journalist must have a high pain threshold, for the agony can last a long time. It is more than a quarter of a century since, in August 1962, I made the front page lead of *The Observer* with a story that began: 'The Chiang Kai-Shek family, which controls Nationalist Formosa, has reached a secret agreement with China's Communist leaders in Peking. This provides for a truce in the Straits of Formosa, and for the future autonomy of the island itself under the continued rule of the Generalissimo and his Kuomintang successors for at least ten years...' Neither side would launch any serious attack against the other during Chiang's lifetime, and after his death the accord would be officially ratified as quickly as possible; Taiwan would become an Autonomous Region of the People's Republic of China, and in time a referendum would be held to decide whether it should be an independent state or part of China proper.

The agreement was the outcome of 'seven years of tenuous contact hampered by mutual distrust', and in Taipei Kuomintang officials 'still protest that so far the exchanges have consisted exclusively of a flood of proposals from Peking which have been met with a wall of rejection in Formosa'. That was not surprising. The negotiations were conducted mainly by two sets of 'peace brokers', one working from Taipei to Hong Kong, the other from Hong Kong to Beijing (a forward 'post office' had recently been set up in Canton). Only seven communist leaders and four Nationalist leaders were officially in the know, and of these the most important were Zhou Enlai in Beijing, and Chiang Ching-kuo — the son of the 'Gimo' — in Taipei. Neither side wanted to gamble on a showdown by invading the other, and the understanding was to their mutual interest. For Beijing it would put Taiwan inside the frontiers of communist China, while for Taipei it would guarantee the island autonomy — and 'an autonomous Formosa will still be a better base camp for the Kuomintang than no Formosa at all'.

My piece led the front page of *The Observer* on 12 August — the 'glorious twelfth' that opens the season for massacring grouse. But now there was something else to shoot down. In Taipei and Washington and points between, Kuomintang spokesmen led the attack by dismissing my report as 'absurd, ridiculous, and impossible'; neither Chiang Kai-shek nor the Americans would for one moment contemplate doing a deal with Beijing; the Generalissimo was dedicated to the cause of 'returning to the mainland', and this tale of an undercover compromise was nothing but an unscrupulous communist fabrication designed to destroy his credit rating with his American backers.

These protestations ignored the two main attractions of the scheme. The first was that for the Chinese face would be saved on both sides: Beijing would be able to call Taiwan part of the People's

Republic of China, while the Kuomintang would remain its actual bosses — and this by virtue of an agreement between Chinese and Chinese that the Americans could not veto without being charged with interfering in their 'internal' affairs. The second was that it might be high time to hedge bets. The Americans might back the 'Gimo', but would they back his son after he died?

'Although America supports the Nationalist challenge to Communist China today, she may not do so tomorrow,' I wrote the following week. 'The next few years may see Communist China join the United Nations and emerge as a nuclear power, the Kuomintang wither further, the status of Nationalist China inevitably decline, and Washington seek a peaceful settlement of the Formosa problem.' By 1972 not only had all of that come to pass, but the United States had recognised Communist China, and President Nixon had visited Beijing. For once I had been wise before the event, but that was all I had to cling to as time continued to slip by. For by 1988 both Chiang Kai-shek and Chiang Ching-kuo were dead, but Beijing and Taipei had still failed to announce their forthcoming marriage.

That would seem to justify the derision showered upon me at the time for trusting the unreliable sources that the sceptics then proceeded to invent for me. Washington pooh-poohed the story as a black-and-white remake of an old script that Maoist agents had been peddling for years. The Hong Kong press remarked that rumours of secret negotiations had already inspired wildly speculative local reports, and went on to speculate wildly that mine was a pastiche based on 'facsimiles of old correspondence of dubious authenticity'. One subsidised publication with more dollars than sense nevertheless picked off one of my contacts: it suggested that I had been taken in by a self-styled Chinese middleman in Hong Kong notorious for pretending that he was involved in hush-hush negotiations between the two Chinas — Tsao Chu-jen.

My Chinese wife Ping and I had had breakfast with Tsao Chu-jen, making our way one Sunday morning past a pile of squawking chicken coops to the ramshackle roof-top penthouse in which he lived — a penthouse which had far more in common with fowls than fancy living, and suitably capped the slums of Hong Kong strewn below it. Tsao cooked the vast Chinese breakfast himself, and Ping and I ate it as he talked. A well-known historian, author, and fellow-traveller, he gave a lucid account of his role as go-between. He normally reported to Beijing through a confidential agent the communists had established near Canton. But for anything important he would go on to Beijing and see Zhou Enlai personally. His contact with Taipei was a classmate who had become a secretary of Chiang Ching-kuo, and who visited Hong Kong once or twice a month on his behalf.

To Chinawatchers I may well have seemed a gullible correspondent who took Tsao on trust, and simply published what he told me. But for me Tsao's account was only the skin of the story, not the sinews beneath, and the irony of it all was that when my report hit the headlines, he wrote a long and irate letter to us and we were never to see him again, although I had been careful to preserve his anonymity. No one trusts a double agent, and through no merit of my own I did not have to put my faith in Tsao any more than did Zhou Enlai or Chiang Ching-kuo. I had other sources.

The man who had given us an introduction to Tsao (in order to find out what he would tell us) was a protégé in Singapore of a Cantonese general named Chang Fa-kuei. Chang Fa-kuei was a veteran warlord of the revolutionary era in China whom no Western reporter could normally see. But we had dined with him in his huge rabbit warren of a house in Hong Kong the day we had breakfasted with Tsao, for he had in turn been a protégé of my father-in-law. And Ping's father was the key to the story that could not be told. He had been a close friend and lieutenant of President Sun Yat-sen, and at the centre of the web of political power that stretched across China south of the Yangtse River. He was highly respected, and to drop his name in Kuomintang circles for whom Canton had been the heart of the revolution was to see the tracery vibrate and set it humming. Long since dead, he was the source of our *guanxi* in Taiwan, the 'Chinese connection' without which contacts are no more than a tangle of loose ends.

We flew to Taipei where it did not take us long to discover that beneath the coats of official whitewash that gave it a suspiciously smooth surface, the Kuomintang was disfigured by a wall-to-wall crack between two main factions. One of these was led by Vice-President Chen Cheng, the other by Chiang Ching-kuo. Chen Cheng had inherited through my father-in-law what the southern Kuomintang considered the legitimate line of descent from Sun Yat-sen. Our *guanxi* therefore ran through the right-wing Chen faction, which would have no truck with the communists, and took in a latticework of political and military contacts leading up to the vice-president himself.

These included not only my four brothers-in-law (two senior generals, the former naval commander of Quemoy, and the quondam fiscal controller of Canton), but a prestigious Kuomintang commander named Hsueh Yueh, who had twice given the Japanese a bloody nose during World War Two despite being let down by Chiang Kai-shek. Like Chang Fa-kuei, Hsueh Yueh had been a protégé of my father-in-law, and Chen Cheng had been a close friend of the family. When my mother-in-law died in Taipei that year, Chen Cheng himself pronounced the eulogy at the memorial service. More name dropping? Yes, but like hard porn in a good novel, it is very much part of the plot. For this was an inner circuit of power that Ping could tap as naturally as I could tap a public relations officer. With the difference that she would be told it as it was.

While I skated across the hard face of the political scene in a series of routine interviews, she plunged through the surface to the reality beneath, coming up for air at the far side of each day to brief me on what she had learned from her talks with her seemingly numberless contacts. The message began to emerge with increasing clarity, as if a reagent were working on secret ink: Chen Cheng would succeed the Generalissimo as president, but he was old and weak and losing ground with the army and Chiang Ching-kuo would wield the real power; Chang Fa-kuei was notoriously insecure, and looked upon with mixed feelings, even suspicion, but there were those inside and outside the Kuomintang who wanted him back in Taiwan to help challenge that power once the 'Gimo' died.

Why? Because Chiang Ching-kuo had been feeling his way towards a contract with the communists for more than six years. He had (it seemed) been using a man called Tsao Chu-jen in Hong Kong as one intermediary, and sending his personal courier to see him at least once a month. But he did not altogether rely on Tsao, because he had learned that Beijing regarded him as an opportunist and did not completely trust him, and he himself wanted a firm understanding with Zhou Enlai. The terms for an agreement were tentative, and would come into effect only after the Generalissimo's death, but there was no doubt that his son was reinsuring with the communists, and a sell-out could be expected within ten years.

Chen Cheng (whose workaday relations with Chiang Ching-kuo were harmonious enough) had therefore begun to spend money in a bid to win back influence in the army and rally support around Hsueh Yueh, so that when the Generalissimo died they would be powerful enough to mount 'almost a sort of bloodless coup' to stop his son from implementing his agreement with the communists. This was the background to my talk with the Vice-President, at which his even temper snapped over the possible sacrifice of Quemoy. Two days later I was taken by night and a devious route to a lamp-lit meeting with the skull-faced General Hsueh Yueh, who saw Chiang Kai-shek himself as the main obstacle to any earlier move against his son. 'I have been waiting for ten years for that man to die,' he murmured softly.

But Chen Cheng died before the 'Gimo', and Zhou Enlai died before the senile Mao. China had been shaken by the terrible paroxysm of the Cultural Revolution, and the fragile synthetic substitute that had done duty for trust between Beijing and Taipei had dissolved. The story had been solid, but it had been washed away by the tide of events. History is full of such sandcastles. And the reporter who describes them may be left with his feet wet and no proof that they had ever existed.

I had protected my informants, however. I had, I must confess, misled my readers by citing as my only sources nameless men in Hong Kong and Macao, and documentation 'in the hands of certain responsible overseas Chinese' (Ping's notes), and it was this scratch list of references that aroused the wrath or mirth of the sceptics. I said nothing of my visit to Taiwan, let alone of the contacts that might have won my copy more respect, and I have continued to say nothing until today. But this gross deception had its lighter side.

A secretary at the Japanese Embassy in Singapore whom I did not know rang me up and asked me to come and chat about my piece. He then had the impudence to face me on my arrival at his office with three more strange Japanese, who — after a little perfunctory bowing and hissing — proceeded without preamble to interrogate me on where and how I had got the story and from whom. I lied, I am happy to think, most convincingly unconvincingly.

20 TREES OF KNOWLEDGE

Pull one end of a thread…you never know where it will lead.

IF PUBLIC facts and public figures provide the surface tension on which a story floats, informal contacts provide the water beneath that enables the correspondent to report in depth, perhaps even get to the muddy and malodorous bottom of things. And despite our marriage vows, Ping could still be classified as an informal contact. She not only guided me (deaf to all my kicking and screaming) through the murk of Maoist revolutionary politics, but on occasion used her 'connections' — as she had in Taiwan — to corner the fleeting truth.

The year before that, Zhou Enlai had visited Rangoon with an enormous cultural delegation whose members immediately went into purdah when not performing and, as far as the press were concerned, might just as well have stayed in the invisible extension of Asia from which they had come. But the delegation included a theatrical troupe, and the theatrical troupe included an opera singer whom Ping had known well before the Liberation. It was the one fingertip contact made between the communist fourth dimension and the capitalist fourth estate on the neutral ground of the Burmese capital, and our one insight into what life in a sick and emaciated China was like in 1961, following the failure of Mao's Great Leap Forward.

The Great Leap had flung China into the stumbling descent that was to end in the Cultural Revolution five years later. In 1966 the Red Guards went on the rampage, the revolution spread to Hong Kong, and by October 1967 I was cabling London from the crown colony: 'In the past seven days overworked explosives experts have detonated or defused 180 genuine bombs planted in the colony, but four people have been killed and 80 others injured.'

Ping had already vanished into the underworld of her personal *guanxi* in Kowloon, for she had excellent references: despite her family background, she had twice been arrested in China for student activities, she was an old girl of the revolutionary university of Canton, and a former classmate of its more inflammable alumni. My notebook began to fill, and among the insider accounts of Red Guard agitation, the connivance of secret societies, but the refusal of Hong Kong workers to strike even if paid, I see one significant jotting — '*secret*: organisation man to get people mobilised went Canton, locked up, but returned'.

This was the nub of the story. Beijing was already curbing the Red Guards, but the Cantonese had got the bit between their teeth, and I could write: 'Southern Chinese extremists, led by a Cantonese cadre who is now the hidden boss of the Anti-Persecution Struggle

Committee, today dominate the Communist revolutionary movement in Hong Kong. The powers of Peking's "moderate" appointees have been drastically curtailed. Repeated Maoist instructions from the mainland to "fight with words, not weapons" have this month been flagrantly flouted. The harassment of Hong Kong has entered a new phase…'

'Left-wing students are sure that if they fight imperialism and go to jail for it now, the more secure they will be [when Hong Kong reverts to China in 1997]. Their Communist leaders reject all proposals for improved social conditions or democratic reform as British bribes…(They) are hostile to the moderates in Peking and look to Canton for support. Many of them believe that Hong Kong's future may lie within a semi-autonomous Kwangtung, the big adjacent province of 50 million people with Canton as its capital, in relation to which the British crown colony is like the pearl in an oyster — beautiful, precious, but ideologically irritating.' Communist China *split in two*? The hostility between Beijing and Canton had been dramatically described by a close lieutenant of the 'organisation man' in my notebook, 'the hidden boss' in my lead. But a splashed story gives the game away in more senses than one. When Ping — who had once known him — then tried to reach the boss himself, everyone suddenly began to lie and look the other way. It was time for her to withdraw.

Connections need not always be so uncomfortably close in order to work for one. The postscript to the Cultural Revolution came to us in 1977 in a letter from an old, half-destitute contact in Canton who was heavily dependent on a few dollars sent to her by relatives overseas. 'When the money arrived this month,' she wrote, I rushed out to buy a bunch of chrysanthemums to celebrate the downfall of the Gang of Four. 'This frivolous bourgeois extravagance on the part of a woman whom the Cultural Revolution had reduced to scraping a living by sweeping the streets said more than a thousand-word cable, and the quote went straight into the lead of a syndication piece.

Another revealing postscript to a revolutionary struggle reached us in a letter smuggled out of capitalist Saigon one year after it had been reborn — by ideological caesarian — as communist Ho Chi Minh City. The writer came of a Vietcong family that had deliriously cheered the triumphant North Vietnamese as their tanks burst into the presidential palace in April 1975, having put the last whirring American helicopters to flight like a covey of startled partridges. The long agony of the Vietnam War was over, the imperialist aggressors had been routed, the patriotic forces of liberation had won, and this was the ironical epitaph:

'The myth is shattered. A year ago we welcomed them as victors, but now we realise that it was we who were the vanquished...' The northerners were taking over everything, elbowing aside valiant southerners who had fought the French and then the Americans over the past thirty years under the inspiration of 'Uncle Ho' and his promises, promises. 'We southerners are terribly disappointed... we find them very ugly in many ways, struggling for power, jealous of each other, dishonest, petty...They have spies everywhere, worse than the CIA...' Like our copy on the Kuomintang split in Taiwan and the communist split in Hong Kong, it was another tale of south against north. The Vietcong had been callously betrayed by their venerated leaders in Hanoi.

For me the letter was the unhappy ending of a running story I had followed for twenty-two years through a proliferating grapevine of contacts that had grown from a single cutting — a cutting I had taken 8,000 miles away in Paris back in 1954. Just one year before that, I had broken into the Italian Communist Party simply by banging on the door and shouting my wares (a projected full page feature in *The Observer*). But more often than not the reporter looking for a way into a wary, even hostile political movement must make an oblique approach through its soft outer skin of supporting intellectuals — perhaps becoming a patient of the doctor who patches up its members after a scuffle with the police, or a client of the lawyer who gets them off on some convenient technicality.

Finding myself acting as long stop for our correspondent in Indochina, and faced with the task of writing a profile of Ho Chi Minh, I asked a left-wing Turkish journalist in Paris if he could introduce me to someone I could talk to among the secret sympathisers of the Vietminh in France. He gave me a name and an address, and not long afterwards I was slipping a note under an obstinately locked door five flights up a dingy block at the wrong end of the Left Bank. The next day Pham Huy Thong phoned, and we met several times thereafter. Peering shortsightedly through his horn-rimmed glasses, he looked like an undernourished medical student struggling through his fourth year. But he was to prove the source of sources.

When I heard in 1954 that I was to be transferred to Vietnam, I asked him if he could give me a contact there. He stalled, saying he would let me know after a few days, and then produced a piece of paper with no name on it, but the address of a paint shop in Saigon. 'Go there and ask for the Professor,' he said simply. That was all. In the movies this sort of thing is all too easy. We are flicked halfway across the world in a second, and no continuity is lost. But in real life we cannot 'cut to Saigon', and the time lag takes its own toll of credibility. Four weeks and forty-eight hours of laborious flying later, Paris had faded into the non-existent past, and when I turned a corner in a strange, unreal Saigon and saw the paint shop, just where the scribbled address said it would be, it had the flat, deceitful air of a mirage. It was impossible to conceive that if I walked through the door and spoke the words I had been taught in that other dream world on the Left Bank of the Seine, someone would actually know what they meant.

'Good morning. Could I speak to the Professor?'

'Certainly. Come through to the back.'

The slim, smooth-faced Vietnamese with a glint of humour in his jet-black eyes introduced himself as 'Lucien', and from that moment a broad net of Vietnamese connections began to unroll for me like a trawl in the wake of passing time. The 'Professor', his elder brother, had been the underground political boss of the Vietminh in South Vietnam during the French Indochina War, and was now in the communist North. I was soon to meet him as 'Gaston' in Hanoi, and through him the four ministers with whom I dined out on the predictable demise of the Geneva Agreement, progressing to Pham Van Dong and finally 'Uncle Ho' himself. Lucien had brothers and sisters and cousins and in-laws with more brothers and sisters and cousins, some in Hanoi or with the North Vietnamese army, some half-submerged in the South as the Vietminh became the Vietcong, and some conscripted by the government of South Vietnam, so that the extended family found itself on both sides of the non-existent front line when fighting resumed in the late fifties.

Each had his piece of the puzzle to fit into place, but in the years that followed Lucien would also arrange for me to see emissaries from the Vietcong and the National Liberation Front who had slipped into Saigon secretly from their hideouts in 'War Zone D'. We would meet late at night, perhaps in a dim-lit room above a radio repair shop, or at the back of a deserted restaurant. Their half-whispered talk over a warm beer while the cockroaches rustled but the city slept would be all the illumination I needed.

'Senior officials of the National Liberation Front accept that the guerrillas in South Vietnam cannot win a purely military victory,' I reported in November 1964. It was news with a capital N. They had told me that they had two options. The first would be to overthrow the Saigon regime with a combination of guerrilla war in the provinces, insurrection in the towns, and mutiny in the National Army.'...The Vietcong has started by suborning junior officers and small units in danger areas, persuading them as good Vietnamese to desert to the guerrillas or stay passively at their posts and be ready to surrender when given the signal.' The troops of an entire military region were now ready to lay down their arms when ordered, one undercover contact told me down in the Mekong Delta, and the spectacular Vietcong raid on the American air base at Bien Hoa in which twenty-eight aircraft were destroyed or damaged had been successful thanks to 'our inside knowledge from men in the Vietnamese unit (there). That enabled us to make a model of the base, mount a trial attack elsewhere against a mock-up of its installations and defences, and direct accurate fire...'

The alternative to this formula for victory (I continued) was to 'beguile the Vietnamese leaders in Saigon into negotiating, and the Americans into departing peacefully of their own accord'. That would turn on the offer of a settlement between Saigon and the National Liberation Front which 'might throw up a broad, largely non-communist Coalition Government and mean that South Vietnam would remain a separate state for several years to come". Here it was again — the snare or the solution I had already been shown from different angles in different lights by Colonel Thao, Wilfred Burchett, and President Pham Khac Suu.

Why? Possibly because Thao was 'Albert', the brother of Lucien and Gaston. He had been the secret intelligence chief of the Vietminh in South Vietnam during the Indochina War. When I first met him he was living incognito in a village in the Mekong Delta, but he moved about at night, and Lucien had taken me to a clandestine rendezvous with him in an empty house in Saigon. Thanks to a wartime understanding that neither would hurt the other, Thao had a powerful protector in the episcopal brother of President Ngo Dinh Diem, and as he had sidled into the city after dark to see me, he would soon sidle into a position of trust under Diem with the nominal rank of major in the new South Vietnamese National Army.

But Thao was the servant of neither Hanoi nor Saigon. As his letter to McGeorge Bundy was to indicate, he was a middleman bent on an endless conspiratorial quest for a leader and a government that could rally all true Vietnamese nationalists behind it, whoever they were fighting for. It was a formula for peace that could arguably give victory to either side, even both. In the military coup of November 1963 in which Diem was butchered, it was Thao who seized the radio station with a detachment of Vietnamese marines and called on the President to surrender. But it was also Thao who coolly told me after the first coup that there must be a second, for the men who had succeeded Diem were not much better. He was working on it. Khanh duly took over with Thao's ostensible support, but when Khanh did not measure up, Thao plotted against him in turn, and went on plotting in his pursuit of excellence until he was finally murdered by

Khanh's successors. None of them had been the man for the job in his estimation, and he was to be proved right.

In his company I would find myself squeezing through the maze of tunnels under some lonely 'strategic hamlet', struggling through the swamps of the Mekong Delta in marinated shoes, or peering over the buckled gunwale of a steel-plated assault craft as we threaded our way through its backwaters in pursuit of the elusive enemy — or was it friend? We confronted captured guerrillas, counted captured arms, pored over captured documents. He saved my life once, pulling me away gently as I was about to tread on a Vietcong booby trap hidden under a fallen palm frond.

It was Thao who revealed that the killing of Diem had involved a false coup within a coup — troops had been brought into Saigon to thwart an imaginary revolt so that they would be on hand to mount the real one themselves — and kept me posted on all the coups that followed. And it was he who told me with a wall-eyed grin that when the mobs came out against Nguyen Khanh in August 1964, five senior generals, ignominiously trapped in the Saigon headquarters from which they notionally directed a six-figure army and the destiny of South Vietnam, were reduced to telephoning the Archbishop and pleading with him to use his spiritual influence to get them out of the place safely. (The disobliging prelate failed them, but Khanh was rescued by helicopter, and the rest of the top brass sneaked out by the back door).

Thao, Lucien, Gaston…It was, so to speak, all in the family. The reporter who thinks of his contacts as isolated informants radiating from the hub that is himself is left with a wheel where he should have a web. Following up news was essentially a matter of following up sources — sources that were already linked to each other in a complex mesh of human relations. The old boy nets, whether of clans or communists or phi beta kappa, could carry the correspondent forward from one contact to the next in his pursuit of the running story. And if it was true that the antediluvian hatred of brother for brother could suddenly tear a hole in the web through which the reporter could fall, it was equally true that the incongruous friendship between enemy and enemy would sometimes enable him to jump frontiers.

****

I first met Wilfred Burchett when the Vietminh marched into Hanoi in November 1954, for he had been with Ho Chi Minh in the field. Later that month Burchett — branded a commie dog to whom the South was off-limits — paid a clandestine visit to Saigon, where he looked me up and introduced me to a ferociously anti-American French geographer named Charlie Meyer. Meyer invited me to a discreet tea party of Vietminh sympathisers unwise enough to call themselves the Vietnamese Peace Movement. Since 'peace' in quotes was the exclusive prerogative of communists the world over, all the Vietnamese members of this little coterie were very understandably arrested within forty-eight hours, but not before I had exchanged cards with a few of them, including a 'progressive' Buddhist named Du. I wrote a piece about the arrests which *The Observer* found room for on the front page. I doubt if that made any difference, but the co-chairmen of the Geneva Agreement called foul, and Du (among others) was quickly released.

For the next fourteen years Du was an unfailing source on the Vietminh, the Vietcong, and the militant Buddhists who entered into a catch-as-catch-can alliance with them, their common ground being not only their hatred of the Catholic Diem, but the belief that each could control the other. He was to lead me to pious Superior Bonzes at the Vien Hoa Dao Pagoda, where the Four Noble Truths inspired so much righteous if bloody rioting, and to my exclusive interview with President Pham Khac Suu and an evanescent scoop about his 'conspiracy for peace'. He also sent me to a series of midnight meetings with a group of dissident intellectuals in Hanoi whom the Hungarian revolution of 1956 had inspired to demand more democracy from Ho Chi Minh (until 'Uncle Ho' closed down their magazine and introduced them to the democratic life of a re-education camp).

The Vietcong-Buddhist connection had a certain logic. But it was at first not clear why the left-wing proclivities of Charlie Meyer had persuaded him in 1954 to become an adviser to Le Van Vien. 'Bai Vien' was the execrable boss of the Binh Xuyen mafia which had acquired its licence to run both the cops and the robbers in Saigon as a reward for fighting against the Vietminh during the Indochina War. However, it appeared that he had now decided against his better judgement that it would be to his advantage if he gave his vile depradations on the Vietnamese public the cachet of a political programme.

At the Binh Xuyen headquarters in Saigon, accordingly, Meyer introduced me to another, mild-mannered political adviser to the illiterate, pockmarked 'godfather' who was his new chief. His name was Ho Huu Tuong, and he contrived to be simultaneously a leading lay Buddhist highly regarded by the hierarchy, and a Trotskyist with links to the Vietcong and Hanoi. He was accompanied by a second Trotskyist called Tran Van An. Their common denominator was — once again — their abomination of the obstinate President Diem, which had meanwhile drawn Bai Vien into a partnership with the

Cao Dai and Hoa Hao sects. Strange bedfellows? They included a Cao Dai general whose two wives had to sleep on either side of him to see that no harm came to his magnificent waxed moustache. But there were to be even stranger.

'Hanoi has announced the formation of an opposition fighting front of the Cao Dai, Hoa Hao and Binh Xuyen sects, backed by the Vietminh,' I wrote in an *Observer* end-lead published on 14 January 1955. Ho Chi Minh had offered to stop pressing for the unification of North and South Vietnam for the next five years, but the main condition was that Diem and the Americans must go. Otherwise there would be an armed insurrection in the South supported by communist troops infiltrated from the North. 'The Vietminh have underlined this threat by consolidating their alliance with rebel sect forces,' I went on. 'Two regiments of former Vietminh resistance fighters are being formed to support the Hoa Hao maquis.' Four years later those 'former Vietminh resistance fighters' — the Vietcong — would kill their first Americans, firing the opening shots in what was to become the Vietnam War.

But by then the sects would be out of the game. For only three months after my piece was published the Binh Xuyen had been driven from the burning streets of the capital by the mortars and machine guns of Diem's battalions, and Ho Huu Tuong had been captured and sentenced to death. I was among those his son appealed to for help, and (doubtless with others) I wrote to Diem, emphasising that Tuong had always urged Bai Vien not to use violence. His sentence was suspended, and he spent the next seven years on Poulo Condore, the Devil's Island of Indochina.

I thought I had seen the last of him, but in 1963 Diem himself was 'executed', Tuong was released, and — like Du before him —

became a loyal source on the labyrinthine politics that threatened to bring the warring Vietcong and the rioting Buddhists together against the latest American protégé at the top of the pile in South Vietnam. Both, moreover, were to be cross-indexed with Thao, Burchett, President Suu and my Vietcong contacts on the subject of a 'nationalist' and 'neutralist' equation for ending the war and sticking the two halves of the country back together again. My experience with Du and Tuong had taught an important lesson: keeping faith with sources is more than just its own reward.

By April 1968 President Johnson had stopped all bombing north of the 20th Parallel in Vietnam, and called for talks 'on the substance of peace'. To the surprise of some, the communists had accepted the offer. What was the real mood in Hanoi — and among the Vietcong? After thirteen years I could still call at the two diminutive, almost identical houses at opposite ends of Saigon in which Du and Tuong lived, with their separate windows on to the other side of the war. Tuong was not only in constant touch with the Vietcong, but had recently seen an emissary from the North. 'The bombing has affected the situation,' he told me, 'especially the supply of food. They need a pause.' So the communists had agreed to talk. Why not? According to Hanoi and the Liberation Front, the Americans had proposed peace moves knowing that they would have to ditch President Nguyen Van Thieu, their latest anti-communist puppet, and that there would have to be a new, 'convenable' government in the South which the North could deal with and Washington would have no obligation to defend. That could mean a coalition in Saigon which would include the Liberation Front. The ants would then be in the sugar.

It appeared that everything would be done to make things easy for the Americans. The Vietcong would be dissolved or merged with the South Vietnamese army, and the South would even agree to accept economic aid from the United States (sic). 'We want to save Washington's face,' Du had told me five days earlier. 'So we shall not insist on key jobs in the new government for members of the Liberation Front; we shall get the ministries we want later. The Front is ready to defer unification with the North, and we shall not demand the immediate withdrawal of American troops. We are not going to push President Johnson into a corner...'

Ironically, Richard Nixon was to succeed Johnson within months, and the war to go on for seven more years (before the communists were to march into Saigon to be duly greeted by a 'neutral' coalition). But they were seven years during which the running commentary from Du and Tuong could have continued had I continued to cover Vietnam. This, though I did not know it, was my last visit. To keep my balance, I asked to see the Minister of Information in the 'pro-American' government of President Thieu — only to find that he was Tran Van An, who had been the other Trotkyist adviser to the Binh Xuyen back in 1955. Burchett, Meyer, Du, Bai Vien, Tuong; Vietminh, Vietcong, Buddhist militants and Binh Xuyen gangsters, doomed rebel sects in Saigon, doomed dissident 'democrats' in Hanoi — pull one end of a thread, and keep pulling: you never know where it will lead, or how many leads it will give you.

2I IGNORANCE IS NEVER BLISS

Never write off bars…they are the market places of the media.

GIVEN the promiscuity of politics, there is no limit to the casual relationships and dangerous liaisons from which a journalist may benefit if he takes a little trouble. In 1956 a left-wing Malay in Singapore named Samad Ismail put me in touch with admirable impartiality with Adam Malik, who was to become vice-president of Indonesia under General Suharto, and with Njoto, the number three man in the powerful Indonesian Communist Party that Suharto was utterly to destroy. In 1957, and running true to form, Samad recommended me to a bright ring of politicians in Malaya whose colouring ranged from bigoted Marxist-Leninist to bigoted Muslim fundamentalist and back again. But for a man who was to confess that he had been a militant communist for three-quarters of his life he excelled himself when he introduced me to Colonel Abdullah Hussein Tyrconnel-Fay — a converted Irish (?) Canadian (?) Catholic who reputedly acted as the liaison officer and arms buyer in Singapore of the murderously anti-communist Darul Islam insurgents in Indonesia.

A few months later the 'Colonels' Rebellion' broke out in Sumatra, and 'Turk' took to propping up the bar of the Cockpit Hotel, cadging drinks and money from correspondents in exchange for lurid stories of the latest Darul Islam 'military success' (a shooting-booting-looting routine reserved strictly for unarmed villagers), and turning on any newcomer the black, vitreous eyes of the born liar. The CIA station in Singapore recruited him — and found themselves paying him $10,000 to shut his mouth. (The Singapore government would not have approved, and they both knew it). But his luck could not last. He was thrown into a remand prison for being on the island without a passport, no one would give him one, and after whiling away the months reading Keats and writing verse in Outram jail, he was finally shipped off to Mexico (the only country that would let him in) where he was found knifed in a cheap hotel one sunny morning the following year.

Yet the most deceptive thing about Turk was his lack of deceit. He may have told less than the truth, but he rarely told more. He was what he said he was, the liaison officer and arms purchasing agent for Darul Islam. In his flat I met a Bugis blockade-runner from Sulawesi, a rebel Achinese 'general' from Sumatra, and one of the men behind the Tjikini incident from Java. Turk told me he had smuggled a Darul Islam 'minister' up to Kuala Lumpur and taken him to a highly compromising meeting with the Tunku. He had.

Never write off bars, whatever the politicians say, for they are the market places of the media, and — as I have shown — I have found good contacts and copy in bars from Panjim to Phnom Penh. Sam White, the respected doyen of foreign correspondents in Paris, held daily court at the bar of the Crillon Hotel for so many years that when it was done away with they cut off and gave him the corner his elbows had worn smoother than smooth. And never write off rascals. They can be infinitely more trustworthy than regular guys. It takes the unsavoury to know the unsavoury, and rascals have the dark meat of the story to give — which is the meat all editors want (and more likely to contain the truth).

In 1973 a former bodyguard of Mao Zedong testified in Washington that the Chinese had been manufacturing heroin in Canton and shipping it out in crates through Macao. Since there was no confirmation from the Macao end, his statement was understandably treated as fragile and handled with care. Reporters tended to avoid all risk of contradiction when writing on the subject by quoting the opinions of fair-haired Anglo-Saxon officials whose misinformation was at least authoritative. There was, in consequence, loose talk of a monstrous Chinese communist plot to enslave the American people as addicts. But this made no sense, if only because the American people could be left to do that for themselves. What did these 'unimpeachable sources' really know? Where was the who-what-when-where-why? It was all suspiciously vague.

So it seemed only logical to turn to the eminently impeachable. And that — as it turned out — set the record straight. It was common knowledge in the underground (a reassuringly disreputable left-wing Cantonese in Hong Kong told us) that the poppies were grown in the eastern part of Guangdong province in South China by the Hakka and Chaozhou inhabitants. The raw drug, which was of inferior quality, was processed in two factories on the south bank of the Pearl River at Canton. The output of heroin and refined opium was slipped across the border into Macao, or smuggled into the New Territories of Hong Kong by fishing vessels. The object of the operation? Nothing sinister. Just money. The communists had nothing to do with it. And why should he lie? We weren't paying him anything.

In many countries of the Third World the political opposition is the devil by definition, but no reporter can earn his keep by sticking rigidly to the side of the angels (who tend to rotate anyway, as if on the point of a needle). It is from the dissident and therefore disreputable that one will learn what the government wishes to hide, for men tend to study their enemies more than their friends, and if they lie about them, they are also experts on them. It was a former Singapore editor who broke the news of the Sino-Soviet rift, and he acquired his notable scoop not in Moscow or Beijing, but Taipei. A cynic would automatically have written it off as a bedtime story fabricated by the Kuomintang, but he realised that while the Nationalists in Taiwan might spread disinformation as a regular nine-to-five chore, they also knew more about communist China than anyone else, because above all others they had the means, the motive, and the opportunity.

The easy way out is to put one's faith in well-groomed contacts who look, sound and smell conventional, especially if they speak English (even if they have not yet been raped). But I have been leery of English-speakers since I was with a British division in Sicily and Italy during World War II, when middle-aged natives would rush up to us in every village we captured from the Germans to offer their services as 'interpreters' (i.e. political informers and procurers). It only slowly and painfully dawned on us that all the members of this touchingly Anglophile brotherhood spoke English in the same streetwise American idiom because they had all been deported from the United States as gangsters and bootleggers. Stamped 'He's-okay-he-speaks-English', these minor Mafiosi were a menace — until we were wise to them and could turn 'Cosa Nostra' into 'cosa nostra'

Similarly, Chinawatchers covering the Cultural Revolution from Hong Kong who lifted reports from Japanese correspondents in Beijing could discover that they had been thumbing rides to ridicule. In theory (and often in practice) the Japanese had two advantages: they were on the spot in quantity, and they could read the most revealing sources of news then available — the ubiquitous big character wall posters. But posters with a real revolutionary message were often half-hidden in a collage of polemical rubbish that could range from the political manifesto of a nineteen-year-old crackpot with a following of five other jokers to the ideological equivalent of 'Charlie Brown is a fink'. It was therefore necessary to sift the fine from the fool's gold, and this could be beyond the collective wit of the less able and more programmed of the Japanese, whose flair for making a personal judgement was about equal to that of their cameras.

When they did sort through the evidence, they were usually influenced less by the realities of the Cultural Revolution in China than by corporate policy in Japan (an editorial line fostering better bilateral relations and thus a bigger trade imbalance), for they were essentially 'bureaucrats on a promotion ladder', as a colleague wrote in 1987. The consequent distortions — and nothing distorts like the urge to conform — were aggravated by the fact that while the Japanese use Chinese characters in their writing, the characters do not always mean quite the same thing in both languages, nor are they pronounced in quite the same way (cf French 'endive' equals English 'chicory', and *vice versa*). Those with only a little learning in Chinese could therefore make dangerous mistakes, and among the canards put about in this way, I understand, was a sensational report that Jiang Qing, the termagent wife of Chairman Mao and leader of the notorious Gang of Four, had been purged at the height of the Cultural Revolution. For 'Jiang Qing' read Kang Sheng (China's elderly security chief). Some Japanese had done the opposite.

As a Chinawatcher myself, I followed closely the ups and downs of fellow palmists, crystal-gazers, thaumaturgists, gypsy queens and investment counsellors dedicated to the same study, and their record left me with mixed feelings about them. The most reliable of accredited experts can become consistently misleading once he thinks he is infallible, and the reporter must above all have a nose for nonsense when it is presented as incontrovertible truth. The decoy, by definition, looks like the real thing, and it was important to be diverted rather than deflected by pundits like Maria Yen, director of the Union Research Institute in Hong Kong, who categorically declared Mao dead years before his time. Like another cocksure pronouncement that the wily old Chairman had ninety-nine doubles, the report was, to say the least, 'an exaggeration' (as Mark Twain cabled AP on their premature story of his own demise). Experts? When in peril of being persuaded against my better judgement, I remind myself that Sir Joshua Reynolds, probably the finest English painter of his century, believed until his death that he had the real Mona Lisa, and the one in the Louvre was a fake.

Before my colleague Gavin Young set out on a long, gruelling and chancy journey through the jungle to find the rebel Naga tribesmen in the wild hills on the Indo-Burmese frontier, he took the risk of asking the only expert on the subject then available in London whether there was something light but welcome that he could take them as presents (the beads that bought Manhattan island inevitably spring to mind). 'Safety-pins' was the instant and only answer. It seemed that these primitive but ingenious fellows could put the pins to a hundred uses and thought them worth their weight in gold. Gavin therefore packed a thousand or so, and after six weeks of self-inflicted exertion and hardship finally arrived at the remote headquarters of the lucky recipients.

Somewhat disconcertingly, this did not resemble a wigwam of Canarsee Indians so much as a British regimental hill station, with its disciplined barracks and drill square, its saluting base and lazily flapping flag, its offices and information centre filled with typewriters, steel filing cabinets and documents (orders of the day, battle reports, news bulletins — all in English), its uniformed staff officers and stamping and saluting sentries. At mess on the first evening (and beneath a sign reading 'Praise God from whom all blessings flow...') Gavin nevertheless raised the subject of safety pins, to be regarded with utter bewilderment by the Naga general presiding. 'Safety pins?' exclaimed the astonished old soldier in an English so precise that it was a reproof in itself. 'Mr Young, what on earth would we do with safety pins?' Gavin might as well have tried peddling the things at Wellington Barracks before leaving London. He had forgotten that his 'expert' had been a woman.

But that is only the reverse side of the coin. Everyone is an expert in something, and if he sticks to what he knows, can be worth his weight in words. First, there are the journalists themselves. The passing correspondent who does not consult native and resident newspapermen is simply not doing his job, for they daily pound the political pavements where he is merely window-shopping. My quick

if slippery grip on the Goa story owed much to patient briefing by
the editors of the *Statesman* in Calcutta and the *Hindustan Times* in
New Delhi, and my first safe if stumbling passage through the maze
of Japanese politics to the Tokyo correspondents of Reuters and the
London *Times*.

Journalists are only a point of departure, of course. In a city of
two million souls there are two million potential sources. But the
natives may be afraid to talk, and — as in Mao's China — you can
find yourself floundering in a morass of silent citizenry with whom
a conversation will yield no more than the time of day and a reel or
two of straight propaganda. In those circumstances not only foreign
correspondents and diplomats but expatriate teachers and students
and technicians can lift a corner of the blackout curtain and let
through a little forbidden light. The reporter must find contacts in
as many walks of life as he can, because the specialist is an expert
witness who cannot be blinded with science. Chinese cadres could
boast to me that thanks-to-the-Thought-of-Chairman-Mao their
pigs were bearing litters of up to twenty farrow, and get away with it;
it took a blasphemous British agriculturalist to ask how they managed
to breed sows with ten pairs of teats, and would they please show
him one? Simple when you know.

And somewhere there is an expert on everything, even when it
does not exist. When a hysterical epidemic of the dreaded if purely
imaginary disease *koro* swept through Singapore in 1967, fathers,
friends and neighbours were to be seen in streets and coffee shops
hanging on hard to the exposed male organs of hapless victims until a
doctor could be called. If their grasp of the subject was not sufficient,
they would truss it with wire, or clamp it between chopsticks, for it
was believed that the afflicted member would otherwise shrink into

the abdomen and kill its mortified owner. There was, in fact, no such disease as *koro*, but I found a specialist in it nonetheless, and was therefore able to write the best-selling story of my entire career.

The correspondent must constantly look at people as possible sources, just as — to paraphrase an old Chinese aphorism — the coachmaker thinks of them as customers and the coffinmaker as corpses. Nor must they be taken at face value, for they tend to be disguised by the labels we pin on them, and are rarely just what we see. An Australian High Commissioner in Hong Kong turns out to be an atomic physicist by training, and therein lies his real significance as a Chinawatcher — at least to me. An old army friend last known as a gem-polisher in London appears in Sarawak in 1964 as a senior officer in MI5. A local British police chief met in Sabah in 1965 is transmuted by 1978 into an American Foreign Service officer in the State Department in Washington. A somewhat aloof Chinese general suddenly reveals that he was educated at Cambridge and took law at the Inner Temple. His father was a British civil servant, and he feels himself a 'two-passport man'. Now we can talk.

It has to be remembered that a man is many things simultaneously — perhaps British, a Quaker, a Liberal, a stamp collector, a Prokofiev addict, a tennis buff, a bank manager — and a contact. When I went to see my bank manager about an overdraft during the Vietnam War, and he casually mentioned that the Americans were buying steel from China through Singapore (and even cement from Haiphong) I made the mistake of concentrating on my role as a needy customer, not a reporter, and of thinking of him as a bank manager, not a source. In consequence, I had walked out of his office hugging to myself my right to spend my way into the red before I realised he had thrown in the first half of a front page story as a bonus. *Just where was this steel going, and for what?* I turned on my heel and ran back in again to ask him for more details. But I had almost failed to recognise the news when it was thrust under my nose, as a Londoner may fail to recognise his local butcher if he meets him on the beach in Bali — with the difference that the butcher is out of context, but a possible source of news should never be.

A reporter must be switched on twenty-four hours of the day, for while the 'photo opportunity' is a sitting duck to be shot at leisure, the 'story opportunity' is a swiftly moving target, and calls for quick reflexes. In the Mekong Delta I suddenly find myself squeezed into the back of a converted jeep with General Paul Harkins, Ambassador Cabot Lodge, and Mr William Bundy, none of whom knows who I am. (Shut up and listen). In Manila a car stops to offer me a lift, and the only other passenger is Vice-President Pelaez. (Start asking questions fast). Above all, the pop-up target calls for instant recognition, whatever the camouflage.

This point was well made by my *Observer* colleague, Neal Ascherson, in his account of how in 1913 an editor in Prague called Egon Kisch shook the known world with a scoop about a sensational spy scandal. Kisch had got on to the story because a star player on his Sunday football team had failed to turn up for a match. The man was a locksmith, and he presented himself apologetically on the Monday to explain that he had dropped out because some army brasshats had banged on his door on Sunday morning and ordered him to open all the desks and cupboards in an empty house. What? Oh, yes, they had found some papers in Russian and some photographs of military plans. But, look here, terribly sorry about the match…(The team had lost 5-7).

The fuming Kisch suddenly came to and forgot about football.

He knew the house. It belonged to Colonel Redl, chief of staff and head of intelligence, whose 'tragic death' had been announced in an official bulletin that morning, accompanied by much wringing of hands over a hero who might have risen to become commander-in-chief of the Austro-Hungarian army. The unthinkable truth dawned on him. The bulletin was a cover-up, and in reality the impeccable Redl had been a Russian spy who had been graciously allowed to shoot himself. Kisch ran the story, which was to inspire a play by John Osborne, and a film in 1985, nearly three-quarters of a century after the event.

Estelle Holt was less lucky. When the corpulent Babal Angelbal told the Air Opium pilots at the Rendezvous cafe in Vientiane how he and his aeroengine had dozed off together in mid-flight, leaving the apologetic Ms Holt to contemplate an approaching mountain peak, one of them came over to talk to her. He was a quiet, pleasant-mannered Frenchman, and she was to see him from time to time until he was killed when his plane crashed two years later. It then emerged that he had been not only a quiet, pleasant-mannered Frenchman, but an outstanding hero of the Resistance during World War Two, and an intrepid agent of the British intelligence service. His funeral in Vientiane was well-attended, and among others two solemn British service attachés in uniform were on hand to salute his grave. Estelle wrote the obituary, ignoring a tasteless objection from Reuters that he had been deported from Britain for gold smuggling. *De mortuis nil nisi bonum.*

It was not until 1986 that the full heat and glare of the British media were turned on to his fabulous exploits. As indefatigable as he was fearless, it seems, he had worked not only for the British Special Operations Executive (SOE) but the German Sicherheitsdienst (SD) and had blown to the enemy a vast network of undercover agents in France, most of whom were executed. Why? To help the Germans win the war? To sell the Germans a very expensive British dummy? At the hollow heart of the mystery was a third, far more startling suggestion that he had not been acting on the instructions of either his immediate British or German masters, but of no less a patriot than the head of MI6, who (being only human) hated the rival SOE more than he hated the Sicherheitsdienst.

Whatever the explanation, he had powerful enough witnesses in Britain (and Germany) to ensure that he was honourably acquitted of all charges after the war, and left at liberty to kill himself in Laos while everyone covered up for him. Rumour had it that he had faked his death and was now living in Spain — but not, of course, under his own name: Henri Dericourt. To Estelle, however, he had been nothing more than an airline pilot. That was his label, and for lack of a clue to contradict it she had perhaps lost a story of stories, even a blockbusting bestseller. 'I think I could have got the whole thing from him; he was pretty lonely in Laos,' she sighed twenty-five years after he had taken it with him. For the reporter, ignorance is never bliss.

22 CATCHING IT LIVE

An immoderate demand in Communist China for Darkie toothpaste?

THE 'story opportunity' is a chance that must be taken, even if it means taking a chance. I suppose Ivansong's dissertation on the loneliness of long-distance reporters could have been prompted by my first encounter with four of them in World War Two, when I myself was not playing the journalist, but the soldier with the pillow-breasted nanny. It was November 1942. Forward elements of my division had landed on the beaches west of Algiers and had raced 500 miles across North Africa in a bid to capture Tunis, too, before the Germans got there. But by the time we reached Tebourba, only fifteen miles from our objective, the going had deteriorated abruptly. The Germans had flown in crack parachutists to block us, and acquired complete command of the air:

Our fighters were by then operating at extreme range, their machines from a base only twenty miles away. In consequence, a regular shuttle service of Stukas had been dive-bombing us all day, sirens blaring, and the main road was littered with the corpses of men and trucks riddled with bullets as the Messerschmidts came screaming down out of the sun to strafe them.

These army trucks were, of course, camouflaged, and most of them had moved up to the fickle front line in convoys, each with its own spotter standing up and scanning the sky nervously for hostile planes. It had done them no good. But now, by way of contrast, down the road from the rear came an improbable apparition, a gleaming black Citroën saloon, its chromework flashing and its low-slung bottom waggling saucily at an ill-tempered Nemesis as it skirted the smouldering wrecks and the bomb craters. Inside were four American war correspondents, who attached themselves to me for rations as if by instinct. They then proceeded to extract vivid first-hand copy from battered but battle-high British soldiery who had just come out on top in a point-blank brush with German tanks, but had not yet been warned against newspapermen.

Towards sunset more German tanks appeared on the skyline behind us, and we were cut off, at least until nightfall. Armed only with their pens and pads, the journalists had driven a hundred dangerous miles into this trap without an aircraft spotter, a lick of camouflage, a toothbrush, a tin of Spam, or a thought for tomorrow between them. I almost blushed for the opulent clutter of guns and packs and blankets and compo rations and petrol cookers in the middle of which we lounged. But at least I could give them supper, and after dark we "withdrew" together, Citroën and all, to leave the enemy empty-handed. Anyway, they had to go back and file.

The armchair commentator who seemed to be taking Neil Davis to task for getting killed in Bangkok while on camera might have given an I-told-you-so nod at such feckless behaviour. He had quoted a book 'which showed that politically astute correspondents, with good connections to the high command, could often get more accurate information on the progress of the war than their more courageous counterparts, who wrongly extrapolated what they saw in one sector of the front to apply to the entire war'. But four correspondents whose 'good connections to the high command' were 500 miles away back in Algiers could have told him that this was manifest bunkum. And it could still be bunkum if the distance was 500 yards.

As I wrote in protest at the time, good contacts at general headquarters too frequently mean men paid, programmed and patriotically motivated to distort the truth to suit their own side. A correspondent must go to them to get the strategic picture as best he can. But he must also go to the front to see for himself, to get the smell and feel of the fighting, its agonies and absurdities. One may be the head, but the other is the heart of the matter. If reporters are 'astute' enough to come through the minefields of misinformation back at base with the truth unscathed, they should be astute enough to avoid 'wrongly extrapolating what they saw in one sector of the front to apply to the entire war'. If their idea of covering an act of violence out in the country is to pick the brains of pundits in the capital, they have no business to be in the business anyway. You cannot report a war (famine, fire, or flood) as a succession of 'talking heads'.

Every reporter knows that it is easier to write about what he has seen than what he has been told, that the facts on paper are no substitute for the facts on the ground, even though he earns his living by transposing them from ground to paper again. And this holds good whether he is reporting a war or a baby doll beauty contest. It was one thing to listen to G. K. Handoo theorising with subcutaneous menace on the future of Goa after the Indians marched in. It was quite another to see what the Goanese thought about it in the great, grim church of Bom Jesus.

As in past times of foreboding, the mayor (in place of the governor) led a pilgrimage of the devout from Panjim to the church to ask St Francis Xavier for protection against the calamity that hung over them. Once inside, a solitary Caucasian, I found myself hemmed in by a stifling crush of men in white and women in saris, many of them with children in their arms, and sensed like a sharp odour the fervour of this close-knit Catholic community. Together we edged towards the emaciated cadaver of the saint in its open silver coffin in the middle of the aisle, and as they filed slowly past it, the Goans reached out to touch the glass case over the robed corpse (eerily preserved after 409 years, although never embalmed), or bent to kiss it, or pressed bread and rosaries against it to be blessed. They had to make do with the glass, for the body had not been exposed since — in an excess of misplaced ecstasy — a woman had bitten off one of the saint's big toes. I took in the straggling strands of hair, the gaunt fading sketch of a face, the old, old skin, and the missing toe. But the fleeting sense of farce was like black blasphemy in the face of the almost suffocating piety of the frightened thousands around me. This was the Goa story.

The church of Bom Jesus was only six miles from Panjim, but the further away the action is from the talk, the greater the need to cover it, for there is no substitute for seeing, even if all one sees is the lie of the land, the reality that separates the ground from the map.

'On the map it was reassuringly marked"landing zone",' I wrote from Sarawak during *Konfrontasi* in 1963. 'On the ground it was a sloping 20-yard ledge above a dark river, a tiny clearing of brushwood and tree stumps backed by a high wall of mountain jungle...' Without experiencing the chaotic geography in which the incongruous partners — the clattering Royal Navy choppers above, the Gurkhas sweating it out under the green canopy of the forest below — worked together to pinpoint and destroy their Indonesian enemy, I was not fit to write copy on this war.

You had to fly over Singapore in a light aircraft to realise that the jostling island outposts of the Indonesian archipelago were scarcely a spit away, that the guerrilla base on Pulau Batam a thousand feet below was just nine miles from Raffles Hotel. In Laos 'the strategic roads marked boldly on the maps turn out to be narrow pot-holed tracks in the mountains', and the government battalions that look formidable on paper are 'weary units of fewer than 500 men which can only advance in company strength along narrow defiles made for defenders skilled in ambush'.

If Hong Kong was living on the rim of a gigantic human volcano during the Cultural Revolution, you had to drive to Laufaushan in the New Territories to smell the sulphur. Communist China was just across a narrow strip of water, whose oyster beds were claimed by the peasants on both sides. The peasants belonged to the same clan, but the village on the Chinese side was now a people's commune, while the village on the Hong Kong side was a tourist trap that was expected to pay dues to it. After two attempts to kidnap their defaulting cousins over the way, Red Guards crossed to Laufaushan on a foray, but were repulsed, baffled, by the bureaucrats they foolishly tried to bully on the basis that the British crown colony was part of China. It was here that one could sense the nightmarish lack of an objective identity that made Hong Kong every man's no-man's-land, like the small Martian in the story of Ray Bradbury who changed into the child of whomever happened to be looking at him at the moment.

Conversely, the reporter must be on the spot to record the non-story when distant colleagues hungry for bad news are putting together knock-down copy out of the clichés of doom. In May 1961, for example, I was obliged to report that 'war-torn, embattled Vientiane' was turning a disappointingly bland face to the world. Under the fiery blossom of the flamboyant trees lining the quiet streets, the *cyclos* were gently pedalling to and fro at their accustomed Laotian speed; public buildings were being languidly repainted white and blue, and the expected intervention of American troops to stop the communist rot had triggered an explosion of commercial rather than warlike activity: Instant tailors were proliferating ('Ladies and Gents made to order delivery within twenty-four hours'), a nightclub was advertising 'Fifteen fresh girls from Bangkok'. And then the Marines did not come, after all.

There is a strategic and a tactical side to almost every big story, and the lone correspondent is often torn between them if they are too far apart. Faced with an earthquake upcountry, does he hang around the health ministry in the capital waiting for the latest casualty lists and emergency plans, the appeals for blood plasma and the foreign aid figures, or get out there to watch the rescue teams sweat and the people die? In one sense the choice is simple. He must take to the field. It he is afraid that news may break at the base while he is away, he can cover himself by asking his editors to 'pick up off agencies' (if he has no stringer). But if he is to write tailor-made copy in the style that suits his newspaper, he cannot leave the story in the field to wire services selling the same reach-me-down reports to 2,000 other customers.

His real problem is how to make sure that he is not stuck out in the sticks and unable to file his copy to meet his next deadline, whether his paper is published ten or 10,000 miles away. Either he must find reliable pigeons, or time his sorties so that he can himself get back to the nearest lifeline to the outside world — telephone or telex — in time to beat the clock. But that is going by the book. Too often he must jump at a chance of a lift into the action without knowing when he or anyone else will get out of it again. This means that once the story has taken shape on the spot, he must be as quick to seize the first chance to return to base as he was to seize the first chance to leave it. Great as the temptation to fatten it further may be, greed for more copy will ground him. And the greatest scoop is dead before it can be killed on the news desk if a correspondent is left clutching it in limbo because he stayed there a day — even an hour — too long.

Or because he is dead himself. No editor (creditor, mother, or wife) has any use for a dead correspondent, so — one might ask — should he risk his life for a few lines of copy? There is no answer, for the question is a mathematical non sequitur. Risk is an imponderable that cannot be equated with column inches, any more than talent can be bought by the yard. Most hazards are incidental. At the mountainous 'front line' in Laos I was more afraid of the cold than the communists. Covering a sweep by Vietnamese troops across waterlogged ricefields in the Mekong Delta, I suddenly spat blood; I had not been hit in the lung by a Vietcong bullet, but by TB. Back intact and about to land after a tree-top swan over the Sarawak jungle that had taken us right up to the hostile Indonesian border during *Konfrontasi*, I froze with fright as our chopper struck a cable stretched across a main street in the state capital of Kuching. Was this to be the ridiculous, irrelevant end? The cable snapped. 'Wasn't there yesterday.' shouted the RN pilot, faintly resentful, as we dropped into the airport. Excuses, excuses. But we were alive again.

Even when the hazard is a matter of choice, the choice has usually been made for one. The most prudent reporter must take calculated risks to get good copy at first hand, because that is what reporting is all about, just as steeplechasing is about jumping fences in order to win. The story is always ahead, not behind, and he must push on until he is stopped, his instinct telling him to move towards trouble, not back away from it. But just one thing has higher priority than copy: Staying alive to file it. If a journalist takes a chance beyond the call of journalism and is killed out of context, he is guilty of unprofessional conduct. When a correspondent started talking casually of his breathtaking exploits in the Korean war while drinking in the Foreign Press Club in Tokyo, someone would jam on his head an old, battered American steel helmet with one strap hanging loose à la John Wayne to shut him up. It was kept there for the purpose. Journalism admires the guts that get the story, but derides the rashness that is beside the point.

Luck must nevertheless be caught by the lapel before it turns us back — an unrepeatable offer to make the first leg of a long trip to the rebels in Sumatra hidden in the back of a truck; a chopper taking off for an inaccessible battlefront in Laos (only while stocks last); a lift by night into Hanoi just before the last curfew comes down and the Vietminh march in; standing room in an assault boat in the Mekong swamps; a spare car seat to the disquieting Cambodian frontier, where after a modicum of American bombing hatred of the white man can be felt between the shoulder blades. No journalist could throw away opportunities like these, for when Fortune smiles, we must smile back.

There is always a risk. A helicopter carrying seven correspondents on a tour of the front in Laos stalls and falls three thousand feet. The pilot slams the engine into neutral so that the rotors can freewheel in the uprush of air, cushioning and stabilising the descent, and the journalists hit the ground unhurt — only to find that they are in enemy territory. But there was nothing foolish about their decision to fly in the first place. On the other hand I would have been a lunatic to accompany the defeated Bai Vien when he proposed to escape from Saigon in a flying rustbucket piloted by a French floosie — a floosie too young to have driven an antique like that before, but who thought she could probably get it off the sodden field in which it sat all right, *cheri*. (I declined the offer, and Bai Vien himself slipped away through the swamps in the end).

Only common sense can draw a line between the acceptable and the unacceptable face of danger, and even then it must be lightly pencilled in, especially where mobs come into the story, for mobs can be as moody as they are many-legged. It was as safe for me to push my way through a sea of yelling Chinese to reach the British Embassy in Beijing in 1958 as it would have been foolhardy for me to have done so in 1967: The first time they were play-acting, the second out for blood. Fair, tall, blue-eyed, and white. I have hovered unhappily on the fringes of mobs that were screaming for vengeance against fair, tall, blue-eyed, white men (English or Dutch) from Trieste to Jakarta, and got away with it by not plunging in too far. Fear is a good guide, and the first thing to fear may be your own appearance. In Trieste a *Times* stringer tells me that the British-officered police have shot an Italian demonstrator dead in a downtown church. We rush to the scene. There is blood in the aisle, a terrible sense of sacrilege. The crowd begins to murmur, and I suddenly realise that while my colleague is small, dark and Latin, I look the epitome of a British police officer. On such occasions, never break into a run.

In taut situations a correspondent should go only where he has to go to get the news, if he is to survive to tell it. To wander aimlessly through a city in search of copy in the middle of a revolution is to gamble wildly, and almost certainly lose. When times are hard the bystanders are ignorant, the shops are shuttered, the main roads empty or a solid mass of stalled traffic or full of flying bullets. Quiet streets can cheat, buildings block off sound. Turn the wrong corner and you can miss a riot by fifty yards — or be needlessly trampled by the mob. If there is a coup, the stepping-stones to the story will be obvious, and only the fool will get his feet wet unnecessarily. The actors and the action will (for example) be at the palace, the army headquarters, the police barracks, and the other objectives the rebels will have set out to seize — the airport, the radio station, the telecommunications centre. But wherever possible the prudent reporter will still telephone ahead to find out the latest form, rather than just drop in on danger (or dead calm).

However, if a private contact of proven worth pointed to a target and said 'Let's go', I almost invariably went, for fear of losing not only the story but the source. Nothing endears one more to one's fellow men than falling in with their plans (as long as it does not involve money), and Vietnam was an excellent testing ground for this readiness to scramble at the sound of a siren voice. The impetuous Vietnamese excelled at turning up suddenly with a drop-everything demand that you meet someone or go somewhere at a moment's notice. If you pleaded another engagement, they would look at you in astonishment. You had commitments to the *future*? But surely life was something you made up as you went along? It made a kind of sense, but it meant that they would arrive at dusk just as you were sweating over a hot lead to tell you that you must come *at once*, the long-promised meeting with the Vietcong leader was on *now* — no, not in Saigon, of course, out in the provinces at Can Tho. The car was waiting below, and we must take off *immediately* to beat the curfew. *Vite! Vite! On y va!*

Die for one's paper? There were fates worse than death. I chewed betel nut as part of the ritual when acting best man at a Vietnamese wedding in the Mekong Delta, and tried to preserve a pious demeanour while it burned its way through my cheek. In my eagerness to please my Vietcong contacts I found myself eating raw-chicken embryos in the shell in a pitch-dark garden outside Saigon, and raw turtle eggs in a 'love village' outside Phnom Penh, as we talked (if rather intermittently) of Hanoi and the war. These 'fortifying' diets, they told me, with a wink and a nod, would do me a power of good. But their concern for my youthful vitality could at times be a trifle obsessive. As part of the convalescence after my rhenal colic in 1964 they gave me a lavish Chinese dinner in the company of a decorative young *poule* who was supposed to be served after the equally lacquered pressed duck; it was as if they expected to kill one stone with two birds.

I have smoked bad opium in dim dens in Saigon in order to meet Cao Dai rebels on the run, hunted hypothetical tiger as a guest of Bai Vien (in a jeep mounted with machine-guns and a searchlight), and climbed after Charlie Meyer into the palm-thatched Cambodian *maison* of the great Madame Choum, where strict dress protocol demanded that one put on a sarong at the entrance after forsaking all else. At one end of the world I have been soaked through in a swamp forest in Malaysia tracking an elusive Sumatran rhino with a bag of salt. At the other I have been jammed into a celebration at the thin end of Chicago where Black Panthers handed out minatory leaflets in the lobby, Jesse Jackson yelled 'I am somebody. I am black. I am beautiful, I am proud' (he had just become a father), and the sable audience around me screamed back 'rite on, rite on'. And all because some get-up-and-go well-wisher left me no choice.

A journalist should never have to regret lost chances. But how far does he connive? I have a compromising photograph of myself releasing a Nationalist propaganda balloon carrying goodies from Quemoy to the starving hordes of Communist China. (There seemed to be an immoderate demand there for Darkie toothpaste). No harm in that, perhaps. But I have carried aid and comfort across other battle lines between north and south, east and west. I have delivered a swordstick bought at Wilkinson's in London to a rebel colonel in Central Sumatra. I have taken private mail and old clothes from pro-communist intellectuals in Saigon to their needy friends in Hanoi, and so won a new circle of clandestine contacts. I have passed a letter from Thao to the Americans who were backing his enemy Nguyen Khanh, and — ten years earlier — a message from the Americans who were backing Ngo Dinh Diem to his enemy Bai Vien.

The message to Bai Vien was simple enough. If the godfather of the Binh Xuyen wanted the United States to take him for a politician instead of a pirate (and so become eligible for slush), he must drop his gun and start talking terms. On the verge of throwing his 5,000-strong army of thugs against Diem, Bai Vien paused. It was a mistake. The American ambassador discreetly withdrew to

Washington, and Diem then struck at the Binh Xuyen while their boss was still sunk in what passed for thought. Was I used by the Americans to make Bai Vien hesitate, and so give Diem time to reinforce his embryo army by buying up Cao Dai turncoats before pre-empting the Binh Xuyen onslaught? Was I used by the Chen Cheng group to leak the story of secret contacts between Taipei and Beijing as part of a smear campaign against Chiang Ching-kuo?

A marginal fall guy? The only thing I can be sure of is that the Americans and the Chen Cheng group both believed what they said when they said it. The lesson is clear, however. What a journalist must remember as he is dragged into the latest live soap opera is that whereas he may think of himself as a voice-over, other characters may see him as a player. By the time he is not only describing the plot to his readers, but talking to both sides — often about each other — he is a piece on the board, a potential pawn. The day came when Gaston was posted from Hanoi to East Berlin, and William Colby, then head of the CIA station in Saigon, suggested that Thao go to Germany and try to win him over for the South. (Inevitably, Thao was one of Colby's contacts, and vice versa).

'I refused,' said Thao, 'because I knew Gaston would never rally to Diem. But I told Colby that if he wanted to make the approach, I could recommend someone else who knew him.'

'Who?'

'*You!*' We were south of Saigon, and it was as if the treacherous mud of the Mekong Delta had sunk, suddenly and softly, under my feet.

I did not go to Berlin, and could not have gone even had Colby asked me, of course. (In 1987 Colby said he did not remember Thao mentioning my name). The correspondent cannot control his sympathies, but he must not be drawn into the plot — become *engagé*, as Graham Greene put it in *The Quiet American* — beyond a certain point. It is not always a question of dodging propositions. Covering Cuba during the Spanish-American War of 1892, William Randolph Hearst apparently regarded taking prisoners as part of the assignment, and eighty years later, it seems, a Western correspondent led the Royal Laotian Army in an attack against an enemy outpost (and took it). In Vietnam there were quasi-military American reporters wearing not only 'greens' but guns. They would have done well to remember that they had not been drafted, and were not being paid to play soldiers. We forgot that in Trieste, where anti-British rioters burst into a bar taken over by the assembled correspondents and were most unfairly beaten up with somebody's golf clubs. (It was a Saturday afternoon, and only the *Sunday Times* man and myself had anything better to do).

It is easy enough to fall into the trap. Patriotism and objectivity are, on the face of it, mutually exclusive. The soldier and the scribbler on the same side of the struggle are not brothers-in-arms, but they are brothers, and it is the enemy (with luck) that is shelling them. The war itself cannot be reported with detachment, for it has become a family affair ('and where are you from, Corporal? Wife and kids? You don't say. Let's have your name'). Over the Sarawak jungle, a helicopter crewman writes in my notebook: 'Lot of heat haze. If you want to take pictures you may use safety strap and sit on the step.' I signal my thanks as he hooks me up, and he adds in neat capitals: 'NAC D. BROWN 845 NAVAL AIR SQDN HMS ALBION C/O GPO LONDON'. Twenty years earlier on a hill above Tebourba I was the other half of the bond, and dictating to Drew Middleton of the *New York Times*, 'Captain Dennis Bloodworth. that's two "n"s…'

Empathy at the tactical level does not exclude objectivity at the strategic, however. For every gung-ho American reporter at the front in Vietnam, there was a savagely critical correspondent at the rear who was to be accused of losing the war for Washington. But they could be the same man. And when they were, he was among the best and the brightest. For all the tricks of the trade mean nothing if a journalist cannot keep his passions out of his perspective, and look truth in the face the morning after — despite the wrinkles.

23 THE BARE FACTS AND THE NAKED TRUTH

The South Vietnamese were accused of feeding prisoners alive to tigers from underground cells beneath Saigon Zoo.

THE Judgement of Solomon would doubtless have gone against me. Among my most satisfying memories are those of pieces I wrote with almost mathematical fairness about divided countries, only to have them ruthlessly cut in two in their turn by the opposing governments — Hanoi or Beijing quoting one half in their favour while damning the other, and Saigon or Taipei doing the reverse. It is particularly reassuring to be vivisected by the propagandists of both sides, for it is proof that one is not a propagandist oneself. It is a paradox that while propaganda is meant to be persuasive, nothing could be more tedious than to know what someone is going to say before he says it, unless — perhaps misguidedly — the listener thinks it a good thing at the time ('I love you; marry me'). Papers may have their policies, and take a consistent line in their editorials, but the tub-thumping correspondent is no better than a barker in a television commercial, and is asking to be switched off for the sake of everyone's sanity.

On *The Observer* we had, at different periods, an aviation correspondent and a financial columnist whose weekly imprecations against the Concorde and Mrs Thatcher's economic policy respectively — predictable as Sunday lunch — had readers reaching for the rival *Sunday Times* in self-defence as if it were Goering's gun. It has been said that by endlessly repeating the phrase 'Carthage must be destroyed' like the mantra of some tiresome pop song, Cato the Censor finally talked Rome into starting a Third Punic War it did not want. Personally, I suspect that he bored the exasperated Senate to a point where even war seemed preferable to hearing him say it just once more.

But what of the alternative to blatant bias? On a memorable occasion 18O years later Pontius Pilate asked 'What is truth?' yet (so it is reliably reported) 'would not stay for an answer'. Not surprisingly. One has only to look at the people who claim to know what it is — like the dean of a brainwashing camp in Taiwan who waved an arm towards a column of political prisoners and told me, 'Our object is to persuade the *students* to surrender voluntarily to the *truth*.' The trouble is that the face value of facts is false. They have no validity in themselves, but only in relation to one another. And then, as one Indian journalist once remarked, 'they seem to be neutral, but their presentation is conditioned by the correspondent's cultural and social values.' (This means that although Asians fondly believe that they would report Asia more fairly than Caucasians, the reality is that they would merely report it differently. By definition, impartiality is not a matter of colour).

The most dishonest thing a journalist can do is to pick only the facts that fit his case, for that converts them into fiction. If he does not guide the reader, on the other hand, he may only confuse him. How did the Singapore race riot in July 1964 really start? Do we accept the gospel according to Lee Kuan Yew, who said that during a procession on the Prophet's birthday Malay stragglers out to make mischief attacked a Chinese policeman? Or the gospel according to Tun Abdul Razak, who said that someone in the crowd began it by throwing a bottle at the Malays? The truth is too intricate to fit into either of these down-stage declarations to the audience; it remains discreetly in the background, which must therefore be explained if the reporter is to shed light on the subject, and not darkness.

If he does no more than repeat the statements of interested parties without prejudice or comment, he may simply be passing on lies, damned lies — for statements are as dangerous as statistics. How far does he go in the cause of a totally misleading objectivity? The Vietcong claimed that in the first six months of 1970 they had killed or captured nearly 250,000 of the enemy, including 70,000 Americans. They had also shot down more than 4,000 aircraft, knocked out 6,000 tanks and armoured cars, and sunk 250 boats. But since even bubblegum statistics can be dull fare, their propagandists enlivened this twaddle with flesh-and-blood marvels.

During one fortnight in July the South Vietnamese were accused not only of plucking out the teeth of prisoners with pincers, but of feeding them alive to tigers from underground cells conveniently located beneath the Saigon Zoo. In neighbouring Laos the Pathet Lao had meanwhile alleged that the Americans had tried to conceal the illicit presence of US troops in the kingdom by ordering that any soldier who was fatally wounded in the field should be systematically mutilated to prevent his being identified. There was nothing new about the atrocious American. In 1966 Hanoi had reported that in South Vietnam GIs had disembowelled 5,000 innocent villagers and cut out their livers for immediate consumption. Was the reporter to quote verbatim these assiduous purveyors of old wives' tales that were not only redder than red, but grimmer than Grimm? And if — as he should — he gave the Americans the 'right of reply', how many sceptics would still echo that most pernicious of proverbs. 'There's no smoke without fire'?

Speeches? 'No force on earth can disrupt Sino-Soviet unity,' said the Russian ambassador to Beijing in 1962 at the height of the world's most significant fraternal quarrel since Cain took against Abel. All attempts by the lying imperialists to detect a schism within the Soviet camp were, of course, doomed to failure. Yet nearly twenty years later his embassy in the Chinese capital was still a closed fortress in hostile territory, importing Russians to perform even the most simple tasks behind its locked gates.

Where a story has two sides, the reporter must rescue the reader from the raw facts and quotes by cloaking them in his own ifs and buts. There is no such thing as the *naked* truth. To fall back on the excuse that 'I can only tell you what I saw and heard myself can be deceitful when not naive. It was the plea of all the distinguished intellectuals from the West who drooled over Stalin's Gulag USSR in the thirties, and drooled again over Mao's regimented people's communes in the fifties. On the principle that only the best was good enough for their foreign guests, their solicitous Chinese hosts fed them model work brigades, happy smiling faces, proletarian solidarity, and Peking duck. The façade was most elaborately rigged, and the more purblind of the academic innocents simply accepted it for what it was not, babbling as intellectuals will of the 'active and voluntary participation of the majority...the happiness and contentment of the peasants' while millions starved behind their backs.

The wider China opened her doors to these gentlemen, the more difficult it became to know just what was happening in the People's Republic. Blinkered eyewitnesses came back to Hong Kong to answer questions about rumours of dire want with titbits of accurate, first-hand misinformation like 'I saw no evidence of food rationing'. (Technically correct: he saw no evidence — although rice, oil, cloth and other commodities had been strictly rationed for years). Yet these casuists would have been the first to explode when the French pseudo-fascist politician Jean-Marie Le Pen made his monstrous contribution to history by throwing doubt on the entire Holocaust because he did not witness it personally. 'I ask myself a certain number of questions,' he said. 'I am not saying that gas chambers did not exist. I have not been able to see any myself. Do you want me to say it is a revealed truth that everyone has to believe, a moral obligation?' Check all facts, say our editors, but a journalist is not a journalist if he does not know that reality is often under the rug. Where the advertised data add up to a confidence trick, therefore, it is up to him to caution the good men and true that buy his paper, not merely sum up the evidence.

The impeccable references of observers may deceive. In 1970 a Frenchman who had accompanied his brother to Hanoi told me: 'The people are smiling and helpful, they look fed and healthy, they are decently clad, and above all they radiate an extraordinary confidence and serenity. It was sometimes hard to realise that the Vietnamese were at war.' The cadres who had dined with them had joked, sung, dropped into the familiar second-person singular, wept on parting. The waitress who served them had shot down her first American jet with a rifle, they were told. His brother had been equally impressed. His brother was Marcel Marceau, the famous mime and illusionist. It was a classic case of the biter bit.

Myths are the mirages before the reporter's eyes as, parched for the truth, he stumbles towards his story. They must not lead him astray. On 3 February 1965 it was announced at the 'Five O'Clock Follies' (the US daily press conference in Saigon) that January was 'the most successful month of the war'. But a back door American briefing one week later told me that the Vietcong now dominated in Central Vietnam and could switch men right across the country from the Laotian border to the sea: they 'are doing to us what the Vietminh did to the French'. Ominous words in view of what was to come. On the other hand a Saigon politician reported that resentful peasants were dismissing life under the Vietcong with the pithy aphorism 'No food when alive; no coffin when dead'. But his sources were refugees — and the tales of a refugee are as dubious as fishing stories (if in a different sense accounts of 'the one that got away').

The visit of Zhou Enlai to Rangoon at the beginning of 1961, and the draft border agreement between China and Burma that marked the occasion, were celebrated in press and radio as a trig point in the 'most cordial' relations between their two countries. That was the mirage. The clue to the reality lay in the way Ping had to break through strict communist purdah to see her friend the opera singer. The Chinese had behaved insufferably. They had complained that their accommodation was beneath their dignity, objected to having to pass through hotel lobbies and so mix with Burmese hoi polloi, indignantly refused to be housed in a villa next to the residence of an American diplomat, imposed exaggerated security controls on their delegation to prevent them from being contaminated by their hosts, and generally conducted themselves as ill-mannered boors. They had meanwhile pushed the Burmese into formally ceding territory they had already stolen from them, and when shortly afterwards Burmese troops launched a campaign against Chinese Nationalist opium smugglers near the Sino-Burmese border, they found themselves facing Chinese communist troops as well.

Political tags may provide a convenient shorthand for the reporter pressed for space, but they can draw a silhouette of the story that conceals more than it reveals. The government of South Vietnam might have been 'anti-communist' and therefore 'pro-American', but when writing I had to bear in mind that President Diem thought it absurd for Vietnamese to fight Vietnamese when their two systems 'had much in common', while his brother saw the Americans as grasping colonialists to be cultivated solely for their money and their weapons.

To depend on such clichés was like entrusting oneself to a rope bridge thrown over a chasm by an Indian fakir. The Chinese Communists and Nationalists were 'implacable enemies'. Yes, but they, too, had 'much in common', starting with their Chinese blood. The Communist Party and the Kuomintang were both revolutionary organisations with comparable cell structures. Each ran a totalitarian state barely softened at the edges by the existence of one or two minor political groups which obeyed the rules laid down by the regime. In consequence, both ran reform camps whose inmates were taught to 'surrender voluntarily to the truth'. And they were not the only ones to be brainwashed. The visitor to Taipei met with the same eagerness to show him only the best in the best of all possible worlds — model factories, model farms, model reform camps — that he had encountered in Beijing. Both were out to make sure that he, too, 'surrendered to the truth'.

In the sixties neither 'anti-American' Beijing nor 'anti-communist' Taipei wanted the tension between them to relax, for that might weaken their territorial claims against each other. But both insisted that there was only one China, and that Tibet, Hong Kong and Macao were an inalienable part of it. Any argument based on a denial of that premise was ipso facto the unscrupulous invention of treacherous foreigners. Both felt their quarrel was a strictly family affair, and looked upon their sponsors in Moscow and Washington with fierce distrust. The communists wanted to take Taiwan — 'if necessary by force' — without the Soviets getting into the fight. The Nationalists wanted to reconquer the mainland without having to call on a single American bomber. Both therefore maintained large armed forces and kept them under tight political control. And by the same token they were capable of coming to an 'internal' secret agreement from which all outsiders would be rigorously excluded.

The Kuomintang talked endlessly of 'returning to the mainland', but every now and again the enamel would crack and the tired wrinkles show through. It is March 1968. Ping and I take a taxi to a private dinner with the mayor of Taipei. The taxi driver mutters a few obscene insults as we climb into his cab, so we climb out again. He then jumps out himself, runs back to the boot, takes out a large tyre lever, and tries to brain Ping. I interpose myself and chop him in the neck. An unfriendly crowd collects. 'She's my wife,' I shout defensively, and the warm summer night relaxes. Everyone starts talking at once, and an explanation of sorts emerges from the tangle of voices around us. The taxi driver thought Ping was a tart out with an American; he's from Hunan on the mainland, an ex-soldier, and he knows he isn't going to see his family again whatever Chiang Kai-shek says; it's frustrating, it drives him crazy, and suddenly he couldn't take any more. He's sorry; please try to understand. And, just for once, I do.

****

Some clichés are carved in stone, but others are written in the soft sand of history. The solidarity of the communist bloc was a cliché — until Belgrade quarrelled with Moscow, Moscow quarrelled with Beijing, Chinese communists went to war with Vietnamese communists, and Vietnamese communists with Cambodian communists. By 1976 the sworn enemies of Western imperialism in Beijing wanted the Americans to stay in Asia to offset the power of a Soviet Union that was 'stretching its aggressive talons' in the Pacific. The object of eternal friendship yesterday had become 'the biggest peace swindler of our epoch' today, and the revolutionary Chinese Maoists were earnestly courting the capitalists of the West in order to isolate the Marxist-Leninists in Moscow.

Buddhist monks — locked in transcendental meditation — are holier than thou. Chinese communist guerrillas are prudish and ascetic, Laotians want only peace. Malays ('Nature's gentlemen') only quiet…These are familiar stereotypes. But in Burma monks cheat in their written tests, and bring daggers into the examination hall along with their cribs in order to frighten invigilators; in the Malayan jungle the Maoist insurgents give hands-on demonstrations of the art of penetration to each new female recruit; in Vientiane a minister tells me that Laotian generals are fudging their accounts more than ever because the prospect of peace is giving soldiers 'a sense of insecurity

— they are getting afraid the fighting may end, and they will find themselves on the shelf'; in the 1969 riots hot-blooded Malays seize their parangs and annihilate both peace and quiet as they set out to exterminate the infidel with seemingly inexhaustible energy.

White New York taxi drivers are the rudest in the world, so are American kids, and to stroll in Central Park is to ask to be robbed. Yet the only rude American taxi driver I remember was in Washington and black (and he was just being matey), the only house in the world where the small daughters of my host greeted me with a curtsy was on 62nd Street, and the only people I ever met during my dawn exertions in Central Park were not muggers but other mugs like myself.

But it would be ridiculous for me to pooh-pooh stories of mugging in New York, pleading that I 'can only tell you what I saw'. An exception may prove a rule; it does not disprove it. If clichés often deceive, it is because they are caricatures of reality, and therefore exaggerate its salient features. But that means that while they must be modified to give a true likeness, you reject them at your peril. The Chinawatcher in Hong Kong who always wrote the precise opposite of 'received doctrine' because he wanted to be the only man in step inevitably ended up by reporting rubbish — that Zhou Enlai, not Mao Zedong, was responsible for the Cultural Revolution, for example. On the other hand, the qualifying clause puts the story in perspective. 'Dog bites man' may be a cliché, but if we wait for Rossetti's bottom line — 'The dog it was that died' — it becomes news. Journalism is 'literature in a hurry', and sometimes a story cannot wait but must be filed on flimsy evidence. But the more time the correspondent can take to reach that bottom line, the more accurate his copy.

Given the elusive nature of reality, however, all will be in vain unless the reporter can recognise it when he sees it. And that demands two things of him: he must first throw out all his own prejudices — and then fill the space with everyone else's.

Nothing shows up a journalist as either a knave or a fool or both more than blind bias. In 1986 a fringe figure called Percy Seneviratne reviewed a book of mine in the Malaysian *New Straits Times*. Apparently it offended his political tastes. Picking, therefore, on a passage in which I had referred to the father of a left-wing Chinese doctor in Singapore as an 'illiterate' fishmonger (I was in fact only quoting the son), he wrote: 'even more unfair is his contempt for the Chinese-educated...I suppose the only explanation Bloodworth can give for making such a disparaging remark is that to any Englishman, anyone unable to speak English must be an illiterate.' For those who knew me this was a ludicrous insinuation.

My family consisted of one 'Englishman' (myself) and ten Chinese. My wife was Chinese-educated and born in China, as were our three adopted sons. They spoke Cantonese as kids, and learned Mandarin and English only later. They then married respectively a Chinese-educated Taiwanese, a Teochew from Hong Kong, and a Hakka from Singapore, and we soon had three Chinese grandchildren as well as five Chinese dialects in the family. But there is more. A senior teacher of Chinese history and literature in Mandarin at a Chinese girls' school, Ping imbued not only her students and our boys but also myself with her own enthusiasm for the Chinese tradition. I could hardly have held aloof, for from the day we married she refused to teach me Mandarin until I had first studied (in English translation) the history, philosophy and literature of her country. And that was back in 1957.

If she was giving me a course in Chinese culture, she was also giving me a lesson in journalism. For if pandering to one's own prejudices leads to wild distortion, even wilful deceit, so does a failure to pander to the perspective of others. The Western correspondent moving into Asia must shed his straitjacket of alien concepts about democracy and freedom, Greek logic and a Jewish God, good and evil, sin and guilt, human rights and human wrongs. And he must shrug on in its place the traditional patterns of thought of the East, so that he can recognise the motives of those around him, and understand what shapes events. Ping had her priorities right, for the danger of getting it all wrong does not dwindle, but grows, when knowledge of the local language is matched by ignorance of the local lore; it is only too easy to believe that because you understand what people say, you understand what they think — or, even worse, *how* they think.

To study Chinese civilisation was to acquire rudiments of the one 'language' that would enable me to understand the Chinese when they talked to me in English but their own mental idiom. And that went for all other cultures in the region. I had to learn that in the different countries I covered people believed in mutual cooperation rather than competition, consensus rather than the casting vote (even when consensus was achieved by big boys bullying small ones into agreement); in the divine right of god-kings, the sanctity of the hierarchy, the grid that fixed the duties between father and son, pupil and teacher, subject and ruler; in submission to fate, even if one's fate was to be a murderer — or his victim.

Democracy? Western Chinawatchers shook their heads with mock sorrow over Mao's zig-zag revolution in which this year's gospel became next year's blasphemy, and today's heroes tomorrow's villains. Even as Labour alternated with Tory and Britain zig-zagged between nationalisation and privatisation, it never seemed to occur to them that in Asian eyes an electoral system that allowed rival parties to dislodge each other every few years in Westminster and Washington might appear to provoke infinitely more convulsive changes of policy at home and abroad. In much of the East elections were merely a means of making sure the right men came to power again.

Was Lee Kuan Yew autocratic? Once the Emperor of China inherited the 'Mandate of Heaven', he did as he thought fit. Anyone who had the effrontery to protest was a rebel to be cut down. But a bad emperor was said to have 'lost the Mandate' if the discontented rose in their millions and cut him down instead. Lee renewed his right to govern at regular and fair elections. If the majority objected to his policies, they could vote him out next time around and he, too, would have 'lost the Mandate'. But as long as he held it, he might behave like a benevolent emperor. That was his concept of democracy. In Europe men voted as a matter of right, in Japan as a matter of duty. But in Tokyo the opposition had been known to block legislation by staying out of the House (since it would have been 'undemocratic' for the ruling party to vote on a Bill without them). In Seoul, on the other hand, the ruling party had been known to lock the opposition out of the House precisely because it wished to pass legislation without undue fuss.

Equality? The Tunku was a prince; you were either below him or (rarely) above him, and the most obnoxious thing about Lee Kuan Yew was that he had the cheek to behave as if they were on the same level. There could be no question of anyone being equal to Sihanouk either, however 'democratic' his meet-the-people sessions and the plebiscites that unfailingly returned him to the post he had no intention whatever of leaving. If he suddenly proposed to open seven universities for a million students (in a country of five million struggling peasants), or a factory whose assembly line could switch from trucks to tractors overnight, that was his affair as long as the peasants backed him. And they did. Sihanouk was not expected to behave like ordinary men, or his factories like ordinary factories.

This was a region whose peoples could reject all Western standards of sinning as mere hypocrisy (an art in which they were well versed themselves). Piracy? Graft? Squeeze? Protection? Concubinage? Polygamy? But a little well-ordered piracy could take the place of a customs service, graft the place of taxation, 'squeeze' the place of a living wage, secret society 'protection' the place of insurance; concubines kept infidelity in the family, and polygamy was not only a form of charity when it took care of a surfeit of girls, but (according to Lee Kuan Yew) eugenically sound: the high IQ that earned a man the money to support more wives was automatically perpetuated in more children. 'We introduced monogamy,' he said regretfully in 1986. 'It seemed so manifestly correct. The West was successful, superior. Why? Because they were monogamous. It was wrong, it was stupid.'

Only yesterday Laotian generals drew pay for dead soldiers in order to provide for army widows who would get no pensions; in the Thai provinces a governor who could not finance his fief by graciously accepting 'gifts' in return for his patronage was considered a failure; in Bangkok the latest military boss was expected to make millions out of the commercial franchises he awarded himself, so that his bounty could trickle down to the meanest of his minions before he made way for another fortune-hunter. The European might call this corruption; to the Asian it was simply another way of meeting obligations and spreading the money around.

Nor would the *grand patron* in Bangkok be doing anyone a favour, for Buddhists believed that it was indeed better to give than to receive: one not only gained merit with Heaven, but ran others into moral debt at the same time, so that it rapidly became unclear who owed what to whom. Nepotism was an extension of filial piety, truth had to be 'appropriate', face had to be preserved — including the face of gods and demons. In Indonesia and Malaysia the *kramats* must be respected, in Laos and Thailand the *phis* placated. Political events waited upon ceremony and superstition. The 'communist' Pathet Lao could not attack Luang Prabang in 1961 because the body of King Sisavang Vong lay there pickled in a jar of formaldehyde, and the *phis* would have been displeased. So much for Leninism in Laos. Conversely, perhaps nothing showed so clearly the ruthless determination of Ne Win to bully the Burmese into shape at all costs than his order that all stray dogs be destroyed. For the Lord Buddha forbids the taking of life, and the more pious Buddhists can react violently to the *visible* killing of any living thing (apart, possibly, from their fellow men). If you run over a cat in a Cambodian village the sensible thing is to keep going — fast.

To the righteous Westerner, Asians sometimes seem to take an unwarrantably slant-eyed view of the Occident. While humanitarians were horrified by the holocausts of Hiroshima and Nagasaki, fellow-Orientals who were happy to see the atrocious Japanese blown out of the war nevertheless rounded on the Americans for dropping their atomic bombs on *Asian* cities. Why not Berlin and Dusseldorf? It had obviously been a fundamentally racist operation.

But — racist operations? In 1970 many white men were outraged by the verdict passed in a divorce case in Malaysia, the grounds for which were alleged sexual perversion on the part of the Chinese husband. 'I had always thought,' Mr Justice Yang remarked in the High Court, 'that this abominable practice was exclusive to Europe and that it had not reached Asia. I do not think any Asian husband would lower his dignity (sic) so much as to have such an improper sexual relationship with his wife. I do not believe the allegation on this disgraceful charge.' Case dismissed. Self-evidently, he would have believed the allegation if the defendant had been a European. Yet, paradoxically, he was in the time-hallowed tradition of British judges who, while dealing in guilt daily, were themselves able to remain so irredeemably innocent.

That might not be the way the Western newcomer would see it, but he is paid to report Asia, not himself. A correspondent who writes it all from his own point of view is like the wife of an Australian diplomat in Saigon whom I caught stitching the initial 'F' on a white handkerchief as part of her welfare work for refugees from the North. It was all very laudable, except that Vietnamese peasants did not use handkerchiefs, white was for funerals, and there was no "F" in the Vietnamese alphabet. Ignorance itself is a matter of perspective. In a hotel on the Bay of Along in Tongking, Burchett asked for Pernod and water. The Vietnamese waiter brought a bottle of Pernod and a bottle of water from an old battered fridge at the back of the bar. When the water was exhausted Burchett shouted 'bring us another bottle, comrade' in the peremptory tone only communist intellectuals reserve for the proletariat. The waiter was no ignoramus. He understood French. But — 'another bottle'? He brought us another bottle of Pernod.

The Asian at the grassroots is understandably hazy about more than the way Westerners drink. Half the peasants in Vietnam could not tell an American from a Frenchman, and many Land Dyaks in Sarawak had never heard of Sarawak. When the war brought the aeroplane to Papua New Guinea (relates Lee Kuan Yew), it also brought a new perspective — distance. If you had earlier asked a native 'How far away is that?' he would have replied 'Two and a half hours'. He could talk only in terms of time, for he had no conception of space.

This is where political understanding begins. It explains the cynical contempt of the despot for democracy, even Lee Kuan Yew's suspicion of the one-man-one-vote system when it works against him in Singapore. 'How do we protect the illiterate masses from the demagogues? Perhaps it will be necessary to have a weighting of votes according to qualifications,' he said in 1962 (and it could almost have been 1985). But that is only one of the keys on the ring, and to unlock the Far East, the reporter needs the whole bunch. Lee's durable ruthlessness sprang from a struggle to forge a nation-state out of a pinpoint of an island and a babel of immigrants in the face of hostile neighbours and an even more ruthless communist challenge. Sihanouk was always teetering in mid-wire, balancing one power against another, because he was obsessed with the need to preserve the fragile frontiers of his kingdom, with keeping out of the quarrels of a cantankerous world to a point where he shied away from joining a 'neutralist' bloc for fear that it would compromise his neutrality. Sukarno was equally obsessed with the frail unity and fuddled sense of identity of his broken necklace of islands, and therefore more concerned with razzmatazz than rice for the masses.

A reporter could not 'read' Thailand without feeling the invisible power of Theravada Buddhism and the throne that coursed through the country. He could not understand Mao's China until he realised how the revolution had saved millions from misery and starvation, but had given the 'good earth' to the landless peasants only to take it away from them again. He had to see the lopsided parliamentary system in Jakarta under Suharto for what it was: not a misshapen by-blow of Westminster, but an extension of the great Indonesian tradition of *gotong royong* — mutual cooperation. He had to hear ministers in Vientiane tear the latest labels from their country — '"*Neutralist* Prince Souvanna Phouma"? But we are all neutralists.'

Most of it was obvious enough. The whiz-kid Chinese who marbled the demographic maps of the subcontinent with their industry and wealth were objects of envy and suspicion, especially among the Malays. Knowing this, I should have foreseen that the union of a predominantly Chinese Singapore with a predominantly Malay Malaysia would not stick. But the Chinese were not the only focus for fury because — as usual — everyone distrusted everyone else. That meant that the struggle between the 'imperialists' and the 'communists' was no more than an overlay on the historical hatreds between one country and the next, and the failure of the Americans to realise that they were not just fighting 'communists', but a fiercely independent people in Vietnam who wanted the place to themselves, deservedly cost them the war. Given the right keys, their defeat was predictable — like the defeat of the rebels in Sumatra, of the communists in Singapore and Malaya, of the Gang of Four in China.

The horseman, it has been said, should stop and dismount to smell the flowers. The trouble with the journalist is that he is always riding roughshod over the country he happens to be in in order to run a specific story to earth. But the more he can find time to abandon the chase and enter the homes and lives of ordinary people, the more will he get the pungent smell of the land itself. That smell may have little in common with the false scents laid by the sly statistics and semantics and statements that so often mislead the pack. And never is that more true than when the bewildered correspondent starts quartering China in search of reality.

24 THROUGH A GLASS DARKLY

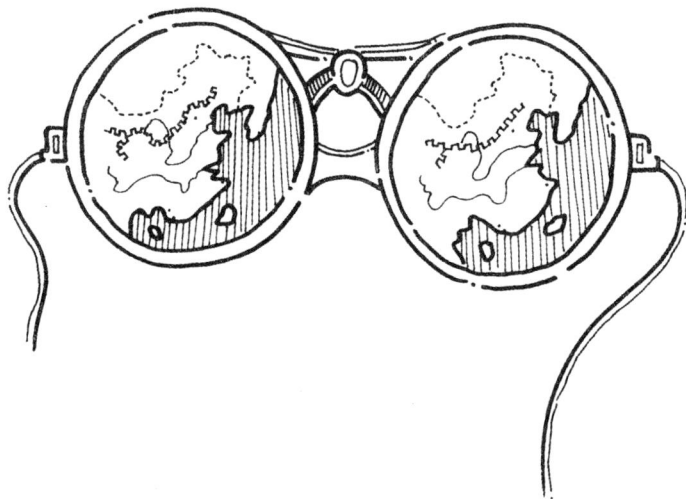

Chinawatching in Hong Kong was a cottage industry, and the Chinawatchers were not only newspapermen, but diplomats, academics, trade commissioners, priests and spooks.

DONALD Wise, then of the *Daily Mirror*, once said that reporting Mao's China in a few column inches was like 'shovelling fog into a bucket'. But those who had studied the background at least had a scoop of sorts. I have seen born losers take on the job with their bare hands, hacks to whom Confucius was just a name, a mandarin was an orange, a communist 'cadre' something one would like to know the meaning of but did not dare to ask. Yet perhaps nowhere in the world was it so important to perceive, however dimly, the roots of the present in the past, for perhaps nowhere in the world were people so aware of the gnarled tangle of fact and fantasy that passed for their history, and believed it to be the truth.

For some 2,000 years (allowing time out for popular uprisings to exchange one lot of despots for another), China was ruled by a divine emperor, and administered by a hierarchy of mandarins in accordance with the official doctrine of Confucianism. There was no democracy, for this was government by one man, one party, one ideology. For those in power, there was no 'loyal opposition' to be given a hearing; there were only rebels to be given a hiding. In this sense communism was in the imperial tradition. The correspondent who kept that in mind did not make the mistake of believing that the campaigns of all the dissident bill-stickers and poster artists from the fifties to the eighties who were foolhardy enough to demand more Chinese *glasnost* than the communist system could bear would come to anything but an ignominious end. There could be no rival political parties or adversarial newspapers in China, for when 'democratic freedom' stepped out of the socialist framework, it became depraved 'bourgeois liberalism' as surely as prince becomes frog.

Since insurrection was the only answer to misrule, China's history is punctuated by bloody rebellions led by heroes who came out of the greenwood to champion the poor against the powerful, the last of whom was Mao Zedong. However, the communist revolution yielded not one, but a rash of regional uprisings, and rebels in different bands bound together by local loyalties evolved their own idiosyncratic form of *guanxi*. After the Liberation, in consequence, communist China was seamed and fissured with conflicting patterns of allegiances that linked generals and commissars and party bosses from the same part of the country, or who had been comrades-in-arms on the same 'Front' or in the same field army. And no correspondent could cover the incessant infighting that passes for politics in all one-party states if he did not tackle this maddening and often misleading maze of fraternal cliques and connections.

Nor was that the only complication. The Chinese ancients taught a form of warfare so flexible that it was said that there were thirty-six stratagems for dealing with danger, but 'the best is to run away'. Reprehensible as that might appear to the Up-Guards-and-at-'em school of suicide, the object was to stay alive to fight again another day. This was the guerrilla doctrine that Mao himself borrowed from the past, and brought into politics. He was, above all, a revolutionary to whom steady advance smacked evilly of mere reform. As a result, the revolution yo-yoed through the years as he flung the breathless Chinese millions into the disastrous Great Leap Forward, but fell back before the protests of his more pragmatic comrades when the economy collapsed, only to throw the country into another headlong dash for the ultimate Utopia as soon as it picked up momentum again.

And the men yo-yoed with the revolution. Deng Xiaoping himself was twice disgraced and thrice risen, and many meritorious Chinese 'stepped aside' when the political tide ran against them only to re-appear when it turned. Not that it was easy to make a comeback, for it was part of the ritual for those with their feet on firm ground to 'beat the dog in the water'. A communist leader praised for imposing a rigid revolutionary policy on the resentful masses while on top could be charged with deliberately scheming to alienate the people from the party once he was down. When the Chinese threw the book at a comrade, moreover, it was often the same book, no matter whose side he was on. In September 1976 the moderate Deng Xiaoping was being cursed from end to end of the country for a 'counter-revolutionary revisionist capitalist-roader' who 'worshipped foreign things'. Just one month later it was the turn of his ideological enemies, the extreme left-wing Gang of Four, to be publicly reviled for 'worshipping foreign things' and pursuing a 'counter-revolutionary revisionist line'. To understand the language, one had to bear in mind that in this game of ideological snakes and ladders, the snakes were always the same snakes.

And countries yo-yoed with the men. In 1967 a Beijing mob burned down the British Embassy, and the communist press attacked the British in Hong Kong for 'perpetrating sanguinary atrocities against the Chinese inhabitants'. Five years later a Chinese military band was playing the 'Eton Boating Song' for the British Foreign Secretary, Sir Alec Douglas-Home, at a banquet thrown in his honour in the Great Hall of the People. That was worth a line of copy. But the real interest of the correspondents present had been fixed upon the receiving line of Chinese dignitaries with whom Sir Alec had shaken hands on arrival — as it had been the day before when the Chinese threw a similar banquet for Norodom Sihanouk to celebrate his fiftieth birthday. For an old face absent, a new face present, an old face present after five years of absence— these could be straws in the high, invisible, frolic wind of Chinese politics, silent signs of change suggesting that yesterday's heresy had become today's gospel.

We were lucky to be there, for foreign correspondents were not immune to the yo-yo syndrome. The 'China expert' who was warmly welcomed in Beijing one day could find the door slammed the next, and be left with no choice but to cover the often inscrutable People's Republic for years on end from a listening post outside. American journalists, in particular, were kept out in the cold (by their own government as well as the Chinese) for the first twenty-three years of existence of the People's Republic. Unable to see the show live, they were reduced to dissecting what reports of it they could lay their hands on in Hong Kong, and examining the entrails for omens.

****

Nowhere is the silly face of the human race more cruelly exposed than in those society magazines that are filled with photographs of the famous 'sharing a joke' with a 'friend' (when not posing with a slightly affronted horse) at some frivolous function or other. But the fun is all in the family, for the readers themselves are for the most part bit players on the fringe of the social board game who riffle through the glossy pages to smile knowingly where they have scored (snapped with the Duke; jump three places) and laugh derisively where their friends have been caught baring their canines beside some similar nonentity.

When the *Hong Kong Tatler* first appeared in the seventies, however, I liked to think that it had a wider readership, that it must be knitting alien brows in Beijing, where I imagined earnest Chinese analysts of the political rat race scrutinising the pictures and captions for hints on current form in the class-conscious crown colony. For much of the first *Tatler* I saw was devoted to parties and party men — men to be seen at this cocktail party, that champagne party, the other 'romantic party' — and party women, among them one listed as the leader of the 'opposition party' in England.

'Opposition?' Yes. But why (the Hongkong-watchers in China must have asked) had the word 'Conservative' been dropped? Mrs Thatcher looked faintly Russian and was dressed in a rather revisionist number. Was that significant? Again, the Commander of the British Forces in Hong Kong was standing on her left, not her right, and unhappily holding his hand to his stomach, as if unwell. Would he be on his way out if the Tories came to power? If so, the confidently smiling colonel in the foreground could be a fast-rising 'helicopter' and a man to watch. It was to be observed, moreover, that the name of Dr Henry S. Y. Fang was embellished with a string of initials — OBE, MB, BS, M.Ch (Orth), FRCSE, FACS, FRACS, JP — whereas the Queen's understudy was merely 'His Excellency the Governor, Chancellor of Hong Kong University', and there was no photograph of him. What did that signify? Nearly everyone was smiling, but one apparently doomed quartet looked as glum as the Gang of Four. Who were they? At this point speculation doubtless ran rife in the Chinese capital (as they say), and one expert must have started listing the names of the unfortunates who did not appear in the magazine at all. It was obviously important to know who had been dropped. For if there was any object at all to this parade of party personalities, it must be to show the world who stood where in the hierarchy. As in China.

Those puzzled cadres in Beijing poring over the meaningless mugshots (like Japanese students counting the commas in *Macbeth*) belonged to a cherished daydream of mine, the revenge of the exiled Chinawatcher in Hong Kong who must scan the magazines of an even more class-conscious China for hints as to who was on the way up and who on the way down. In what order did the captions to the groups of grinning comrades in *China Pictorial* list their names? Had any of their titles been dropped? Who was on the right and who on the left of Chairman Mao? Whose picture had been tarted up, whose left untouched, and whose cut out altogether? (The notorious Gang of Four were ingeniously excised from post-Mao reproductions of photos taken when the old man lived, for instance, and the gap left neatly closed, for they were now non-persons). Who was missing? Who had come back from oblivion? And who was the 'foreign friend' with whom the Chairman had been caught 'sharing a joke' in an 'informal moment'?

There were field days for this pitiful scramble for straws, notably three dates in the year when the watcher in Hong Kong, squinting anxiously through the bars at the blurred political scene a thousand miles to his north, could hope that it would jerk into focus. One of them was 1st May, for the list of Chinese leaders who emerged for that annual one-day stoppage by the international labour movement was like a roll-call of survivors from the seven months of political mud-wrestling that had followed the last public line-up on the preceding 1st October, China's national day. And the national day line-up showed the survivors from Red Army Day on the previous 1st August.

Pictures — all pictures — were as closely studied as any *Playboy* centrefold, and with an even sharper eye for detail. If a foreign guest attending one of these shindigs then came out through Hong Kong with colour slides, a special seance might be organised at which members of the Chinawatching fraternity would murmur hushed comments as the images flicked across the screen — 'The picture of Stalin has gone from the front of the Great Hall'; "That slogan on the Tiananmen only calls Mao "The Great Helmsman" — what's happened to "The Red Sun in Our Hearts"?' 'Zhou's not wearing a Mao button in his lapel'; 'I don't see Kang Sheng on the rostrum at all'; '*And*' — triumphantly — 'what about Lin Biao? He's on Mao's left, instead of his right!' (Bored voice from the back: 'Nuts, they've got the slide in the wrong way round').

This, of course, was in the blind sixties, and long before a dazed Chinawatcher could scream, 'That poster of three gigantic revolutionary heroes skewering a little green Uncle Sam has gone, and look what's in its place — a Coke ad!' It would be some years before God, in the truncated style of Deng Xiaoping, would say

'Let there be light'. I was in exile myself, and carrying a membership card of the 'China Experts Club' which our one-time stringer Guy Searls had given me with a wry grin. In small letters at the top a legend explained: 'I couldn't make a living any other way...'

Anxiously recording all sightings of the shifting constellations in that distant galaxy to our north, we were reluctant political astrologers, dabbling in signs and portents. Lin Biao and Marshal Yeh were in conjunction in July? Naturally, Yeh is behind Lin; they were both in the old Fourth Front Army together, and then Yeh was chief of staff when Lin Biao got the First Field Army, so they have been working closely for twenty years...Glib stuff — too glib when it emerges that familiarity has bred not comradeship, but contempt, and Yeh cannot stand the sight of Lin Biao.

Well, how about Li and Chang? They seem to point to a new trend. Both are in the ascendant, both on the same funeral committee, which probably means they were both 'intellectuals' at the same university in the thirties, and therefore anti-Japanese rather than pro-communist; they are both from Anhui, they were both in the Third Field Army, both...It all looks fine on paper — until some killjoy discovers that Li pinched Chang's wife, and Chang is not as grateful as you might think. In a satire I wrote about Southeast Asia I invented a disinformation department in Beijing whose sole job was to mislead Chinawatchers by switching names about on official lists, publishing pictures back to front, and similar ruses. But I had an uneasy feeling that it already existed, that we were not shovelling climatic fog, but man-made smog.

There were nevertheless times when the system, like picking horses with a pin, came up with a winner. Watching absences could pay off, and in April 1967 I cabled *The Observer*: 'The present army chief, Marshal Lin Piao, has gone into apparent eclipse as Mao's heir to the political leadership, for while lip-service continues to be paid to his title as Mao's "closest comrade-in-arms", he is neither seen nor heard...' It would be five years before Lin Biao was formally denounced, and by then there would have been other signals, some of them putting Mao himself in his place. In 1966 an entire issue of the *People's Daily* was apparently withdrawn so that a news report that had downgraded Mao by referring to 'The Party Centre and Chairman Mao' could be amended to read 'Chairman Mao and the Party Centre'. But by the early seventies Zhou Enlai was speaking publicly of the 'Party Centre and Chairman Mao' in that order, and no one touched the text.

That was straightforward enough. But nowhere were semantics more treacherous than in China. When learning to read English in a London kindergarten, I began with 'the cat sat on the mat' before moving on to four-letter words. Chinawatchers learning to read the English of Beijing, on the other hand, began with a list of the polysyllabic obfuscations that concealed the four-letter words before moving on to more esoteric concepts, for a spade was never a spade. It was necessary, for instance, to know that when press and radio boasted that there were 50,000 'broadcast receiving stations' in Hubei, they were referring to 50,000 cheap wireless sets, and that 'new-industrial elements' rationalising metal supplies in Fujian could mean a few old men walking along a beach picking up bits of scrap iron with a magnet.

'Democracy', of course, could not be translated into Anglo-Saxon democracy; 'freedom of religion' was not freedom of religion; 'the people' were not the people, but peasants and workers and party-cadres — for the rest, China was full of non-persons like intellectuals and similar riff-raff. 'Genuinely independent' did not mean that a country was genuinely independent, but that it had gone communist; and if its industrial plan had been 'basically fulfilled', it had failed. It was necessary to study the finer shades of this very idiomatic language to avoid crass mistakes, to know that while a 'bourgeois reactionary' or a 'right-wing revisionist' might be cleansed of his sins without a change in the party line, a 'counter-revolutionary' could not; that when crossing a frontier enemy troops 'invaded', but Chinese troops only 'punished'. According to party cadres I spoke to at different times, there were no jobless in China but only 'those awaiting employment'; there were no juvenile delinquents, but only 'those who don't know how to abide by the law'; no prostitutes, but only 'women who do it for money'.

In the seventies you had to remember that if a campaign was allegedly sanctioned by Mao, that could mean Mao or 'Mao' — the Chairman himself, or the Gang of Four acting in his name; that as policy yo-yoed, so did terminology: a peasant who kept two pigs might be 'cultivating a proper sideline' one year, but brazenly 'indulging in spontaneous capitalism' the next. After Mao died in September 1976 an ultra-leftist became an 'ultra-rightist' not only because he was out of fashion, but on the principle that one who travels far enough to the east ends up in the west: his extremism had been a device for discrediting the party line by caricaturing it — 'destroying the red flag by waving the red flag'. Ten years later the ultra-left had become 'conservatives' again, this time because they had once more fallen out of step by demanding a return to the unprofitable socialist dogma of their Maoist past.

There was nothing odd about this. In the West, too, language wriggles like a rattlesnake, and the Big Bang slogan 'risk is caution,

caution is risk' rings as false today after the stock market crash of October 1987 as 'China will overtake Britain in fifteen years' did after the Great Leap Forward collapsed in 1959. (It is true that in 1980 a Beijing daily could report that 'the sulphur dioxide in the air at Shenyang is sixty-five per cent higher than in London, and in Lanzhou there is twenty-six times as much soot', but that was already twenty-two years later; obviously the plan had been only 'basically fulfilled'). Meanwhile the fluidity of the semantics did not make the work of the Chinawatcher any easier, and it was small wonder if there were those who mistook *endive* for endive.

In ancient China, doctors were not allowed to lay rude exploratory fingers on the body of a sick female; the lady would extend a forearm through her bed curtain, and the quack would have to content himself with holding hands in order to make his diagnosis. And for years we, too, were not allowed to lay our rude exploratory fingers on a sick China. In consequence, Chinawatchers flocked to Hong Kong to tell what they could from that wrist poked through the bamboo curtain — fascinated, intense, bored, or forever on the edge of a nervous breakdown.

They fought their way daily through Xinhua (the New China News Agency bulletins), through radio monitoring reports, through communist papers and posters smuggled across the border, through the analytical bumph put out by everyone from the British to the Jesuits. They faced hazards like the fiction peddled by the professional refugee who made a living by pretending he had just come from China and would tell all, and the false trails laid by the Chinese Nationalists and the Russians. (The hazard was all the greater, as I have indicated, because the Nationalists and the Russians often knew more than anyone else, and sometimes told the truth). And if one avoided all the snares, there was naturally no difficulty whatever in finding honest experts who would flatly contradict one another. In short, the analogy with the doctors held.

But diagnosis was possible, if only because communist propaganda had created a China so flawless that the slightest symptom of a dysfunction shouted for attention. A correspondent could travel from one end of the republic to the other and receive precisely the same answer to the same question from two cadres 1,000 miles apart— an answer that would begin 'Thanks to Chairman Mao and the Chinese Communist Party...' This meant, however, that China was like a whitewashed wall on which every blemish showed. And since on one side there were twenty-nine provinces, each putting out news and propaganda in accordance with its own local version of the party line, and on the other an exotic subspecies of newshawk in Hong Kong waiting to pounce at the drop of an ideological flyspeck, no discrepancy went unheeded.

Did Canton now urge the masses to 'make revolution *economically*', although Shanghai still talked of 'putting revolution *before* production'? Obviously Xu Shiyou, military boss of the south, was rebelling against the extremists in the north who were ready to ruin the country to satisfy Mao's latest political whim, in which case...Reporting a pronouncement of the Politburo, Hunan would omit an adjective that Hubei underlined, Shandong miss a paragraph that Shanxi put in the lead. Ghostly patterns emerged of provinces for or against the latest twist of the garotte, of some military regions courting and others crushing the obstreperous Red Guards.

Chinawatching in Hong Kong was a cottage industry, and the Chinawatchers were not only newspapermen, but diplomats, academics, trade commissioners, priests and spooks. They made up an international 'intelligence community' so accommodating that it took in the other side, the communist journalists and unofficial representatives of Beijing in the colony: when more than two or three were gathered together you had to know whether you were talking to Chinawatchers or Chinawatcher-watchers or both at once. The club was forever briefing itself over lunch, drinks, dinner, or an office desk, swapping theories and flying kites so that a figment of the imagination whispered to a fellow-sufferer as a joke in the morning could come boomeranging back as fact in the evening, having made the rounds by changing hands as fast as a dud ten-dollar note.

There were sources outside this incestuous circus, of course. There was Hong Kong itself, lapped by the red tide, where on China's national day in 1966 the public portraits of Chairman Mao far outnumbered those of the Queen, and the communist bookshops were crammed with his little red breviary of 'Thoughts'. There were the genuine refugees who sneaked across the land frontier or swam the sharkskin gauntlet to the colonial excrescence the Red Guards had renamed 'Get-Out-Imperialist City'. (The Hong Kong post office accepted mail from the mainland so addressed). There were the businessmen who poured in and out of Canton for the annual trade fairs, the lucky journalists from elsewhere who had drawn a visa to China, the diplomats from Beijing and the foreign engineers, technicians and teachers working in China who came out to Hong Kong for a week to breathe the free, polluted air of the 'Fragrant Harbour' the communists now translated as 'Stinking Port'. There were ship's captains and scientific delegations and overseas Chinese visiting their ancestral homes on the mainland, and there was even my own mother to be debriefed on arrival back in the colony after she had taken a Polish freighter to Shanghai. (She was a mine of astringent feminine observations — 'all those women in badly-cut trousers').

But the information was too often unreliable and contradictory. 'It seems that when two men meet Mao Zedong personally and on the same day a White House official once complained to me, 'one will inevitably say he was in full possession of his faculties, while the other will insist that he mumbled incoherently.' It was true. Visitors were either 'amazed by his grasp of everything' or found him positively gaga. 'Zhou Enlai only looked sick if you knew he was sick,' one told me with limpid opacity. Bewildered correspondents peering through the fog at their looming deadline would turn away and head for a safe anchorage among the resident experts in the 'Fragrant Harbour' itself

The most impressive of these was the US Consulate-General, whose rows of consulting rooms were staffed by analysts specialising in every area of mental confusion in the China watcher's alphabet—in Chinese agriculture, the Chinese army, aviation, economy, education…I felt secure in their soothing company and reassured by their authoritative interpretation of what was going on across the border. But then the terrible day came when the American political adviser asked to see me (instead of the other way around), and I arrived at his office to find ten in-house experts perched around the room on all the available flat surfaces, waiting for *me* to tell *them* what I thought was happening in China. 'Now this is interesting collateral,' one would say, 'because we were just working along the same lines ourselves. Could you tell us where you got that idea?' I would then remember that where I had got it was exactly where I was sitting, and realise despairingly that we were moving in ever-decreasing circles. Before we could perform the celebrated disappearing act which is reputedly the climax of that evolution, however, it looked as if the Lesser Hong Kong Chinawatcher, flapping his way through the mist, had become an endangered subspecies and would soon be extinct.

For by the end of the seventies the dawn had come, and the China we had watched as if on a radar screen in Hong Kong could be seen with the naked eye. The Americans were in Beijing in force, tourists were streaming through the turnstiles, oil drillers, couturiers, ballet dancers and businessmen, teachers and students were poking their way into nearly every corner of the People's Republic. The enigmatic fortress had been thrown open to the chattering mob, and the Hong Kong Chinawatcher, looking a little foolish, seemed to have become as irrelevant as binoculars in a bordello. This was to be the final humiliation of the correspondent who, unable to enter the country for lack of a visa for so many long lean years of isolation self-imposed upon an angry young China, had picked up what he could from the other side of the bamboo curtain like some latter-day Polonius — and been frequently knifed for his pains.

In theory. But when China first began to open up, his ratings were in fact revised. He was, after all, a free agent in an easy-going ideological no-man's-land. In Hong Kong he could talk openly to anyone who came out of China, including all those who would not have dared to speak frankly while still inside the country. And he could feed on as much as he could absorb from the big professional agencies in the colony that collected every newspaper published in China, monitored every provincial radio station, paintakingly interviewed every refugee and renegade, and ran vast filing systems on everything and everybody of note in the People's Republic.

The resident correspondent in Beijing, on the other hand, could not leave the city without a special permit, which would be valid only for one of a few places of passing interest (in the fifties the Great Wall, the Ming Tombs, the beaches at Beidaihe, and little else). When allowed further afield, he was shepherded everywhere by indoctrinated cadres who gave stock answers to his stock questions and dodged the offbeat ones to which there were no official replies. He was otherwise surrounded by millions of smiling Chinese who much of the time would hesitate to be caught directing him to the nearest bus stop. Since he had no immediate access to the provincial press or to monitoring services, he was unwillingly stuck with the view from the capital. And there his main sources were Radio Beijing, a limited number of publications, and another club of even more frustrated Chinawatchers who, like himself, lived in a guarded ghetto and were marooned for most of the year.

I was in Beijing in 1958 when Nikita Khrushchev paid his historic visit to Chairman Mao in a last bid to patch up their differences man to man before the Sino-Soviet split. Neither I nor the two resident Western reporters in the city — the correspondents of Reuters and Agence France Presse — knew that he had come until he had gone again, any more than did the entire diplomatic corps. Nor had we any way of learning that at that very moment hundreds of millions of peasants were being dragooned into people's communes in a revolutionary quantum jump towards the ultimate classless society. I found out about all this only after I got back to Hong Kong. The men who were on the spot did not know; the men who knew were not on the spot. They could coexist, therefore, for they complemented each other. And there was plenty of room in the dark for both.

25 THE PAINTED SCREEN

Things tended to be — yet not to be — exactly what they seemed.

ANTHONY Lawrence, veteran Far East correspondent of the BBC, once said to me: 'For fifteen years I cool my heels in Hong Kong, studying the official Chinese statements in provincial radio reports which tell me, for example, that steel production in Fujian province has increased by seventy per cent since 1967. And when I finally get a visa and can go into China, all agog, what do I learn? That according to official figures steel production in Fujian province has increased by seventy per cent. And this, mind you, is read out to me by a bloke in a Mao suit with the air of giving me an enormous scoop.' The joke had a sharp point. Like his fellow-sufferer in Hong Kong, the analyst moping in China itself might be reduced to political astrology much of the time. Even when he could move about the country, cease to be a paperwatcher, and actually become an eyewitness, he could still fall victim to the echosystem in a country in which truth was fabricated out of endlessly repeated slogans. And statistics.

The Chinese were masters of the meaningless percentage. During the First Five-Year Plan, a cadre in the State Planning Bureau once confided to me, industrial production increased by fifty-six per cent (good), agriculture and water conservancy by 8.2 per cent (well, all right), but — culture and education by 5.9 per cent? How did you measure off 5.9 per cent of culture? Transportation and postal communications by 8.7 per cent? (Buses or birthday greetings?) Urban utilities by 2.8 per cent? 'Others' by 8.4 per cent? What was that supposed to tell anyone? '…and Shanghai phosphates by six hundred per cent.' That jerked me out of my doze. '*Six hundred per cent*? How many tons were produced in 1952, then?' After some semantical squirming the cadre (it was a different one by then) raised the fingers of three hands. Fifteen. I was lucky to have pinned him down. Years later another comrade was to boast that 'during the Cultural Revolution' a Shanghai shipyard had built eleven vessels where only one had been laid down before it started. Impressive — but what he did not say was that they had all been built after 1970, when the worst four years of destructive frenzy that reduced China to near-chaos had already passed. It the statistics were not boring, it was because they had been juggled, and if they had not been juggled, they were usually boring.

That could hardly be said during the Great Leap Forward, however, although the same story was repeated (with local variations) wherever I went. In Chongqing a plant that had produced 250,000 tons of steel in 1957 would produce 500,000 tons in 1958 and two million by 1960, I was assured; a Shanghai chemical factory that had produced 21 million yards of plastic in 1957 had been scheduled to produce 26 million in 1958, 'but the workers themselves' had raised the target to 106 million yards and the number of new products to be manufactured from eight to 130; in the Shanghai diesel factory 'the workers themselves' had decided to increase production from 1,400 motors in 1957 to 5,600 in 1958 and 'no one could yet say' what it would be in 1959. It was the same down on the farm. Output in 1958 would be nearly 70 per cent higher than in 1957 — in 1958 the wheat yield around Xian was 302 *catties* per *mou*, but in 1959 it would be 4,000 *catties* per *mou*; for rice the yields were 618 *catties* per *mou* in 1957, 3,600 in 1958. and 'no idea' for 1959. The figures were for the façade, and bore no relation to reality. The overworked land and machines and men would in any case collapse from exhaustion and so end Mao's hop-skip-and-jump into the purely imaginary future to which they belonged.

But meanwhile there was much genuine — if misplaced — enthusiasm for the Great Leap Forward. The Chairman had spoken, and the Chinese were dutifully fooling themselves that the dream could become the reality. A cadre, however sceptical, dared not cry that the production targets were crazy. His one concern was to win kudos by outbidding the cadre next door, thus pushing the baseless estimates of output even higher— 'thanks to Chairman Mao and the Chinese Communist Party'. The correspondent, caught up in the illusion and hearing the same chant echoed all around China, began to have a horrid feeling that there was only one source in the country — the well-drilled chorus of 650 million Chinese.

His powers of personal observation were his greatest asset. Roaming backstage, he could see the unvarnished lath-and-canvas facts behind the painted façade of the Great Leap Forward, and hear what he could not see. His hotel was dirty, the staff forever yawning; the incessant call for all to work longer hours, to make more of everything 'faster, better, more economically', was creating a nation of sleepwalkers. Fuddled officials were repeating themselves during interviews, children were slumped over their school desks after rising at three in the morning to fit part-time factory work into a twelve-hour day before they began their lessons; doctors and nurses were abandoning their patients to make their quota of unusable back yard steel. Quantity was all, quality came nowhere, work was slipshod, and workshops full of rejects; lifts were built askew, doors did not fit, new ceilings fell in. Somnolent factory workers were putting in record hours as if their mere presence was a form of output in itself. The jealous ardour of many cadres was beyond praise or blame, but China had rings under her eyes.

It did not need a Great Leap Forward, however, to persuade the peripatetic reporter that in China he was living a gigantic whiter-than-white television commercial as, visit after visit, he continued to be served the mixture as before: the friezes of smiling faces, the glossy statistics, the tours of showpiece farms and factories, the stories of soaring production and bumper harvests, the workaday adulation for Chairman Mao. And the adroit evasions: Why had the Chinese press failed to report the American landing on the moon? 'There are more important questions to be solved on earth.' Why have the Chinese people not been told that Lin Biao tried to murder Chairman Mao? 'Because everyone knows about it already.'

In 1972 nothing symbolised 'seeing China' for me so much as one of the first things I saw — an imitation panda hearth rug made out of dyed goatskin, displayed for export at the Canton trade fair.

The Chinese did not pretend it was a real panda, any more than they pretended that the 'model' commune they were showing to the latest group of visiting journalists was not the same one they had already shown to all the other batches of barbarians they had processed. As they perceived it, their half-truths were half true, and their deceptions were not expected to deceive unless you were mug enough to believe them. It was only after Mao's death that a spade began to be called a spade, and a 'bumper harvest' became 'a fairly good crop'.

Even then, hospitable cadres might take one around a freshly-painted two-storey peasant house equipped with both TV and radio, or a magnificent 1,400-year-old Buddhist temple that the communists boasted they had rebuilt themselves. But if any journalist bought the illusion that all peasants lived like that, or that Chairman Hua was 'Defender of the Faith', that was his affair. (Matters were complicated by the fact that poverty as well as progress played a part in the overall 'production': China was officially poor; otherwise — for one thing — how could she claim to be the leader of the Third World?). Foreigners were fed what was good for them, and were expected to know what they were swallowing. 'One should never believe men on account of their words,' a cadre once told me sternly, after decrying Lin Biao as a practised deceiver. 'But we have to deal with a China in which millions of people do not know that.' He may have realised a moment too late just what his remark could imply — not against Lin Biao, but against the entire communist regime. But it would have been pointless to try to impale him on this. Lin Biao was a loser and therefore a liar; winners did not tell lies: they were merely protective about the truth.

As little as possible was left to chance. In the early days a visiting correspondent had to submit in advance a list of all the people he wanted to interview, and a list of all the questions he wanted to ask each one. This could take up the whole of his first day in China. Once an interview was set up, the minister or department head would read out his answers, and an interpreter (whether wanted or not) would translate them into English. The questions had to be artfully phrased to circumvent the mirage — not 'What was steel production in 1965 and how did it compare with 1964', but 'How many *tons* of steel did China produce in 1965, and what was the actual target?' Not that it always helped, for the minister could still come up with a handful of digits as flavourless as frozen fish fingers.

The interpreter could prove another hazard. For one thing, he served as a fire screen between reporter and subject; his presence did not necessarily mean that the man talking through him could not speak English. I have known Marshal Klementi Voroshilov, later President of the USSR, to shout suddenly 'That's not what I said', and dismiss his interpreter as a 'drunken fool'; and I have heard Zhou Enlai gently correct the not-quite-word-perfect Nancy Tang in mid-flow in Beijing. With reason: when an American correspondent asked him a delicate question suggesting that China might be meddling with the peace prospects in Vietnam, he replied cautiously 'a little' (*yidianr*), which Miss Tang translated very freely indeed as 'you could say so'. I have caught Chinese interpreters rendering a *mou* as an acre, and a *li* as a mile, although there are six *mou* to an acre and three *li* to a mile, and this poetic licence could yield startling statistics on everything Chinese from agriculture to athletics without anyone even having to fudge the figures. ('A summer vase for pouring tea' once stumped me in Singapore, until I realised it was a translation of 'samovar'.)

Beguiled by all the stagecraft, the hapless foreigner had above all to make sure that his own interpretation of what he saw and heard was correct, for only thus could he cut through the charade. Things tended to be — yet not to be — exactly what they seemed, and it was dangerous to trust first impressions. (The newcomer to the East who is saddened by the sight of a dutiful wife walking meekly three paces behind her turbaned master must realise that this is also an excellent position from which to nag).

Since in Mao's day it was impossible to visit a Chinese home informally without exposing the family to suspicion, interrogation, harassment, perhaps arrest, formal tours that took us into private homes as well as factories and farms had to be turned to good account. There was much to be learned — even in the presence of an official guide. When crude Anglo-Saxons armed with notebooks and cameras plunged into the two-roomed flat of a textile worker, prying into corners and poking into cooking pots, the inmates would look on with placid smiles in accordance with China's universal 'cheese' syndrome, and meet their impudent questions with stock answers. But every detail told a story. Did the father wear a Mao button? Was the daughter in a boiler suit or a flowered blouse and jeans? Was there a picture of the Chairman on the wall? In every room? And were the *Selected Works of Mao Zedong* on the solitary bookshelf? If not, what was? Meanwhile the questions had to be as secretly pertinent as they were seemingly impertinent. 'What is the first thing you do when you get up in the morning?' 'Switch on the radio for the news, and then go and wash.' So what? *So she did not bow to the portrait of Chairman Mao.*

The weakness of the façade is that it is only a façade. Trudging through one section of the vast labyrinth of tunnels and chambers that made up the complex of air-raid shelters under Beijing, our ears were assailed by echoing statistics once more — 'three kilometres in length...ninety separate entrances...eight metres deep...get 10,000 into this section alone in five minutes...connected with other networks and the underground railway...the whole system takes eighty per cent of the four million inhabitants of Beijing...' The scale was impressive, but was it a giant shelter or a giant trap? 'No danger. People can be led through the tunnels right to the outskirts of the city.' It was at this point that I noticed our guide had lost his way. Action had contradicted words, and — if the Russians dropped a bomb — the rest could be left to the imagination.

****

Reality was not to be found in the sweeping statistics of myopic bureaucrats; it was down in the markets and shops and pay packets, in the cost of a cabbage and the ration of pork and the wage of the worker, the factory hand's budget and the farmer's diet. I haunted department stores and restaurants, pricing everything and peering at everyone's food. Nothing paid off as well as simply wandering about, watching points — a group of Soviet citizens held up at the railway station, for example, while Westerners were let through. ('Don't be taken for a Russian' I was warned — and that was *in* 1955). Twenty-five years later, when more of them had found their tongues, I conducted my own mini-poll on how the Chinese were responding to the government's latest ukase that couples should have only one child. A young cadre said he did not have to be told twice: trying to raise a kid in China had become a miserable chore. An old man cocked an ear to my question, grinned mischievously, and raised five fingers. A street hawker handed me a bag of hot doughnuts and said,

'But what if the first is a girl?' I spent time scanning the big character wall posters, the overlapping sheets as close as fish scales, looking for further comment.

But although you were free to nose around the city at will, the authorities looked with sorrow on any ungrateful attempt to opt out of the rat-run when you were attached to a visiting VIP. Eager to show you all that you should be shown, they packed the official programme so tight that the correspondent had to use considerable ingenuity in order to squeeze in anything extra that would take more than an hour. To win spare time for mooching, you could plead a headache; or point out that, alas, you had to stop enjoying yourself and write copy sometimes, and therefore must regretfully sacrifice the chance to visit the Great Wall for the fourth time; or protest that you had seen the school for the deaf and dumb already and reported on it in detail. The cadre might smilingly assent, but then produce his trump: it would be better if you remained in your hotel room in that case, because 'something important may come up'. This might be a much-awaited meeting with Zhou Enlai. Or again it might not. But there was no way that you could tell whether he was bluffing until it was too late, and you could take no risks. He had you pinned down as effectively as a matador 'fixes' a bull.

To get the smell of the country it was best to travel by train or road, not soar over it like some incurious god. The reporter would then see what could not be hidden — the ant-like armies of blue-clad peasants grubbing away the earth on gigantic irrigation or highway projects with picks and shallow baskets; the gaunt cave dwellers in the loess hills of Shaanxi; the glowing infinities of emerald-green rice; the crumbling mud villages and neat brick communes, the great fleets of fishing junks on the shining waters, the bucolic life at muddy wayside halts.

But first he had to apply for a pass which would list the places he was going to visit in date order, laying down a precise itinerary for his package tour. Having mistakenly asked to visit Xian before Loyang on a rail trip from Beijing to Chongqing, I realised too late that Loyang should logically have come first. On arriving there at four o'clock in the morning, accordingly, I jumped train. The station was in darkness, and silent but for the groans and murmurs of several hundred itinerant peasants in black pyjamas sleeping in the courtyard. Not for long, however. A short, fat and startled station master appeared, hastily buttoning up his Mao jacket, and uproar followed. What was this? A foreign correspondent had broken loose and was roaming China. It was an emergency. Where had I come from? Where was my pass? Where was my intepreter? I was told to join the peasants and not to dare to move.':

I half-expected handcuffs, if not a halter, but I was allowed to sit on my suitcase while he phoned some bureau in Loyang, and the bureau phoned Beijing to be told not to talk nonsense, I was on my way to Xian, it said so on my pass. Loyang passed this rebuke on to the baffled station master: 'But, comrade, I assure you…' The sun was well up when a bespectacled cadre arrived with a car to coax me carefully back into the fold. By noon we were a well-adjusted couple, and he was walking three paces behind me on a tour of No. 1 Tractor Factory. I might not be in the train and on my way to Xian, but I was — to everyone's evident relief — back on the rails.

The correspondent was not always accompanied when in transit. Normally, he would be put aboard his train or plane on departure, and collected at the other end. He would then be taken everywhere in an official car with a guide, and there would be no escape. Guides were captive subjects for interrogation, of course, and sometimes their smooth answers to rough questions could be revealing. But I found their presence irksome when I wanted to jot down notes on the more squalid, or possibly secret, sights we passed on the road to the next showpiece — that is, until I applied my left-hand page technique to the problem.

'Tell me,' I might say, as I spotted something of morbid or military interest ahead, 'what has been the increase in steel production in Fujian province during the past five years?' And as he rattled off the unwanted figures, I would nod sagely from time to time and write: 'filthy beggars outside mud hut, people living in caves, skeletal old man in rags pulling cartload of muck uphill single-handed.' Or: 'What do you feel about the latest Vietnamese aggression against China?' ('Convoy of army vehs plus six Russian-built T-62 tanks, 85 mm anti-tk guns, 120 mm mortars parked at roadside, facing south…').'Quite so. And tell me…'It was far better than sitting beside a silent and perhaps suspicious driver as one scribbled guiltily away.

In general, however, I did not cheat. I did not duck my (or our) Chinese minder and make off into town when I was supposed to be visiting a mental hospital. If I wanted to break free of the schedule, I would clear it with him first. After all, he was responsible for me. When, in my ignorance, I went on a picnic to the Great Wall without a pass during my first visit to China in 1955, I confessed my crime the next day. Twenty-five years later I declined a last-minute invitation to a formal dinner in Beijing because I had already arranged to have supper with Sergei Svirin, by then an inmate of the hated socio-imperialist revisionist Soviet Embassy. But I did not simply plead a prior engagement. I told the Information Department I would be dining with a Russian friend.

If foreign correspondents from the capitalist half-world were not regarded as spies by the Chinese, they were at least potential subversives. But the more straightforward you were seen to be with them ('nothing up my sleeve') the more would they be seen to trust you. That suspension of disbelief— the contract between the conjuror and the audience — could not be carried too far, however. The correspondent who openly cultivated Chinese friends at the wrong moment did as much damage as the one who tried to do so covertly, for the contacts of both could end up in the same labour camp. Transparent honesty was no excuse. When prudent Chinese shied away from the more inquisitive reporter, the time had arrived for the prudent reporter to shy away from the more inquisitive Chinese — for their own good. As always, the wall had two sides.

But in Mao's day most Chinese were tone deaf, if not stone deaf, when faced with a hit-and-run correspondent, and for streetside comment he often had to fall back on resident foreigners. That included foreign communists, for the sources are often better (if not greener) on the other side of the hill. Although the sealed lips of one brand of comrade might be compounded by the sealed lips of another as long as they were officially friends ('You can talk about China — I can't,' a chance Bulgarian encountered in a Chinese train said bitterly), it was different when they fell out. The Jugoslavs would reveal facts hitherto hidden from the West when the Chinese were chastising Tito, and the Russians when they were chastising Brezhnev.

It was an old Jugoslav contact from my Paris days named Dakovic who first told me in Beijing in 1958 that the Russians were forgetting their manners and talking of '*cette merde chinoise*', and that a break between Moscow and 'a reactionary, Stalinist Beijing' might be imminent. And it was Svirin in 1979 who painted a picture of the

People's Republic as seen through the pale eyes of the Muscovite, but also gave me my lead: 'The Chinese will agree to hold talks with their Russian rivals before the Brezhnev-Carter summit next week as part of Peking's "fifth modernisation" — a radical readjustment of foreign policy that will put China in the eye of the international typhoon...' And so they did. The foreign communists working for the Chinese in Beijing had their own perspective, and I still have notes recording long talks — half party line, half pithy comment — with comrades like Israel Epstein and Alan Winnington (then filing to the London *Daily Worker*) over a bottle of vodka (or two). Barbarian could meet barbarian without risk, and in 1958 it was easier to walk into Winnington's house than the British Embassy in Beijing.

The embassy (as already noted) was under siege by a vast, nominally hostile sea of Chinese ('just now we are not actually allowed to kill foreigners,' one of the mob confided). Tens of thousands of angry posters covered its high walls and it was estimated that in all a million demonstrators filed past the open gates in the first forty-eight hours of protest, fulminating in shifts against our intervention in Jordan (and doubtless enjoying the break from work and the pleasant change from indoctrination classes). But one still drew a deep breath and plunged through the crowd to get into the beleaguered compound. For in China diplomatic contacts were not only precious in themselves; they led to others in the British (or Indian, or Swiss) community from which one could pan gold.

I remember a British businessman trying to sell a tyre factory to China who had an illuminating ninety minutes with Zhou Enlai. Zhou not only discussed with him the Western limitations on 'strategic sales' to Beijing, the possibility of using Whitehall to put a brake on Washington, and China's preference for the Americans over the Russians as enemies (the Russians were too near), but went on to confide that 'in retrospect the Chinese invasion of India in 1962 was a mistake: the generals had taken the bit between their teeth, and had gone too far. The operation had been counter-productive, since the West and the Soviets had rushed to India's defence.' Zhou also implied that Malaysia, with its heavy Chinese population, 'might be a useful buffer against Indonesia...' A curious kite to fly in the middle of *Konfrontasi*.

I also remember the ageing British *taipan* who perhaps knew more about the daily life of the humble Chinese worker than Zhou Enlai himself. For when the communists closed down his business, he had opted to wash cars in a local garage for a living rather than have to leave his beloved Beijing for England, Home and Beauty. But the communists did not close down all foreign business, as I discovered when I went to Shanghai in 1955 and called on the British Consul-General. 'Splendid,' he said. 'You're just in time for the RAF Association lunch.' The what? He might just as well have been talking about the Mad Hatter's Tea Party; I had played Alice at my prep school (to the vulgar amusement of Gascoigne, Chetwynd, Rathbone et al) and for a moment almost felt that I was back on the boards.

Nor was the illusion quickly dispelled, for he went on to say that as there were only so many foreigners in Shanghai, the membership rules of the association had been slightly relaxed, and it now admitted Britons who had never heard a Spitfire cough. It also admitted not only resident Dutchmen and even neutral Swiss, but Japanese and Germans — one or two of whom at least had *not even served in the Luftwaffe*. In a daze I was marched up seven flights of stairs (the disapproving Chinese had disconnected the lift) and into an anteroom full of loud confident voices in various languages, where

I was given a place at the bar and a stiff pink gin and introduced to everyone present. Lunch was in honour of the birthday of the oldest resident, and — after 'The Queen', of course — we all drank a toast to him ('For he's a jolly good fellow, hear, hear, I say, congratulations, old chap', etc), and when the champagne was finished I exchanged cards with a number of ever-friendlier faces, promising to get into touch within the next few days. It was a promise I had every intention of keeping (for once).

By now my aural memory was a jewel-box of tumbled gems — 'the rectification campaign is getting tougher, y'know; suspects picked up in the middle of the night, one chap asked to write down 400 reasons why the communist system is best, suicides on the increase, the vice-mayor jumped off a roof-top only two days ago…Stiff morality campaign, too. They told you no prostitutes in communist China? They must be joking. Tarts all over the place. Two Swiss fellows got caught with a couple of girls in their hotel, and two Czechs — or was it Hungarians? — nasty business. Lots of women out of a job, y'see — hairdressers, manicurists, dressmakers, masseuses…And they're cleaning up the teddy boys — Oh, yes, they had them, had their own clubs, wore the usual gear, narrow trousers, spivs and hooligans the lot. Don't trust pedicabs, either, they're a bunch of rogues down here…So mind you're not taken for a Russian (this for the second time) — one beaten up on the Bund last week, and even White Russian women have been attacked…' This was the back of the Chinese looking glass, and nobody said 'Thanks to Chairman Mao…'

But it was not a malicious distortion of the truth. Most of these old hands would spell out the good as readily as the bad side of the regime that was taking their China away from them. And they knew what they were talking about. The expatriates were either continuing to manage foreign factories that had been taken over by the Chinese, or were caretakers for foreign banks and business houses. I dined with the solitary boss of ICI at a candlelit table in the middle of his vast lawn, out of range of any microphones and surrounded by dark, empty houses, the expropriated residences of former staff in the company's huge compound. The other guests — astonishingly — were two well-dressed Chinese couples, and we danced to 'blue' records (jazz) played on a clockwork gramophone. The next day I drank dry martinis at dusk with two *taipans* on the roof of the Gloucester Building, while watching Chinese teenagers play baseball on the old racecourse below. And the following Sunday I went to a garden tea party that could have been transplanted from the Sussex-stockbroker belt, including the time-hallowed call, 'Anyone for tennis?' I preferred to talk as we watched. Gossip? But this gossip was gilt-edged.

Three years later, I visited a Swiss aluminium factory and a British spinning mill as the guest of their respective foreign managers, men with facts and figures at their fingertips to back up their stories of — yes — soaring production in the Great Leap Forward: ('They set the official target at 360 tons a month, and that was bunkum and they knew it — but they *did* raise production from 80 to 240 tons; I couldn't believe it. They were dead keen, felt guilty if they didn't put in more work, genuinely happy when output went up. It could only happen in China'). And of soaring political misery: ('The workers hate all this spying and informing on their mates, and endless meetings and self-criticism sessions on top of all their overtime. No breakdowns here yet, but we started late; several suicides in other factories already').

'Monday 11 August. 12 Shell,' says my diary for 1958. The Shell Building was on the Bund. I made my way up the stairs, and the British general manager introduced me to his assistant ('*the* most marvellous person'). She was the widow of his Chinese predecessor (who had died of cancer only a few months before), a slim, handsome woman in a plain, dark cheongsam: I remember large, worried, half-smiling eyes in a long face. She was anxious that I should not quote her, for as a Chinese 'adviser' to Shell she was in a delicate position. Our talk was strictly off the record — her English was excellent, precise — but I still have the notes I typed later, headed simply 'Cheng'.

Once again I was getting the story behind the statistics — details of the vicious stripping of Chinese capitalists and the humiliation of intellectuals, of the now unemployable and penniless teachers and lawyers of the old regime who had fallen back on their families for food and shelter, of mutual denunciations by jealous cadres. She spoke of the thousands of losers shipped down to the country to rake muck on the farm, but also of the good work done for the old and sick and weak by the street committees the communists had set up. She then enlarged on China's reluctant dependence on the Soviet Union for oil, which had prompted the authorities to try to save petrol by converting cars and trucks to burning coal, or ordering drivers to switch off their engines and coast along in neutral as long as the wheels continued to turn, especially when going downhill...

As she had said, her position was delicate, and she was to pay for that. For this was the Nien Cheng who nearly thirty years afterwards was to give us in her wry, chilling book, *Life and Death in Shanghai*, more of the real, raw China than most could have endured. The book describes how she was arrested during the Cultural Revolution as a spy of British imperialism, and thrown into solitary for six years to be beaten and tortured and endlessly interrogated; how her house was sacked by Red Guards, and her only daughter murdered for refusing to tell incriminating lies about her. Nor did the ordeal end with her release, for she was then hounded by security police who shadowed and harassed her, blackmailed her friends into informing on her, and mobilised her neighbours and even their children to spy on her and yell abuse at her in the street.

By the eighties Nien Cheng was in America, and China was no longer the land of smiling masks and painted veils that I had found in the fifties. The Great Leap Forward and the Cultural Revolution were on the horizon of history and receding, and much of the madness had gone out of the story. But if a spade was now a spade, and not an 'agricultural implement' any more than an old man with a magnet was a 'new industrial element', the fog was still fog.

Policies seesawed; the foreign correspondent could still be caught off-balance, even be thrown out of the country as a spy. But he still had to get the fog into the bucket somehow, to reduce the latest arcane twist in this involuted drama with a cast of a billion to 800 words of pellucid copy that would tell the whole story without, preferably, introducing more than three Chinese names. And for this, above all, he had to keep his nerve. For if a wretched reporter could be flayed by supercilious pundits for ignorant, inaccurate, superficial and simplistic 'parachute journalism' when given a column and three days to cover a straightforward riot in Seoul or a coup d'etat in Cambodia, where did that leave the Chinawatcher?

26 CAUGHT SHORT

One of the best ways of keeping abreast of events in Japan is to watch television.

WHERE indeed? According to one disgusted reader, it left me a 'self-styled China Expert, i.e. in the main, a less intelligent journalist who is paid large sums of money and expenses by a press baron to squat on Hong Kong monitoring a lot of irrelevant radio-broadcasts which he has never even attempted to understand properly, for the dual purpose of exploiting the genuine interest in China of Western newspaper-readers and enriching his employer by trying to be the first to wire home that Mao has died for the 57th time'. This was the verdict of a Mr R. S. Jenkins writing somewhat unamiably to my editor from the Universitat Giessen in Germany. Mr Jenkins was in a strong position to deny that he was a 'China expert' himself since he had made only one four-week visit to the People's Republic, but this apparently qualified him to pass judgement on a long eyewitness article of mine in *The Observer* (a paper can choose its staff, but not its readers) and condemn it as 'absolute rubbish'.

Four years earlier, just after the Tet Offensive of 1968, I had written a syndication piece from Saigon in which I had spoken of the fighting qualities of the Vietnamese communists. It seems that Mr G. S. Butler of Cynthiana, Kentucky, USA, objected to this, for it inspired him to write to me: 'It is of little importance how well the fanatical indoctrinated North Vietnamese fights, or just how he does anything else…The USA has the power to destroy North Vietnam in a few short hours, but being a compassionate nation it tries to use just sufficient force to insure freedom for those who wish it. When you write your diatribe to encourage Communism, you are giving aid and comfort to the enemy, the Communist. Are you a Communist? If you are that would explain it. If not, then I am forced to conclude that you are just a plain damn fool. Or is it just that you are a plain cringing coward? It is all too evident that Britain has produced too many cowards in this century…you and your ilk spew your insidious rot over the world where it settles and chokes the nation like a lethal smog…' It takes a man in an armchair 12,000 miles away from the nearest firefight to write something like that, but I wish Mr Butler and Mr Jenkins could have met. Politics apart, they appeared to have much in common.

A Far East correspondent did well to accept with equanimity the sticks and stones of his calling. Otherwise even the words would hurt him. For if covering China exposed him to snipers, so did covering the rest of the region. The problem was that he was expected to report authoritatively on some fifteen fidgety countries, each with its own national language, history, religion, customs, and political system. He might be able to put them all into perspective, to trace broad trends across half a continent over issues ranging from family planning to football hooliganism, to compare one state with another in terms of sex, violence, democracy, religion, and the other fashionable hazards of the day. But his copy would inevitably be figure-skating on the thin ice of his knowledge, which had to be spread so wide that it could not possibly be more than skin deep.

In my innocence, I thought I saw an obvious — even orthodox — solution that seemed to have mysteriously evaded my predecessor. We had far too few stringers. I would build up a network of able and articulate local reporters covering all the capitals on my beat. They would dance attendance on me when I descended on them, book me into a hotel, fix interviews for me in advance, meet me at the airport, and brief me on the action of the moment. When I was elsewhere they would file their own copy direct to *The Observer* and the Observer Foreign News Service (whose backgrounders went to more than a hundred newspapers around the world). They would also feed insider tips and raw information to me in Singapore, for which they would be paid out of a special account. It seemed a good — if not very original — idea at the time, and it still does. But I sometimes think that when we finally engineer our own Big Bang and so put forward what is euphemistically called the Day of Judgement, the only suitable epitaph for mankind will be 'He should have known better'.

Let me say at once that some of my best friends were stringers — hard-working, conscientious, energetic, loyal, altogether admirable fellows who filed for our rivals. But I could count the good men who worked for us on the fingers of one hand caught in a car door, and quickly discovered that prospects of changing this lamentable state of affairs were few and dim. It always seemed to be a stringers' market, and when wealthy American news organisations were bidding for them, *The Observer* was soon out of the auction. A few might still be found in well-stocked fleshpots of foreign reporting like Hong Kong and Saigon, but hunting one down in Djakarta or Rangoon could prove a maddening business.

Nor did one's troubles end when the chase was over. Rare without being endangered, those members of the species who were available in the lonelier corners of the subcontinent appeared to have a strong aversion to writing, and after a showy burst of energy when first recruited, would be afflicted with an insuperable languor if asked for a steady flow of copy. The exceptions were the wordaholics who, seizing on the slimmest of stories, would fire off a glittering lead followed by an interminable tail of gaseous waffle — a sort of journalistic Halley's Comet — on the principle that if a piece is padded enough, even a rate of one pound sterling for a hundred words must pay in the end.

There was, moreover, something feline about their cool, almost insolent sense of independence, their failure to answer when you called anxiously into the night. Even in places where they were usually reliable, you might be let down with a bump that could abruptly kill a beautiful friendship. I remember once trying urgently to contact a Tokyo stringer who had suddenly dropped out without a word. I finally tracked him down through another correspondent in Japan.

'What do you want him for?' he asked.

'He's supposed to be stringing for us in Tokyo. Do you know where I can find him?'

Pause. 'That's not so easy.'

'Oh? Why?'

'Well, right now he's in Pensacola.'

'*Where?* — sorry, this is a bad line.'

'I said he's in *Pensacola.*'

'*Pensacola?*'

'Yeah. You know. The US navy base in the Gulf of Mexico.'

'What the hell is he doing in the Gulf of Mexico when he's supposed to be…?'

'Well, actually, he's been there some weeks fixing up this project of his.'

'What project, for Christ's sake?'

'Well, he's got this idea of getting the US Navy to fund a scheme for him and another guy to be the first men to cross the Pacific in a stratospheric balloon.'

This, I felt, was a worthy ambition — even a newsworthy one — but irrelevant to my immediate needs. Saddened, but unimpressed by his potential for covering snake-dancing student rioters in the streets of the Japanese capital from Florida or 50,000 feet over the Marianas, I was obliged to start looking for a successor who would stick a little nearer to the story. But by then I had learned that you could no more lick a squad of 'our local correspondents' into shape than you could train a Siamese bluepoint to salute the masthead.

The best stringers came plain and coloured. There were the frustrated Western correspondents who, confined to five column inches in their own popular papers or mangled by rewrite men on a formula magazine, turned to us for space in which to tell it all in their own words. Among these I counted a *Time* bureau chief who wrote for us under a pseudonym, a *Daily Telegraph* correspondent called Frank Robertson who wrote for us as Robert Franklin, and a

Christian Science Monitor correspondent called Gordon Walker who wrote for us as Michael Gordon. ('Furthermore, Gordon Walker of the *Monitor* and Michael Gordon of *The Observer* both agree...' ran one editorial in a Hong Kong paper, incontestably clinching some argument. Conversely, Frank Robertson once scooped himself as Robert Franklin, and then got even by refuting the Franklin exclusive with official denials reported by Frank Robertson in the *Telegraph*). And then there were the Asian journalists of standing and experience who were working for the domestic press in this or that capital but wanted an international byline. The first slipped easily into the style required, and knew precisely what was wanted. But the second had the local knowledge and contacts and a news organisation behind them.

The most precious stringers of all, however, were sometimes the least qualified, for they were outsiders taken on in places where there were no newspapermen to suborn. Any correspondent who shunned these enthusiastic amateurs would be making a big mistake, especially if he had no hope of being allowed within 500 miles of where they were himself. A foreign teacher working in a university at the white-hot heart of Mao's Cultural Revolution in Shanghai in 1968, for example, was a prize to be hugged jealously to oneself. He might not be able to write a line of professional copy, but any raw material he smuggled out could still be as precious as rough diamonds.

On the other hand, you should never take on a stringer you know nothing about, unless a newsbreak suddenly forces you — like the little Dutch boy and the dyke — to fill a gap immediately with whatever is to hand. Employing bad stringers was like employing bad house painters. If they were paid by the day, they would be slow; if by the job, slapdash. But if the correspondent was slow or slapdash in handling a good one, he had only himself to kick if he lost him. It was up to him to fight for the prompt and proper payment of the men he took on, to brief them on the idiosyncracies of his paper (filing times, length of copy, style required, policy on expenses), and to see that they were properly accredited, knew the names of everyone they needed at head office (and they his), and was armed with full collect facilities. In short, he had to nurse the stringer at the outset, if he wanted the stringer to nurse him afterwards.

Sometimes callous to a fault, the correspondent also had to bear in mind that a 'native' (the word applied to a local whether in Wonga-Wonga or Washington) was even more vulnerable than he was himself. As a resident, a stringer had his roots where he worked. If he had a family, they were hostages to misfortune. If he was a citizen, a vengeful government could throw him into jail without worrying about diplomatic complications — when his sole sin might be that he was the sidekick of a smash-and-grab reporter who had written his country into the ground before flying off to freedom without a care for the consequences. When tapping out a damning charge sheet against some despot in darkest Asia (whose previous record had also to be taken into consideration), it seemed only fair, therefore, to ask the man who would stay behind and take the backlash to glance at the copy before sending it. If he fell on his knees and begged for a reprieve, it might be necessary to show mercy to the stringer by showing mercy to the despot.

But it would be a delicate decision, for the regional staffer could not allow the native in turn to become *his* hostage to an unfriendly government. When taking the job, the local man had to accept the risk along with the string, for it went — quite literally — with the territory, and he was being paid to keep his eyes open, not shut.

As Gavin Young girded himself with safety pins and set off to find the rebel Nagas in Burma, our stringer in Rangoon, fearful that he would be the scapegoat for the sins of *The Observer*, wrung his hands in dismay. But Gavin was not going to cancel his elaborate if subversive safari, nor was I ready to recommend that he should. In the event, all went well.

The prudent correspondent tried to recruit a stringer wherever a major story might break, uncomfortably aware that he could not be everywhere at once himself, or even within striking distance of it. But he might still land on a lucky square now and then, since for those in pursuit of the fugitive news the snake-and-ladder element is never quiescent. When Vietnamese air force rebels bombed President Ngo Dinh Diem in 1962, I was on the spot in Saigon and saw the aircraft go into their dive. I could not preen myself on having had the local insight to be in the right place at the right moment, however. Two innocents from the BBC who had just arrived from England for their visit to Indochina had timed things far better. Waiting for a guide who was happily late in coming, they were standing about on a street corner just opposite the presidential palace, cameras in hand and (doubtless) curses on their lips, when the bombs fell. Their exclusive newsreel of the event was in London within twenty-four hours. But far too often has a disgusted reporter left a country after the inevitable has refused to happen, only to have a crisis blow up behind his retreating back like a delayed-action bomb.

When news breaks, the regional correspondent cannot always fly to it — for one thing, he may not have the right visa. If stringers are inadequate, therefore, there are times when he must stop dodging about at the net and settle for a little base-line reporting. It may seem unglamorous, slightly dishonest, even downright ignoble to cover a street-fight in Seoul from Tokyo (or the Vietnam War from the US Public Affairs Office in Saigon). But if, for the moment, it is the only way he can get the story and meet the next deadline, it is no good being fussy about it. The reporter is in the business for the copy, not the charisma.

Second-hand coverage? There are countries, like Japan, in which first-hand reporting can be even more frustrating. The foreign correspondent in Tokyo cannot just pick up a phone, say he is from the London *Times*, and expect to find himself talking to an instant source. The Japanese are not babbling springs of cool, clear information. They are suspicious of aliens, and may sometimes have to be coaxed into answering the simplest question (there must be something *behind* it) with a letter of introduction from the reporter himself. They are, moreover, creatures of habit and form, and if you try to short-circuit the hierarchy, or cut through red tape, it makes them uneasy. Their own journalists belong to exclusive little 'press clubs' which alone have the entrée to this or that ministry or industrial giant or trade union, where they will all be told the same thing and then write it. And these closed shops bar outsiders, of course.

Often screened from direct access to the live news, the *gaijin* cannot count on getting it second hand by skimming through the national press either. When in 1976 the Prime Minister, Kakuei Tanaka, was found to have pocketed much of the largesse distributed by Lockheed to persuade the Japanese to buy the Tristar jet, the first report of the scandal was ignored by the rest of the Japanese press as part of an elaborate cover-up — until the story was blown from the outside. But as Richard Halloran of the *New York Times* told me ten years ago, once the news begins to break, one of the best ways of keeping abreast of those events in Japan that are not considered too unseemly for public exposure is to watch television. The channels are so numerous and the coverage is so suffocating (the TV teams often outnumbering the participants) that little is missed. By swallowing his pride and covering the TV teams in turn, the correspondent can rely on twenty eyes instead of two and save himself much exhausting legwork.

Following up a hijacking at Haneda Airport, for example, Halloran combined tactical and strategic reporting by getting his on-the-spot impressions from the box, while tapping his Tokyo sources by telephone, digging through files for background, contacting New York — and writing copy. Having resisted the temptation to rush off and lose himself at the scene of the crime, he could file four stories in one day. 'It may not have been foreign correspondence as it was when you and I were young,' he wrote to me, 'but we did a better job with television…' But that attitude calls for the humility of the hard-bitten professional who does not have to prove anything to anybody any more.

To back up his active reporting in the field, the Far East correspondent needed a base with as many channels of information as Japanese TV, and when I first took on the job, Singapore had them. It was not only a Commonwealth communications centre in which all the main wire services ran regional bureaux, but the headquarters of the British Commissioner-General for Southeast Asia. And his concrete box of an office at Phoenix Park was the hub of a network to which all British embassies from Tokyo to Rangoon filed copies of their telegrams and despatches to London, a miniature Whitehall with diplomatic, military, intelligence, commercial, labour, shipping, signals and cipher sections, and antennae in every capital in the subcontinent and beyond. Caught short by the street-fighting in Seoul, I could pick up the threads of the story in Singapore not only from agency and radio reports, but from a glimpse of the latest flimsies from our embassy on the spot — given friends at Phoenix Park.

Add a good bank of cuttings files and a bookcase of reference works, and from a base like Singapore a correspondent could write three times as much copy as his editor wanted on any subject in the region. But that was the snag. 'Ten inches headlined is 400 words,' a 1968 *Observer* guidance sheet for newcomers curtly warned the prolix; '450 words make half a column: 1,000 words make a column. "Long" means anything over 500 words. The splash is rarely more than 600 words. If you file a new nose five inches long to an earlier 10-inch story, suggest where you think five inches are best cut. The later you file, the tighter you need to write. The later copy arrives in the office, the fiercer its fight for space and place. Know your cable rates; the higher they are, the more careful you need to be. (For airmail syndication stones the normal length is 700 words).'

These exacting standards of brevity meant little to the academic, with his thesis of 40,000 words of borrowed ideas duly acknowledged in even longer footnotes. Nor did they mean much to the regiments of the verbose — the politicians, the intellectuals, the lecturers and lawyers not subject to the rigorous discipline of the column inch. In consequence the journalist who could only reveal the tip of his woeful knowledge was castigated for not drawing the whole menacing iceberg. When I wrote an article on Maoist subversion in Malaysia, a reader promptly accused me of being 'so obsessed with communism' that I failed completely to mention the menace of racial discrimination, which 'anyone familiar' with the country knew about. 'It is not always possible to include in an article of limited length all aspects of a nation's problems,' I retorted with muted sarcasm. But the shot whined over his head.

When cramming the complexities of all China into that 600-word splash, the reporter might try to pre-empt a flank attack by dismissing what should have been another thousand words of fine print with an airy 'against an infinitely more complicated background, two main issues stand out…' It was (and is) a useful device but, as in boxing, the need to sidestep in order to get out of a corner always meant trouble. The Chinese fog was at its thickest when I was attempting to estimate the number of political prisoners whose souls were being redeemed through hard labour. After thumbing through the available guesses of the British Foreign and Commonwealth Office, the International Commission Against Concentration Camps, and the Joint Paper of the UN Secretary-General and the International Labour Organisation, I wrote in *The Observer* that there were 'believed to be about ten million'. I was at once accused of making 'a serious allegation in a responsible paper' without giving my sources. But there just was not room to list them with their individual assessments — any more than there was room to explain that my figure took in both those sent to forced labour camps and those committed to 'labour custody', a less severe form of punishment under which the miscreant had no right of personal…etc, etc, etc.

The Far East correspondent was equally vulnerable as someone who specialised in all things, and therefore had to bear the slings and arrows of those who specialised in only one of them. Whether you were writing about polygamy or pandas, there was always some expert who would put every line of your copy under a microscope to catch you out, and you had to hope he was a subeditor, not a subscriber. For among your readers were the exhibitionists *manqués* who wrote to the editor in order to give their prose and prejudices an airing, and whose syntax was either shaking with ideological fury or ornamented with such elegant turns of phrase as 'Your correspondent seems to be entirely unaware…I am afraid I find it difficult to comprehend…Your correspondent appears to be unable to grasp… May I be permitted gently to point out…It seems to have escaped Mr Bloodworth's attention…' — and the rest of the verbal baroque of those who have not learned that you do not humiliate by being pretentious, but by being humble.

Detractors who called you a fascist or a communist (and sometimes quoted the same parts of the same piece to prove it) were at least warm-blooded bigots in their own right. It was the bluestockings of suburbia and the bogus academics pontificating from the arid heights of less favoured universities (not to mention Universitat Giessen) who — like so many others — tempted you to feel really sorry for God. But you were not writing for them. You were writing for the hundreds of thousands of your fellow men who asked sensible questions or raised reasonable objections or, better still, did not write letters to newspapers at all. However, what you had to bear in mind was that if your editor could spare you space for only 500 words of copy, that was because most of your readers could spare you only the time it took to read them. Provided, of course, that you held their interest.

27 THE EYE OF THE BEHOLDER

The mass hysteria of the koro epidemic caught the sympathetic imagination of readers from Colombo to Calgary.

MEGO — 'My Eyes Glaze Over' — may be an editor's acronym for a story to be spiked, but it should be blinking in the back of a reporter's mind whenever he sits down to address himself to that wayward, exigent subspecies of mankind the Victorians so euphemistically called 'Dear Reader'. For if, as the great 19th century reformer Wendell Phillips said, we live 'under a government of men and morning newspapers', the newspapers like the government must be of the people, by the people and for the people, even if news does tend to perish from the earth within twenty-four hours. And the people? The definition of a reader is a man or woman who may spare five minutes of his time for your past week's work. It you are lucky. When a US congressman had the temerity to ask a man-in-the-street which was more prevalent, public ignorance or public apathy, the man replied. 'I don't know and I don't care'. It was the perfect, point-by-point answer.

Don't know? There is a story that when prime minister of a Britain that was mistress of a quarter of the globe, Stanley Baldwin gazed with astonishment at a map of China and said 'So Peking is up there! I always thought it was' — a finger on Canton a thousand miles to the south — 'down *there*'. Any ill-advised analysis of the average human mind reveals that it is made up of nine parts plain ignorance and one part fact, fiction, colouring material from TV documentaries, and authorised preservatives like schoolbook history. I am insulting the customers? In 1963 my foreign news editor sent me a sobering cable that ran:

WELCOME YOUR ADVICE BEST WAY ORGANISE
SOME 4000 UPWARDS WORDS CURRENT FAR
EAST SITUAT1ON VIEWED EXPEKING BASIC
APPROACH BEING DISMAL IGNORANCE
ESSENTIALS INSCRUTABLE EAST DESPITE LIMPID
BLOODWORTHERS...EMPHASISING PRIME NEED
APPEAL EVEN OUR DIMMER READERS.

This was closely followed by:

FORGIVE ANOTHER ADJURATION BUT PLEASE
KEEP YOUR MAIN PIECE TOMORROW HIGHLY
INFORMATIONAL REPORTING SINCE YOU
WOULD NOT CREDIT GENERAL IGNORANCE
FAR EASTERN AFFAIRS HERE CHEERS NEWSED.

A public opinion poll will quickly establish that — setting aside the vast majority of those who indeed 'don't know' — 95 per cent of American cognoscenti think the president of China is Deng Xiaoping (or Mao Zedong), and 95 per cent of Chinese think (perhaps forgivably) that the president of the United States is Nancy Reagan, if they think about it at all; 57.7 per cent of Britons think Singapore is in China, India, Malaysia, or Hong Kong, in that order, and most of the rest of the world thinks South Africa is (of all things) white.

If that degree of innocence puts a sneer on the face of the Far East correspondent who can tell you the Shiite Muslim population of Zamboanga and the eating habits of Lee Kuan Yew in the same sentence, let him ask himself what he knows about Portuguese politics, who controls Uruguay, where Zambia stands in relation to Zimbabwe, who is killing whom in Lebanon this week, and whatever happened to the Congo. As for whether his readers care about riots in Medan or murder in Manila, what does he himself care about coups in Quito or sabotage in Khartoum? And is he immune from the mathematics of sympathy that divides the dead by the distance, so that when ten thousand are buried in an earthquake six thousand miles away, they arouse less interest than two kids killed in a skateboard collision on the corner of High Street? It may be no easy matter for a man (*pace* Matthew 7:3) to see the beam in his own eye, but the exercise will remind the reporter to write up to his reader's intelligence while writing down to his ignorance.

I would ask myself what questions I would ask if the story I was writing about Tongking was a story I was reading about Tegucigalpa (starting with where is it, and why should I care). I would then try to answer them in my copy. It was not easy to find the space. For the paradox is that although a newspaper may be by people, about people, for people, there is an incongruous gap between supply and demand that is difficult to bridge. An item of straight news on an economic crisis in Jakarta may seem too obscure to an editor to rate more than a few lines in London, yet for exactly the same reason it will lose a reader's attention in five seconds if he is given no illuminating background to read it by. He can no more 'see' the event without the necessary framework than a shutterbug can see Piccadilly as a composition until he has trapped it within the four sides of his view finder.

Under these cramped conditions, adversity must stimulate art if the reader is to keep his eye on the column. But even when there is room for the whole story, the art — to my mind — should often be impressionist. A photographic likeness of the reality on the ground that faithfully repeats every detail is fit only for the iron digestion of the Sunday-morning intellectual. Much of the time the journalist does well to stick to broad strokes to get his copy read — especially by a commuter on the 7.25 from Haywards Heath to London (forty minutes from the front page lead to the classified ads). That means reducing the number of bewildering names to those of the main places and protagonists in the story, and cutting other corners. Pundits may say that a quote should always be published in full, but I am for the ruthless curettage that leaves the reader with the pith without changing the sense. The Old Testament may carry six-and-a-quarter column inches of antediluvian copy from "Adam begat Seth' to 'Noah begat Shem, Ham and Japheth', taking in a cast of eight unmemorable characters on the way, but they lived for 500 years and more in those days. The average reader with a mere three score years and ten wants the wood, and wants it quickly; he could not name the trees it you paid him piece rates.

Statistics call for the same treatment, since so many of them are either boring, misleading, or irrelevant. ('Unemployment [in Britain] is still over three million — 2½ times the level of the entire Singapore work force.' So what?) Figures should be true in the geometrical sense, and preferably carry a straight punch: 'Prices were rising by 1,500 per cent annually' (in Sukarno's Indonesia); 'Those so far arrested include 21 police chiefs, six members of parliament, the former Mayor of Seoul and nine provincial governors.' When writing for the general reader, I put 'one out of three pregnant mothers' rather than '33.3 per cent', and round numbers off. He will only yawn if told that 1.65 fools cross London Bridge every minute, or that a building is 49.87 metres high — it is advisable not to cut people in half below the belt, and 'nearly 50 metres' carries the second message far more incisively by being vague.

A nose for news should ideally be matched by a palate that reflects the reader's taste. Some may protest that news is the product of newspapers, that what they do not print does not happen, that they dictate what the public shall or shall not like from politics to pornography. Perhaps so. But the truth is that if left to himself the reader recoils from much that the editors feel they have to feed him — the 'Oh-not-*again*' copy on a static story whose familiarity has bred growing contempt (Maggie Thatcher on the virtues of the Victorians, the Iranian ayatollahs on the vices of the Americans), or a running story whose familiarity has bred growing confusion (the open-ended shoot-out in Lebanon, the Cambodian problem, the Nicaraguan snakepit).

Yet a serious newspaper is chained to repetitive daily chores as much as any housewife; it has a duty to publish Queen-Anne's-dead news with leads like 'Kim Il Sung was re-elected President of North

Korea yesterday' and headlines reading 'Geneva Arms Limitation Talks Stall'. It cannot sweep the dust and ashes under the rug. Part of the paradox that can divide paper from public is that nothing makes eyes glaze over faster than the intricacies of parochial politics in distant lands, so that the exclusive about the secret ganging-up of the left-wing PPDFP with the DSPAC to overthrow the ruling anti-communist NLCU that the special correspondent has been sent to Ruritania to write (and the newspaper must print because it is a newspaper) may be precisely the one the reader will skip.

The solution, of course, lies in the skilful choice and editing of stories. But that, too, begins with the man in the field. And what is he to choose? In my thirty-odd years of serious political reporting the piece that aroused the keenest interest among those eager to be informed and entertained, winning critical acclaim from all parts of the syndicated world, began like this: 'Strange, hallucinatory scenes have been enacted in Singapore during the past few days… In a coffee-shop lavatory, a small crowd, drawn by cries of anguish, gape helplessly while a middle-aged soap-boiler clamps a pair of chopsticks over his exposed male organ to stop it from retreating into his body. The chopsticks snap. Some quick-thinker substitutes a pair of market stall steelyards, but these prove too unwieldy. Panic! One bystander seizes the reticent gender and starts pulling; another rushes off to dial 999; a third runs for a Chinese doctor…A young fellow is hastily carried down a village main street in his bed while his father jogs alongside, clutching the prostrate youth's masculine member. Another trots down a lane, his retiring nature in the firm grasp of a friendly pacemaker. They are on their way to the nearest clinic…'

The mass hysteria of the *koro* epidemic (the Observer Foreign

News Service headlined it 'A Chinese Clock and Bull Story') caught the sympathetic imagination of readers from Colombo to Calgary. So did the exploit of a gang of artful extortionists who ordered their victim to put half a million dollars into a public trash bin on a main street in Singapore. Relays of armed police staked out the drop hour after hour, but nobody came to collect. Finally, an officer lifted the lid, to discover that — presumably the night before — the scoundrels had slit open the bottom of the bin and then shifted it slightly so that it stood over the uncovered manhole of a main drain…The payoff had long since gone, of course, but the police still had the last laugh, for the bundle of notes had been cut out of old newspapers. The story was in the great born-loser tradition of *The Treasure of the Sierra Madre,* and therefore a natural winner.

The very thought of *koro* may make strong men wince, and not all are amused by the antics of cops and robbers. But a syndication service is like a Gallup poll: the number of clippings of his copy that the reporter gets back from client newspapers tell him at once how well or badly a piece has gone down. And those two stories were bestsellers in their own class. Solid subscribers still demand solid fare, and the first duty of the journalist is to give it to them, of course. But he cannot allow himself to be mesmerised by the major event he was originally sent to report to the exclusion of all else ('Yes. Mrs Lincoln, but how was the *play?*'); he must leaven the diet by keeping a keen eye open for the story that touches Everyman — and that does not have to be the assassination of a president. 'We want to make all our news pages more appetising to the general reader, as distinct from the specialist in foreign affairs,' ran an *Observer* directive. 'The whole field of sociology, religion, crime, trade unions, business, architecture, transport, entertainment and so forth is open to you.'

Covering crucial general elections in Burma in 1962, I found myself writing about 'a huge, full-grown, wildlife expert who had just come out of the hills on the Assam border, bringing down with him a female who was even bigger and hairier than he was. Her name was Budorcas Taxicolor Taxicolor (sic) Hodgson, and he was keeping her in an air-conditioned room at Rangoon airport while he arranged to have seventeen seats ripped out of a KLM commercial aircraft in order to fly her off to Hamburg. This Miss Hodgson was a rare and precious catch, six hundred pounds of monstrous mountain goat in high heels with a face like a moose and a back like a bear...'The result of the election was politically stunning, but I wonder which of my pieces was more widely read. Stories about animals other than homo sapiens never break their promise, and I have found it worthwhile to go out of my way (and everyone else's) to get them.

Slipping out of the hot news into something cool and comfortable may even be a matter of discipline, not choice, and the reporter must therefore be ready to file on the frivolous even in the middle of a major fracas. Facing my fortnightly deadline for a light 'Far East Diary' while reporting the tumultuous and violent rioting that was to overthrow President Syngman Rhee in South Korea, I found myself shouting to the copytaker in London (to the jeers of unfeeling colleagues waiting to use the telephone): 'Kimchi — I'll spell that — sometimes described as Korea's national dish comma is not so much a food as a cuisine in itself stop cabbages comma cucumbers or radishes are soaked for about three days in hot water in large earthenware jars stop then the mixture comma which may contain onions comma hot peppers comma garlic comma dried fish comma salted clams and shrimps and other delicacies is inserted between...'But it went down well. Syngman who?

A reader can always be reached from the other end of the world with human stories if they strike a familiar chord at home, whether they are about pickles or poor little orphan Annie; with stories that mirror the dramas on his own doorstep — pollution, inflation, mugging, vandalism, Aids, garbage collection, Christmas; and with 'international' stories that span continents — about Muslim fanatics, racialism in Japan (cf Australia, Southeast Asia, India, the Middle East, Africa, Europe, Bradford [Eng] and Birmingham [Ohio]), even about sinking cities (Tokyo, Shanghai, Bangkok, but also Venice). It could happen here, if it hasn't already.

Conversely, however, the eye passes over the commonplace and fixes unerringly on the odd man out — the pink punk hairdo in the jury box, the piebald horse in the car park. It is axiomatic that the mind does the same, and will always seize on the strange, the unprecedented and un-heard-of, from news of a landing on the moon to the story of the Taiwanese who painted his own banknotes and passed them off in a brothel. It is therefore worth remembering that when the place and time seem wrong, the familiar becomes freakish and therefore doubly readable. They have gay discos in *Vladivostok*? Bank robbers in *Mao's China*? No one would think twice about gay discos in California or Chinese bank robbers in 1987, any more than they would look twice at a punk hairdo in a pub or a piebald in a paddock. A Love Boat? Millions have watched the television series ad nauseam. But that gives added piquancy to a feature on the *Orient Princess*, which on its maiden voyage to Hong Kong was owned by a Chinese communist state corporation, was based in Singapore, registered in Panama, and had a German cruise manager, a Filipino cabaret, a casino run by a Caribbean gambling syndicate, and a Chinese political commissar known in polite circles as the 'personnel director'.

****

None of that alters the fact that the main story — the crisis, the coup, the war, the tornado — is the raison d'être of the foreign correspondent, and that men will read it eagerly if the reporter makes it readable. My *koro* piece was a one-off lightweight success, but it was the two series I wrote on my visits to China in 1955 and 1958 that were published most widely — 87 syndication customers found space for the 10,000-odd words in the second, and the articles were distributed in booklet form to every British diplomatic mission abroad at the request of the Foreign Office. But then, China was China. How many would have read them if they had been about Canada (outside Canada)? The measure of the journalist is not that he can exploit man's appetite for an Oriental banquet, but that he can beguile him into attacking half a page of geopolitical corned beef hash.

The angle is all-important, and the angle must be acute. A reader's interest is like a locked drawer that can resist any amount of battering with broad generalisations, and is best prised open with the thin end of the particular. Addressing the International Press Institute in japan, Keyes Beech vividly evoked the wretched state of a wrecked Tokyo after World War II, not by fazing his audience with strings of figures, but by describing how difficult it was for the fastidious Japanese to keep clean. Soap was hard to come by and bad; there was no way of getting about; most of the bathhouses had been bombed anyway, and if you found one that was intact, you could not leave your clothes to go and bathe, or they would be stolen…After nearly thirty years, I still remember his speech.

When contrasting the lingering revolutionary ethos in North China after the death of Chairman Mao with the way men shrugged off his memory the further one moved south. I let the clothes of our interpreter Miss Han tell the story. In Beijing she wore a shapeless Mao suit and was hardly distinguishable from a man, but by the time we reached Szechuan this had sharpened into a well-cut dove-grey two-piece, which gave way in Shanghai to a lilac blouse and a black pleated skirt, and by the time we reached Canton she was a girl in a smart cotton frock looking just like her cousins in capitalist Hong Kong just across the way.

In Vietnam, where the story had been worn threadbare by the tread of a thousand reporters, one way of stealing attention was to turn it over and look at the back. Copy that could be headlined 'The View from Hanoi' was worth a hundred rewrites of 'The View from Saigon' ('We can never win this war just by fighting in the provinces. But the people of Saigon are not yet conditioned for an uprising, or even for a wave of terrorism. As things are, the war may go on for years. We are ready to do everything possible to save Washington's face, if only the Americans will go home...'). And, like everything else, the story always has a back.

A leaden report on the anniversary celebration of the Mongolian People's Revolutionary Party, laboriously condensed into copy 3,000 miles away in Singapore, suddenly becomes a story when I learn at Phoenix Park how the jollification was interrupted by an appalling storm. The entire diplomatic corps at Ulan Bator, dragooned into watching an interminable communist 'cultural performance' in the evening, found themselves gazing glassily at patriotic trick-cyclists and listening uncomprehendingly to ideological crosstalk comedians while the water rose inexorably from their insteps to their shins. The show was abandoned before anyone actually drowned, but the agony was not over, for they were torn from their beds at one o'clock in the morning with the glad tidings that the floods had receded and therefore, in the best traditions of the theatre, the show *must* go on. Symbols, metaphors, paradoxes, ironies — they can all concentrate the mind wonderfully, and paint a vivid picture with far fewer than a thousand words. Flying across China 'I receive a series of small, seemingly irrelevant gifts handed out by our air hostesses — an address book, a pair of folding scissors, four key-rings. In the hotels brightly decorated washbasins rest on perennially dripping bath taps, the coloured towels have been elaborately folded to look like huge chrysanthemums, but the lavatory seats have lost both hinges.' A China emerging from the stifling era of Maoism is as long on traditional niceties as it is short on modern conveniences; an uneasy dualism is pulling the Chinese two ways at every turn. Meanwhile the struggle for power in Beijing is evoked by an uncanny electronic talking head that packs the Chinese crowds in at the British Energy Exhibition. Here is a 'Big Brother' never dreamed of in George Orwell's philosophy. But if the party put one in every village, whose head would it be?

Small, sometimes mischievous glimpses of reality, like the snapshots of a voyeur, catch the eye before it glazes. When Robert McNamara visits the Hoa Hao in South Vietnam to bind them closer to the American cause, he presents a hearing aid to the deaf old lady who is the *grande dame* of the sect. Good thinking. Except that no one can make it work, and as large white men with ever redder faces stand around banging the plastic case and twiddling the knobs it becomes a symbol of the blank incomprehension that lies between the Vietnamese and their alien allies (and a comment on the triumphs of technology as a means of winning a guerrilla war).

If symbols are short cuts to understanding, irony can drive a point home with a treacherous smile. In Hanoi, a flock of slender girls in pastel *ao dais* cycle away from their high school like a cloud of gossamer butterflies, after giggling over a collection of photographs pinned up on boards inside the gate. I cross the road to see what amused them. It is an exhibition of French atrocities, and the centrepiece is a picture of a white soldier holding a dripping Vietnamese head by the hair in each hand. In Saigon, a large notice outside a textile mill gutted by American mortar bombs during the Tet Offensive reads 'Church of Christ Salutes You — American Friends'. (A freakish association of ideas reminded me of this twelve years later in Wuhan, when two Chinese girls played 'The East is Red' in praise of Mao on a set of bronze bells cast 2,400 years before Christ, and followed that up with 'Holy Night' as an encore).

Connections make good copy. An entry in the Chinese Almanac that reads 'Beware of Fire' lends point to a routine piece on the opening of the Year of the Dragon in 1976 when 600 homes in a squatter settlement in Hong Kong are promptly swept flat by the worst conflagration in ten years. The zig-zag course the ferry takes between the treacherous rapids of the Yangtse Gorges suggests the zig-zag 'road to socialism' of Chairman Mao and China's own perilous passage down the years since 1949, just as the dead straight lines of the irrigation canals that criss-cross Pol Pot's Cambodia suggest the rigid dogma of the Khmer Rouge who have so soullessly created them.

'The two scenarios were almost identical,' I wrote of rival road shows in 1960. 'The streets were divided into sections by white lines behind which clumps of regimented schoolchildren cheered dutifully and waved cheap paper flags. Large, alien Secret Servicemen prowled in the vicinity of the distinguished visitor, contemptuous of the susceptibilities of his native hosts. There was the usual surfeit of speeches. But in Jakarta the anti-colonialist President Sukarno was receiving Premier Nikita Khrushchev, while in Taipei the anti-communist President Chiang Kai-shek was receiving President Dwight D. Eisenhower.'

Striking parallels — the more incongruous the better — may be divided not by ideologies, but by space or time. When Chinese arrogance, British insensitivity, and ludicrous mutual incomprehension seemed ready to touch off an explosion over the future of Hong Kong in the early eighties, I could lead a backgrounder with the lofty judgement passed on a distinguished British envoy by the Chinese Viceroy of Canton 150 years before: 'The said barbarian is of reasonable intelligence. If he applies himself with perseverance, he may yet distinguish between right and wrong.' (But the British of the day proved as stubborn as Mrs Thatcher, the envoy became 'a lawless foreign slave' and a 'barbarian dog', the Opium War followed, Britain acquired Hong Kong, and that was where we came in).

It requires little skill to capture the reader with a human story, of course; what is more important is to be able to reduce the impersonal to human dimensions, and this has to be done even when the impersonal is about people. 'The Javanese waiter in my hotel earns a dollar fifty a month, the price of a tube of toothpaste' will stick in a mind whose metabolism will pass three paragraphs of assorted economic statistics undigested. The Chinese may run a national campaign against the lax morals engendered by the evil winds of 'bourgeois liberalisation' blowing from the West, and even support it with facts and figures. But the story only starts to breathe when a British woman delegate tells me how, while sitting between two senior Chinese cadres at a grand official dinner in Manchuria, she felt a hand moving up between her thighs — 'And when I say up, Mr Bloodworth, I mean *up!*' After that quote, a reader would not dare to risk skipping a line of the rest of the turgid copy.

The most vital connection of all is the spark that jumps from the report to the reader. Commuters in Hertford, Hereford and Hampshire cared more about the rain in Spain (let alone hurricanes nearer home) than a revolution in a Singapore at the other end of Asia, but 'Singapore, *Britain's biggest military base East of Suez*' could snap the gap shut in the English mind. Few subscribers would have abandoned the lead story on the front page of *The Observer* of 31 May 1959 after reading in the first sentence that 'The left-wing anti-colonialist People's Action Party' had won a landslide general election under a new constitution that gave home rule to Singapore — 'strategic pivot of Britain's defence system in the East'. *Left-wing anti-colonialist…landslide…home rule…strategic pivot* — they were like four jabs from a sharp elbow.

When all Indochina went red in 1975, Southeast Asia became comprehensible to the Western reader once it was pointed out that it was no longer a distant morass of seeping communist subversion, but a subcontinent bisected 'like Europe' into anti-communist west and communist east. China's repetitive ravings against the Soviet Union, which had for long enjoyed the ratings of a TV commercial for the ultimate detergent, earned at least a sidelong glance again in 1980 when Jim Callaghan visited the People's Republic, and one could write: 'Russians in Beijing glumly regarded the arrival of the former British premier as another twirl of the cylinder in China's game of anti-Russian roulette.' Muslim evangelism in Malaysia won space in London after Muhammad Ali had been persuaded to defend his title in Kuala Lumpur against the British contender, Joe Bugner, as a promotion gimmick for Islam.

Paradoxically, the reporter must internationalise his reports just because the reader is too parochial and drawn only by a handful of familiar names. Drag Colonel Ghadaffi into a story about the Muslim rebellion in the Philippines, or Mr Gorbachev into a story about the disputed outer islands of Japan, and the rest of the copy will reel him in. A piece on the Year of the Dragon caught far more eyes if one listed the unlikely band of Western firedrakes who had been born in it as cycle succeeded cycle (Joan of Arc, Bernard Shaw, Woodrow Wilson, Broz Tito, Aleksei Kosygin, Harold Wilson, Edward Heath). Richard Nixon came into this world in one Year of the Rat and paid his historic visit to Beijing in another, and once this was explained, many people were charmed by what they regarded as not one, but two coincidences.

I need hardly add that spot news about a dead mouse in some obscure high-speed digital facility on the most unconsidered of Pacific atolls can rivet attention the world over if it opens, 'The entire global strategic defence system of the United States was paralysed here today when…' But not otherwise. For to persuade the reader even to begin to read what he writes, to switch his skimming eye from fast forward to play, the reporter must first hook him with the lure whose fashioning can be the most fiddling, frustrating, time-wasting, tormenting, and revolting chore of his craft — the lead.

28 THE LEAD AND THE CLICHÉ

'Inexpensive garments for the mature figure.'

FIRST catch your reader...But not all agree on how this is best done, it seems. In 1971 the North Korean government confidently set out to seduce the people of Singapore with an eighteen-page 'advertisement' published in a local tabloid in excruciatingly small print. This was headlined succinctly: 'Brief History of the Revolutionary Activities of Comrade Kim Il Sung, General Secretary of the Central Committee of the Workers' Party of Korea, Head of State and Premier of the Cabinet of the Democratic People's Republic of Korea, Peerless Patriot, National Hero, Ever-Victorious Iron-Willed Brilliant Commander', and ran to about 50,000 more words in the same lively vein. But that was only Part One. Eager and impatient subscribers had to wait until the next day for Part Two, which filled another eighteen pages.

In the same year the soporific Chinese press was shaken by a stern rebuke from on high for printing 'long-winded, empty, stereotyped' copy, when articles should be as short and clear as possible 'so that workers, peasants and soldiers have time to read them all'. It was excellent advice, but when I next looked at a Beijing newspaper, it had inspired a front page news lead that ran: 'Under the great inspiration of the spirit of the second Plenary Session of the Ninth Party Central Committee, the leadership cadres of the Chinese People's Liberation Army at various levels, filled with boundless, deep proletarian feelings for the Great Leader Chairman Mao and in close coordination with the practice of the three major revolutionary movements…' With fifty-five words on the page and no main verb in sight the writer had already lost most of the workers, peasants and soldiers that formed the reading public in the People's Republic. But an overworked hack in Fleet Street might—just for a moment — have envied him his licence to do so.

For here was the paradox. Mao talked endlessly about the need to struggle, while the West talked endlessly about the need to be free. But a 'socialist' reporter in China was free to lead his paper with a stupefyingly mindless intro that could have written itself while he slept, where his Western counterpart would have been locked in a desperate struggle with words and ideas and time and space to produce a vigorous lead of half the length. But there it is: a journalist born in the wild must be forever alert for the sudden demands of the jungle; not for him the comfortable routines of his domesticated cousin behind the fence in communist countries.

The freer the press, the more formidable the challenge, and a newspaperman condemned to a fight for survival against television, radio, and his own rivals must use all his guile to stay in the game. He is not without assets. Television may provide instant news in vivid pictures, but it gives ephemeral exposure rather than durable exposition, sometimes shocking — even distracting — rather than explaining. And then the pictures have gone. Radio can be more frightening, for it is like noises in the dark. In 1960 I watched demonstrating South Korean students advance in a solid mass through the streets of Seoul, to be brutally stopped by the stammering automatic weapons of riot police out for blood. But afterwards I heard an unforgettable recording of the same event made in a first-floor office of Associated Press that had overlooked the scene, the 'one-two' chorus of ten thousand students marching in step — 'I-sha! I-sha!' — the voices and the tramp of approaching feet louder and louder like an incoming tidal wave; then the shouted orders, the sudden roar of the machine-guns, and, almost in my ear, 'GET AWAY FROM THAT WINDOW, YOU FOOL! YOU WANNA BE KILLED?'.

No article could convey the terror of that tape. However, a well-written piece about the same episode could not only recall the violence and bloodshed, but tell the story behind them — not in pictures and sounds that instantly slip away into the past, but in cold black and white, for the record. It could sketch in the personalities involved, analyse, interpret, put the drama into a form that could not just be re-run, but re-read at will with a simple movement of the eye, marked with a comment here, underlined there, pinned to a complementary piece, and kept on a file with others. Above all the press can report the unsaid, the secret side that is hidden from the candid camera's eye and the broadcaster's microphone but can be learned from the off-the-record, not-for-quotation, strictly-for-background contacts of the reporter with his notebook firmly stuck in his pocket. It was a newspaper, not a network, that uncovered Watergate. It could not have been otherwise.

The correspondent nevertheless needs all the professional wit and wisdom at his disposal to persuade the reader to treat television as headline reporting and turn to him for the rest of the story. It is often said that a journalist writes best under pressure, when he will draw the stark lines of the news with a firm and fast hand, without shading or trimming it. But that is no argument for dashing off a piece in fifteen minutes if he has half a day in hand in which to let it gestate, to draft a skeleton, marshal his facts, plunder his files, call on memories, line up analogies, metaphors, the telling phrase and the telling quote — above all to devise a lead that will open today's Pandora's Box with a snap that jerks the reader awake. Only after that may the copy (as they say) 'write itself' — to be read and checked with care before it is confided to calloused hands on the subeditorial horseshoe.

To my mind, the secret of composing the straight news lead is often to avoid trying to tell the whole story in the first main clause. 'Between 27,000 and 41,000 American troops in Vietnam (10 to 15 per cent of the total force) are now using hard drugs, usually heroin' pulled a punch that should have hit the reader with the full impact of just eleven words and five digits — 'At least 27,000 American troops in Vietnam are now using hard drugs, according to...' The rest could have followed. Flouting the pundits, I nevertheless made much use of the 'As' opening in order to put across two ideas before the first full stop. If the two ideas contradicted each other, so much the better: 'As final details for the withdrawal of Indonesian terrorists in Sarawak and Sabah are being negotiated, security forces are in fact bracing themselves to defend these Malaysian territories against intensified attacks'.

The pedantic frown on opening with a quote, but happily my editors did not stifle instinct with a style book, and I was able to get away with: '"Is God white? Is he an American? Has He chosen the free world," asked Prince Norodom Sihanouk of Cambodia'; and 'Mister, I would have promised the Khmer Rouge the moon between two slices of bread...' A good quote can tempt the reader to take on a story he might otherwise turn away from with a shudder: 'You cannot teach a tiger to eat grass' (Khrushchev on the carnivorous colonialists in a speech that went on to leave his audience dozing in the Indonesian sun).

Headlines, of course, can tell the story and allow the reporter to write a more relaxed intro. (Among some of my favourites are: 'Inflation Hits Ritual Buying of Human Skulls', Firewalking can be Fun', and the deliquescent horror of '27 Laotian Refugees Found Eking Out in a Ranch'). But there is much to be said for opening with a short jab that leaves the reader mentally breathless — 'Canton has disappeared'; 'Mount Everest is growing taller' — or a lead that seizes him by the shoulders: 'Hong Kong is fishing for the goodwill of Peking with human bait' (throwing back refugees); 'Is security a British battalion or a Chinese smile?' (on Hong Kong); 'East Asia is filled with the sound of slamming doors, for a killer is abroad' (on cholera).

The lead is a multi-purpose tool that can take the reader from the particular to the general or from the general to the particular, according to need. Where to open with a generalisation about contraband in the Far East might be tedious, a specific intro can report: 'Police have found that demurely-dressed hostesses on excursion buses from Taipei have been giving a strip-tease show once they reach the mountains. This seems to be the first known case of anyone deliberately smuggling out nudity under the cover of clothes.' But where a bag of individual stories with the same message must be pulled together by the neck-string, a simile can produce the generalisation that introduces the theme: 'Like a sharp stone skimmed across the surface tension of Southeast Asia, "student power" has struck successively in Burma, Indonesia and the Philippines during the past two months.' Or a metaphor: 'The Bangkok Pact has suddenly provided the foundation for a precarious scaffolding of international goodwill that has been rushed up almost overnight.' Or a paradox: 'There are disturbing signs in Asia today that…the system of frank enmities which has until now provided a firm basis for international diplomacy may be dissolving into a shifting pattern of peace moves.'

The intro can also deal with the delicate problem of disclosing that the reporter does not really know what he is talking about. My own devices for excusing my bafflement or abysmal ignorance have included: 'From conflicting official statements about the equivocal fighting in Laos, it seems that the North Vietnamese were victorious but President Nixon won'; 'With Chairman Mao and Premier Chou Enlai edging towards eternity, their possible heirs in the Chinese hierarchy bob up and down as inconsequentially as tumblers in a lock, leaving exasperated Pekinologists to interpret their misnamed "power struggle" without holding the key…'; 'How will the death of Mao Tsetung affect China's support for communist guerrillas in Southeast Asia? China's foreign trade? China's relations with Russia, America, Europe, Japan, Australia? These are questions a demanding world is asking, and to which hapless Chinawatchers, unable to plead the Fifth Amendment, have often given flagrantly contradictory answers'; and for a profile on Chairman Hua Guofeng, the relatively unknown heir of Mao about whom distressingly few facts were to hand: 'Hua who?'

There will be those who object that I am breaking the rules. A stylebook or a school of journalism may lay down that the reporter must not use long quotes, must not telescope quotes, must not open with quotes (though he may close with them); that he must not lead with a subordinate clause, or a question, or an unidentified pronoun; that he must avoid repetitive use of the same words, redundant adjectives, words of three syllables, non-specific nouns ('situation'), foreign phrases, technical jargon, pseudo-intellectual gobbledygook, complex sentences, and clichés; that he must write simple, uncluttered copy in the active voice…Just so. Nevertheless, just as 'correct' French is correct, but colloquial French is what Frenchmen speak and understand, so the syntax of the trade is not enough in itself: it must lead to fluent and lively writing that is designed to please readers, not pass exams.

For one thing, the style used for straight news and the style adopted for situationers, features and profiles (with all the problems of putting a man in space), cannot come out of the same mould. Straight news obviously demands short sentences, short paragraphs and plain language; it is the epitome of 'literature in a hurry', and the reporter may have had hardly more time to bang it out on a Dakota flight from Vientiane to Bangkok than the reader will have to read it in the London tube from Tufnell Park to Tottenham Court Road. That does not excuse bad writing, but I part company with the pundits when they denounce the use of clichés and redundant adjectives.

Much nonsense is talked about clichés and stereotypes (I have even read of 'stereotypical clichés'). Both words meant the same thing — an original plate from which to print, and from that an idea or image of which so many copies have now been run off that there is nothing original left. But we are clichés ourselves, run off from Adam and Eve, and so, therefore, are all the elements of our nasty, brutish and short existence that derive from their sordid little drama of archetypal sex and violence. A cliché is hackneyed just because it embodies an eternal verity or misconception ('Everything I tell you three times is true,' said the Bellman in *The Hunting of the Snark*), and as it becomes more and more fashionable for the glibber critics to stick the label on to the characters and the plots of real writers, every quirk of the human condition threatens to become 'cliché-ridden' (or 'riddled' — even the clichés about clichés multiply). The day seems not far off when all art and life itself will be written off as a *'cleeshay'* and there will not be a single recognisably new thought to set down on paper any more. Everything will be on a par with the car chase and the golden-hearted whore.

But there are live and dead clichés, and for the straight news reporter the live cliché not only carries a swift kick where a substitute might fail to make contact, but acts as a form of universal shorthand, a code of instant comprehension that links writer and reader when both have only minutes to spare. It springs to the reporter's mind automatically as he struggles to beat his deadline, and it evokes an immediate echo from the reader at the other end. Furthermore, the force of cliché-ridden copy is often doubled by the use of redundant adjectives (how blasphemous can I get?), for they can lend a sentence strength and rhythm and familiarity. 'The City was rocked by violence yesterday when bloody rioting in which seven died erupted in broad daylight, following a long string of persistent rumours of insider trading.' Take out 'bloody', 'broad', 'long' and 'persistent', and the copy at once seems anaemic. Delete 'rocked' and 'erupted' and try to rewrite the intro without clichés, and it may turn white and keel over before the reader's eyes. Clichés and the otiose ('last of all', 'a new beginning', 'a team of ten workers') may look ugly customers, but to him they are old friends with whom he has an unspoken understanding.

The cliché and cat-sat-on-the-mat English are nevertheless like fast food in the world of grab-a-sandwich journalism, and to be selected with care by those with the leisure to be more fastidious. Much that applies to news reporting may also apply to the Sunday read, but while (if I have it right) 'inexpensive garments for the mature figure' may sound better as 'cheap clothes for fat women', and 'pursuit operations terminated with negative results' as 'we lost them', short words and short sentences can become wearisome if not interspersed with longer ones. And although to use the same word for the same thing all the time can make for monotonous reading ('the party in the first part shall be known as the party in the first part'), it sometimes strengthens the copy where an elegant variation would weaken it: 'We shall fight on the beaches, we shall fight on the landing grounds, we shall fight in the hills…'

Since one should never blind the public with science, it is providential that when he is writing on abstruse technological subjects the reporter is usually as ignorant as the reader, and they therefore speak the same language. But then they must always be speaking the same language, even when it is French. There is a place for the apt foreign phrase: *Savoir-faire* cannot be translated as 'know-how', and Flaubert's *mot juste* is the 'right word' in more senses than one. But while *jolie laide* inimitably describes a pretty-ugly woman (as against a pretty ugly one), it can only be used in the sort of piece that is going to be read by the sort of person who will be familiar with this oxymoronic gallicism — an art review in a literary supplement, perhaps — and will not translate it as an 'amusing lay'. There may be off-the-peg English for news reporting, but otherwise the vocabulary must be carefully tailored to fit the publication and even the page.

And in case the correspondent has persuaded his reader to run right through his piece, the end should not be an anti-climax, but sum up the story with an incisive bottom line: On the worries of the South Vietnamese over cease-fire negotiations — 'For while some of them believe in a just war in Vietnam, none believes in a just peace'; on the possibility that the Americans will bomb the dykes in North Vietnam — 'it could be the next card in the somewhat sinister tarot pack with which President Nixon tells the fortunes of his enemies'; on hints of closer contacts between China and the Philippines — 'It can be objected that these are only straws in the wind, but they are still the stuff that bricks are made of'.

The parting shot, however, must be written in hope rather than expectation. It may always be cut for lack of space, and I took an added risk with that terminal preposition: I could not be sure it would get past the desk. For before he pleases the reader, the reporter must please that other wayward, exigent subspecies of mankind whom letter-writers euphemistically address as 'Dear Editor'.

29 THE THING FROM ANOTHER WORLD

The editor is a weird, even grotesque form of life that he would shudder to meet (as he one day might) in a mirror.

JUST twenty-four hours after I had arrived in Saigon in 1954 to cover Indochina for *The Observer*, I found myself warily shaking hands in a sidewalk cafe with the man covering Indochina for *The Observer*.

'They didn't tell me you were still here.' I said, aghast.

'They didn't tell me you were coming to take over,' said Rawle Knox equably.

We looked at each other for a long moment to see, I suppose, who would blink. Having just spent forty-five hours flying from Paris to Saigon, I saw myself spending another forty-five hours flying straight back. It had taken the combined negligence of our mutual editor, managing editor, and foreign news editor to contrive this egregious encounter. But they did not hold those posts for nothing. They had brought it off.

As some turn to the East to pray, we turned to the West to curse. Then we both forgot about London and settled down to the complex business of planning the coverage of the entire Far East for the most prestigious Sunday newspaper in the world and its renowned syndication service. It took surprisingly little time. 'Saigon's all yours,' said Rawle. 'I've had Indochina anyway. I'll be glad to get back to Hong Kong.' He signalled to a waiter. 'What'll you have?' And that was it. There is nothing like solving problems on the spot.

In his novel *Out of the Silent Planet*, C. S. Lewis describes a repulsive being from another world from which we instinctively flinch — its head 'almost square', its face 'masses of lumped and puckered flesh of variegated colour fringed in some bristly dark substance' — until we realise that it is not a Martian as seen by Man, but Man as seen by a Martian. And to a correspondent at one end of the world with a similarly alien perspective, the editor at the other is a weird, even grotesque form of life that he would shudder to meet (as he one day might) in a mirror.

The London office of this creature contains no charts of time zones. That leaves him free to indulge an atavistic instinct to shoot off cables at sunset, so that they will wake you up in Saigon at three o'clock in the morning with demands for urgent copy. Nor is the office cluttered with maps. That enables him to ask for a colour story about Lon Nol's life in Hawaii when you are in Singapore; but to refuse hot copy from you when you are in Honolulu, because the story should be left to 'our American correspondents' (the nearest of whom is 2,500 miles away).

Sometimes these esoteric methods of warping time and space come very close to putting the correspondent in two places at once. It is done quite simply. An editor of only average cunning can manage it by waiting until the last moment before sending him a cable like this:

> DELAYED ADVISING YOU LAOSWISE BUT
> ENTHUSIASTICALLY FOR YOU LAOSWARDS
> NOW STOP OBVIOUSLY ATTRACTIVE HAVING
> VIENTIANE DATELINE TOMORROW.

Tomorrow? The cable reached me at eleven at night. To file from Vientiane within twenty-four hours I would have had to find a seat on a plane to Bangkok first thing in the morning, apply for a visa on arrival (there was no Laotian consulate in Singapore), wait until it was processed by a slow motion Lao, then catch a hypothetical Dakota to Vientiane in the middle of a crisis that had suspended commercial flights, get my story in what remained of the day, cable it to London at double urgent rates in the evening, and retire to pray.

But the editor is never joking. Matters are so designed that only the victim sees the funny side of it all, and when he laughs it duly hurts. On the other hand let the correspondent who is told to take his time and settle down properly in a new base before filing beware: within forty-eight hours his solicitous editors may show that they have not forgotten him by sending him a first cable screaming:

> BADLY BEATEN BY OPPOSITION ON
> STRANDED BEAUTY QUEEN STORY STOP
> WHERE WERE YOU QUERY.

The Editor's Law of Plastic Time and Space also applies to copy, for which it reads 'The nature of copy is that it requires only half the minimal space it requires'. Arriving back in Singapore at nine-thirty one night after spending ten days in Borneo covering Indonesian *Konfrontasi*, I was met with a cable reading:

WELCOME 200 WORDS PERSONAL
IMPRESSION ETUNEXPECTED FACTS FOOD
HYGIENE PRACTICE YOUR AREA PROWORLD
ROUNDUP RELATED ABERDEEN TYPHOID
STOP MUCH TYPHOID THERE CONNECTED
DIRTY FOOD HANDLING QUERY DO
CUSTOMERS BOTHER ARE SANITARY
REGULATIONS ENFORCED HOW FARE
EUROPEANS QUERY HOW COMPARES BRITAIN
QUERY GLAD COPY OVERNIGHT THANKS.

In 200 words? The cable itself had used forty-five.

But the editor of an *Observer* travel supplement managed to be more exacting, even by mail: 'We were wondering whether you could supply a four-to-five-hundred-word travel note on the high spots of the part of the world you cover,' she wrote, '*including whatever you know about Japan.*' Five hundred words is half a column. I started listing the names on the back of an old cable: seventeen countries or colonial territories, including China, Japan, Hong Kong, Taiwan; then the tourist musts in alphabetical order: Angkor, Bali, Bangkok, Borobodur, down to Sun Moon Lake and the Temple of Heaven; then whatever-you-know-about Japan: Biwa, Fuji, Hakkone, Kyoto, Nara, Nikko,

Osaka…Then I gave up and wrote back asking for reactions to a request for 'a four-to-five-hundred-word travel note on the high spots of Europe, *including whatever you know about Switzerland.*' I added 1,700 words of copy, but they were never published.

Language can be a problem, as some editors tend to communicate in a mental idiom of their own. CAMBODIA LOOKS PROMISING STOP WHATS HUK QUERY WELCOME FEW SUGGESTED NOTEBOOK TOPICS LETTERWISE SOONEST BESTEST is clear enough, but GOT ANY MAINSTREAM TWO PART UNPOLITICAL MALE ET FEMALE IDEAS PRO REVIEW FRONT MID NOVEMBER PUBLICATION QUERY REGARDS floored me for a moment or two. More disconcerting, perhaps, are the occasions on which that mental idiom is applied to a call for action: when eight men were to be hanged together at dawn in Changi jail (they were marched to the scaffold in three ranks of three with one blank file), London asked me to arrange for a photographer to take pictures of the event for a German syndication customer as if we merely had to wave our press passes to get privileged seats, not organise a two-man jailbreak in reverse and risk being next for the high jump.

But even requests for instant bite-size copy cannot rival this well-thought-out bid for something a little longer (or so I assumed) in the next twenty-four hours:

PLANNING SPECIAL DOUBLE PAGE COVERAGE
CHINA SWEEK COULDST THEREFORE FILE
BY THURSDAY ANALYSIS PEKINGS GENERAL
OVERSEAS POLICIES ETINTENTIONS TOWARDS
SOUTHEAST ASIA INTAKING INTERNAL
POLITICAL ECONOMIC MILITARY SITUATION

IN CHINA ETELABORATING SINOSOVIET
DISPUTE ETNATIONALIST THREAT
EXFORMOSA ANSWERING QUESTIONS IS MAO
STILL BOSS IF NOT WHO QUERY DOES CHINA
INTEND ATTACK NEIGHBOURS IF SO WHERE
QUERY INTERVENTION IN VIETNAM QUERY
ATTITUDE OF HANOI QUERY WHAT CHANCE
INTERNAL DISRUPTION CHINA ITSELF QUERY
WHAT LIKELY IMPACT CURRENT CHINESE
AGGRESSIVENESS INDIAN FRONTIER QUERY
SUGGEST ALSO INFILL RELEVANT FACTORS
ELSEWHERE FOR EXAMPLE INDONESIA
QUERY MALAYSIA QUERY SINGAPORE QUERY
THAILAND QUERY LAOS QUERY WHAT
CURRENT SINOJAPANESE RELATIONS QUERY
CHEERS NEWSED. (My italics).

I thought about it for a minute, gritted — no, bared — my teeth, and relentlessly filed and filed and filed. But he had the last word. He countered by using everything I sent him down to the inevitably bitter end.

While displaying a noble faith in the ability of the distant reporter to unravel the whole unsavoury mess of political spaghetti in his region as long as no one contradicts him, the foreign editor is quick to reveal that the last person he trusts is his own correspondent as soon as somebody else says something else. In November 1963 *The Observer* led the paper with my account of the assassination of President Ngo Dinh Diem and his brother, and the news editor cabled: BRAVO FOR YOU SPLASHING WITH SAIGON STORY

STOP, but then tore the smug grin off my face by adding accusingly: ASSOCPRESS REPORT VIA MALCOLM BROWNE SAIGONSIDE DIEM AND BROTHER HAVE ESCAPED ALIVE. Fortunately (or unfortunately) I was right.

Although eager for exclusives, therefore, some editors are inclined to be unhappy when they get one since, scoops being scoops, there is no collateral from the competition. Are they really expected to believe the unsupported testimony of their own man? Many will only be reassured when the big news agencies confirm the story — but by then, of course, it will no longer be a scoop. I was once congratulated on the accuracy of a file after it had been checked in London against a Reuter despatch: to everyone's relief, it appeared, it had proved to be 'substantially correct'. If one fails to echo the opposition, on the other hand, there is always the implication that somehow one has missed something:

> REPORTED HERE AMERICANS HAVE OFFERED
> TRAIN MALAYSIAN TROOPS STOP WELCOME
> MORE DETAILS EXPLANATION WHAT
> SIGNIFICANCE THANKS. (Utter nonsense).

Or:

> WELCOME 650 WORDS CAMBODIA
> EXPLANATIONER BUT HOPE THIS POSSIBLE
> THROUGH USING PERSONALITY SIHANOUK
> CUMSTORYLINE STOP INFORMATIVELY
> TIME MAGAZINE HAS AMUSING SIHANOUK
> COVERSTORY PLEASE ADVISE.

But then there was the black day when rumour had it that the Prime Minister of Iran had expired, and the *Daily Express* man in Teheran received a cable from his editor complaining

DAILY MAIL HAS MOSSADEQ DEAD WHY
NOT YOU?

The most hazardous exploit a self-indulgent correspondent can undertake is not to storm ashore with the Marines — for that you can only get death — but to seek an exclusive interview with the local prince, president or prime minister that yields nothing but platitudes. This gives the editor a wonderful opportunity to spike the copy and so leave the reporter abjectly apologising to minions of the enraged potentate for its failure to appear. And that may do him no good. The potentate may still accuse him of insinuating himself into his presence under false pretences in order to abuse his magnanimity and waste his time, throw him out of the country within the next twenty-four hours as an impostor, and never allow him back. 'Interviews are rarely welcome unless the interviewee says something that either makes news or includes a startling comment on a news story,' reads an *Observer* note on requirements put out in 1968. *Verb. sap.*

It is at least fortunate that the great are more affronted when their words are taken lightly, rather than their actions or even their lives. Otherwise what vengeance might President Sukarno have wreaked on me when *The Observer* counted his life so cheap that it spared only three column-inches for my report on his near-assassination during the Tjikini incident? And for once I would have sympathised with him. I could feel my own jaw drop under the weight of my indignation when I finally tracked my mutilated copy down to the wrong corner of the front page. For journalists, too, are more touchy about their words than their actions or even their lives, and this gives editors considerable scope for driving them mad by mauling their files.

A correspondent must therefore keep his cool, especially when he thinks he has been absolutely brilliant and in consequence is at his most vulnerable. Up in the Central Highlands of Vietnam in 1955, I watched a long line of elephants approach a seated Ngo Dinh Diem and kneel before him, one by one, as an act of fealty. That is, until one big fellow, forgetting his party manners, turned his back on the Prime Minister (as he then was), knelt in the opposite direction, and so presented him with a vast and wrinkled expanse of pachydermatous rump. My more feckless colleagues merely laughed, but I saw at once that this was the keystone to a story that would otherwise be no more than a gaudy colour piece.

For if the dutiful genuflexions of the other beasts had symbolised the formal submission to the Vietnamese overlord of the minority hill tribes who owned them, the great uplifted bum of this behemoth had symbolised their true feelings about Saigon. And to make the point I had the perfect quotation from the lips of the Sultan in James Elroy Flecker's *Hassan* — 'Thine impudence hath a monstrous beauty, like the hindquarters of an elephant.' What insight! What erudition! Hadn't somebody said that genius was an ability to make connections? How they would exclaim in London! They didn't. They cut the entire anecdote, the comment, and the quote, and then — as if to underline the snub — ran the rest of the 1,200 words as straight descriptive copy.

Incomprehensible though their thought processes may

sometimes seem, nothing is more unnerving about editors than their editing. But it is the mark of the professional reporter that, for the most part, he lives with it with equanimity, looking upon the fate of his prose much as St Matthew must (if with ill-concealed disapproval) have looked upon the fate of pearls cast before swine. It is true that in 1964 I composed a note for the foreign news editor complaining that almost everything I wrote was being bludgeoned by the subs into gibbering, unrecognisable, ungrammatical, clumsy, and inaccurate rubbish before it was flung on to the stone and then fed to the waiting public. But I did not send it. In 1980 I also complained that 'a girl with a passion for semi-colons who was not even born when I started working for *The Observer* has been entrusted with the task of editing my copy'. But I did not send that either.

And one sobers up when one starts to write books, for the peccadilloes of the newspaper sub are nothing to the mortal sins of publisher's editors. An American copy-editor once changed my not very original 'Quoth the Raven. "Nevermore"' to 'Quoth the Raven, "Never again"' ('Nevermore' was evidently an inadmissible archaism), and 'armoured fighting vehicle' to 'armoured, fighting, vehicle'. Not to be outdone, a British editor changed 'insalubrious' to 'unsalubrious' (among many other gaffes), adding for good measure: 'This is not to my taste.' Nor, indeed, was it to mine.

But I am not suggesting that the reporter should invariably accept the mangling of his copy with what passes for pious Oriental resignation. For one thing, Orientals only display this pious resignation themselves when they know they cannot change things, and are apt to start a riot the moment they think they can. For another, he must protect his interests — after all, it is his name that is laid on the byline — and the interests of the paper. After accusing the syndication editor of having 'baffled the reader and made an ass of me', I received a reply reading 'We do indeed hang our heads in shame for the maltreatment of your story', and on another lurid occasion, 'Deepest apologies for the mess we made of your story'. That seemed to justify a little niggling.

There can be more to it than that, however. At one point a member of the British Communist Party infiltrated the subs' desk and began to tint the *Observer* copy that passed through his hands an indelicate shade of pink. The journalists who wrote the copy were naturally the first to spot the discoloration, and when they protested, he was blown and fired. Years later, I had reason to suspect that the ruthless cutting and mishandling of my files was part of a ploy by an ambitious foreign news editor to put a younger, more malleable man in my place. One must defend one's patch, and when he began to accept copy from outsiders behind my back, I protested vigorously.

But if editors cabled that they were handing out assignments in my area to restless staffers at home, or peripatetic freelances with an itch to hold the gorgeous East in fee, I weighed the advantages against the disadvantages. It might seem that it was second nature to the enigmatic aliens in London to challenge my territorial imperative whenever they had a free moment. But unless the visitors rewrote stories I had published five years earlier as if nobody had discovered — let alone covered — the subcontinent before they arrived, or broke a confidence (as in the case of the 'Mexicans') and left me to play the patsy, I let them pass. Who was I to object? I must have looked like a poacher myself when I first came to the Far East, to be caught red-handed on Rue Catinat in Saigon by Rawle Knox in his role as incumbent bailiff.

Was I too easy-going? Some deride those who see both sides of a story, the limp purveyors of on-this-hand-on-the-other-hand copy. But if in writing the ability to put oneself in the other man's (if not the other monster's) place is the key to objectivity, in life it is the key to smooth working relations. For the distant reporter, the exercise begins with a refusal to act the Martian, with the recognition that correspondents can become editors and editors correspondents without any gruesome biological change. Look closely at an editor — which means putting yourself where he is — and suddenly he is not a bizarre creature from another world, after all, but just another journalist with another perspective.

It is a perspective the reporter must himself keep in view if he is to remain sane and survive. However earthshaking the Tjikini incident might have appeared to me in Jakarta, to the man on the desk in London it was a remote, slight, momentary tremor that only just made the Richter scale of human tragedy and folly that the past twenty-four hours had yielded. Most editors are selling copy, not correspondents. They must think of the reader's taste in stories, the owner's taste in policy, the advertiser's taste in circulation. The majority have to fit the history of the world into a handful of pages every day on the day, cutting and trimming the news from all parts of the planet to fit their strange and terrifying collage. Resolving the rival claims of correspondents from Buenos Aires to Bombay, they are endlessly at war with time and space in their struggle to beat the competition.

In so far as the drama takes place only on paper, the reporter is no more than his report, and he should therefore adopt the philosophy of the player who must somehow fit in — like his piece — not act the prima donna. And he can do this once he realises that he can turn the idiosyncrasies of the man on the desk to his advantage; that his stories can be improved by good cutting and editing; that the loathsome interloper who arrives in his bailiwick one day, waving an accreditation from head office, can take over the reporting chore for a spell and free him to write all those scintillating analytical pieces he has always meant to write but never had time for. He can spare himself much grief by meeting editors halfway, taking the initiative by telling them where he should be going and what he should be covering, generating his own stories, consulting them in advance before filing, writing to length with the best of the copy up front (the tail will be lopped off first if space is short), and suggesting where cuts could best be made without killing it.

This paragon may seem to bear little resemblance to the dear, familiar figure of the smoking, sweating, swearing correspondent, forever railing at a smoking, sweating, swearing editor on the other side of the globe for screwing up his copy before throwing it away or, perhaps worse, screwing up his copy before printing it. But they must learn to get on with each other, these two, for they are the same animal. And for every animal there is a platonic ideal, identifiable by its basic qualities. Even if Arnold Bennett was right, and journalists are men who tell lies in the hope that with repetition they will come true, that means they are indeed 'the stuff that dreams are made on'. The question is, then: What makes the 'right stuff'?

30 MUGSHOT OF A REPORTER

NO.015647 BLOODWORTH Dennis 6'3" , 190 lbs.

His is the face of a dedicated man.

IT IS no more possible to draw the ideal journalist, of course, than it is possible to draw Euclid's straight line (since, like many articles, it has length without breadth). But as an outward manifestation of an inward form, a police description may do duty where a platonic abstract cannot.

A London policeman first sketches the suspect as a full-length figure — subject is a well-nourished Caucasian male, apparent age exaggerated, hurrying along in strong, scuffed shoes and a shabby raincoat that flaps open to reveal a shapeless jacket with bulging pockets. He wears no hat, and badly needs a haircut. Nicotine stains on fingers of left hand. No rings. What would Sherlock Holmes have deduced?

This man belongs to an inelegant but demanding profession that pays little yet condemns him to a haphazard existence bound by few rules and no set routine. He carries his tools of trade on his body, ready to move at any moment; he is a chain smoker whose job keeps his nerves stripped for action, and the lack of a ring could mean that he is either single or divorced, since his mode of life and his erratic and sudden comings and goings put a strain on marriage. A journalist, my dear Watson. When he is sixty he will be past it all, and perhaps that is what is worrying him. For if I'm not very much mistaken, he is headed this way.

Not all journalists look like that off the screen, but although Shakespeare may have said 'There's no art to find the mind's construction in the face', no matter: this picture of the reporter is built up from a metaphorical rather than an anatomical identikit, and so is the mugshot that follows. They reflect eternal truths, not traits.

His is a thankless calling, the money it earns him is not worth the trouble most of the time, yet unlike nursing or teaching it is regarded as faintly disreputable. The ideal correspondent, therefore, does the job because he loves it, and would do nothing else. He is a maverick who always wanted to write, who seeks excitement, drama, romance, strange places, a byline and a bucket seat on the bandwagon of great events. He is an inquisitive dropout who looks at the regimented ranks of nine-to-five commuters performing their unchanging daily round in their neatly pressed straightjackets and — forgetting his own rigorous regime of deadlines — imagines himself to be the only one not on the treadmill. His is the face of a dedicated man.

In repose, it can be deceptively calm, even resigned. There are moments of crisis when a dozen different ideas — tears, urges, leads, synonyms —jam the doorway of his mind as they try to push their way through it simultaneously, but he must keep cool however stifling it may suddenly seem. A service message I sent to London in August 1964 reads:

> HAVE RETURNED FROM KUALA LUMPUR
> WHERE SUMMONED BY ACTING PREMIER
> ABDUL RAZAK FOR ROCKET OVER OBSERVER
> BACKGROUNDER ON RIOTS STOP HAVE
> ARRANGED MALACCA STRAITS SEA PATROL
> FOR TWO THREE DAYS AS FROM MONDAY
> MORNING BUT HAVE ALSO PROVISIONALLY
> BOOKED DIRECT FLIGHT TO SAIGON FOR
> TUESDAY IN VIEW DEVELOPMENTS...

Razak had talked of kicking 'inappropriate' correspondents out of Malaysia and given me the you-first nod. But one thing at a time. The reporter and the lion tamer have a motto in common: 'Don't Panic'. And for roughly the same reason.

The brow is broad, but not high. The journalist depends on a reliable memory, a quick grasp of the bones of a subject (he will put the flesh on himself), and a good sense of proportion. But he needs a common wit that will keep his interpretation of men's follies on firm ground rather than an intellect that may induce flights of fancy not cleared for take-off. Above all, he must have a ringside view of his own responsibilities.

This accounts for that furrowed forehead and those tangled eyebrows. Without title, braid, or bodyguard, he cuts a slight figure on the fringe of public life, but the narrow shoulders bear an awkward load, for he can tilt the axis of world events, making history and breaking men with a word (like 'Watergate'). He must weigh the 'public's right to know' against the damage and distress the knowledge will inflict, 'considerations of national interest' against a good story he owes his editor. (Keyes Beech sat on a scoop about CIA clandestine operations in North Korea for nineteen years). Wherever there are two sides to a question he must distinguish carefully between the objectivity that is legitimate and the impartiality that is misconceived. And in all this his conscience must be his fulcrum.

But he must be ready to suffer for it, for much of the reporter's business is with knaves or fools. In Sukarno's Indonesia the two outstanding journalists were Mochtar Lubis and Rosihan Anwar. Both were savage critics of the profligate president, but while Lubis flared up fearlessly in his columns and went to jail for his trouble, Anwar trimmed the wick of his copy and stayed free to write more. Lubis upbraided Anwar for betraying his beliefs. Anwar upbraided Lubis for putting himself in jail where he could no longer influence the Indonesian people, let alone their leader. Which was right? Both, of course, for each followed his own instinct — Lubis to become a martyr, Anwar to stay in the game.

The reporter's forehead may nevertheless be creased not by a struggle with conscience, but simply because his eyebrows are raised. And if they are often raised in disbelief, they should sometimes be raised in disdain. For the journalist is the butt of much criticism of uneven quality, and if he should listen to the just rebukes of honest men with humility, he can only survive if he treats the carping of the knaves and fools with contempt ('Your worm's eye view of China... Intelligence should stop paying you', signature illegible and no address given).

There was, for example, Felix Greene ('The only American-based correspondent who has visited China in recent years'), who wrote a book about how all the other journalists who had covered Mao's paradise had made a ludicrous mess of the assignment. After I had filed a critical 'China Today' column in 1968, one woman wrote to *The Observer* sarcastically: 'China today? I would like to enquire whether the Editor and Mr Dennis Bloodworth have read Felix Greene's *A Curtain of Ignorance* — and to point out that some of his readers have'; another added, 'The bulk' (of what I had written) 'has been found to be without foundation by visitors to China (see for example *A Curtain of Ignorance*).' By deriding all of the opposition over 332 pages, the gullible Felix Greene had transformed himself into the sole oracle of a rose-red People's Republic of his own creation. (But history was to make a fool of him).

When appropriate, then, the raised eyebrows of the subject may signal a becoming immodesty in the face of specious censure, and the skin is correspondingly thick (in accordance with Cuvier's Law of Correlation, no doubt). This is a man who must have faith in himself, and let nothing bogus shake it. Since a reporter commits himself to a report, he is not only exposed to attack but can expect to be assassinated at the moment of his greatest triumph. For there is nothing like a scoop to put a man in the hands of his enemies — by definition, it is his word against the world. In 1956 I cabled from Saigon that the first communist guerrilla regiment had been reassembled secretly in South Vietnam, and *The Observer* gave me the front page lead. The Indochina War had been over for two years, and the Americans laughed in my face. Three years later they were less amused. All I had to do was to stick to my story. The laughter was louder and far angrier when I filed my piece on the secret understanding between Beijing and Taipei, and I can still hear the echoes. But although Arnold Bennett's wounding insinuations may apply to the faker, the reporter who does not invent his copy can afford to wait until the truth comes true.

The face of the journalist necessarily reveals a kind of stoical arrogance, like that of a righteous Pakistani with all his papers in order standing in a queue of aliens passing through British Immigration. He may invite suspicion, hostility, even disdain from the officers at the desk, but bloody-mindedness will get them nowhere. In Saigon two middle-aged Frenchwomen on Rue Catinat call me 'sale americain' and spit in my face as I pass. In Singapore a Minister of State for Culture, goaded by the lamentable failure of the international press to confine itself to one long panegyric about his country year after year, declares that all foreign reporting on the republic has been hostile — a statement as fatuously inaccurate as it is sweeping. Between the two extremes stretch three decades of assorted curses and contumely. So be it. A reporter accepts this with resignation as part of the landscape. A man whose life is largely dictated by the daily antics of the human race is inured to its seamier manifestations.

The eyes, therefore, are patient and tolerant, but they share with the (slightly pointed?) ears the characteristics of the Devil's Advocate. They can be sharp, sceptical, quick to detect false coins and notes, to seize on the small, revealing sights and sounds that give the game away. A left-wing student named Tan Wah Piow fled Singapore on a passport with a forged entry in order to escape national service. Were all his stories of persecution by a ruthless anti-communist government to be believed? For me, he answered the question himself when he declared that he ran away because the authorities were planning to put him into the artillery, the 'most dangerous' arm of the service, despite the fact that he 'wore glasses'. The snide implication was obvious. And it was snide because the artillery is not the most dangerous arm of service, and it is quite normal for gunners to wear glasses — Like Brigadier-General Lee Hsien Loong, the son of Lee Kuan Yew. Tan stood revealed for what he was. (It was then that an official at the Ministry of Defence corrected my bias by refusing to tell me over the phone whether a man with glasses could join the infantry: my question was 'too sensitive').

When tribesmen blocked roads in order to stop loggers from stripping the rain forests of Sarawak that were their home, Malaysian Prime Minister Dr Mahathir attacked well-meaning Westerners who sympathised with their refusal to change their way of life, pointing out that plans were being laid for them to be properly housed and educated elsewhere. Although Malaysian politicians were among those privately selling off the forests for cash, it seemed to me (as someone touchy about Western interference in Eastern affairs) that he might still have a valid point. But then he declared: 'They discourage the people from wearing modern clothes and tell them that wearing loincloth is good enough so that Europeans can come and see that these are primitive people living in a zoo.' Once that insinuation sank in, I knew who was in the right.

Dr Mahathir doubtless believed what he had been told. But that is not usually the case. While the downright lie may be the weapon of an honest rascal (e.g. an ambassador), innuendo is normally the weapon of the twister and the coward. And an innuendo may be no more than a matter of a choice of words. A British member of parliament campaigned for a doctor to be prosecuted for rape, and although the doctor's name was unambiguously cleared, lamented when interviewed by the BBC in 1987 that the fellow 'was still walking the streets'. He might as well have called him Jack the Ripper.

In the first paragraph of the Acknowledgements at the front of my book, *The Tiger and the Trojan Horse*, I wrote: 'I would like to express my warmest thanks to Mrs Lily Tan, Director of National Archives…(and) to the security authorities of Singapore for the invaluable help they so readily gave me.' This clear identification of two of my main sources was translated by M. G. G. Pillai, Malaysian stringer for *The Times* and *The Observer*, into: His book was written with *obvious* access to intelligence files', and: 'He *does not deny* his access to intelligence files, and that others, beside him, have a *vested interest* in the orientation of the book'. In the Introduction I noted: "I have on more than one occasion found myself faced with diametrically opposed versions of the same incident.' Having said that I had always given 'the official version uncritically', Mr Pillai turned this into: 'He *admits* that he, often, was given several versions of the same incident.' The introduction was mainly devoted to explaining that the book confined itself to the struggle for power in Singapore between the outlawed communists (the 'Tiger') and the legal People's Action Party (the 'Trojan Horse'); yet when I pointed out to the editor of the Kuala Lumpur *Sunday Star* that much of his reviewer's diatribe was not relevant to this theme, Mr Pillai wrote: 'He *now* says his book is about the PAP Government's struggle against the communists.'

'*Obvious* access…*does not deny*…have a *vested interest*…he *admits* that…He *now* says his book…' (My itals). Mr Pillai tells no straightforward lies here, of course; he simply misleads the reader by using loaded words to make plain statements of mine the basis for malicious insinuations. But when a journalist is the victim, he must usually accept this sort of thing without demur along with the rest of the shit that goes with his territory, and not fight back unless he can wring publicity out of a row. He can raise his eyebrows with impunity, but too much stooping is bad for the posture.

Since language is the litmus test of his integrity, the eyes and ears of the ideal reporter are directed inward as well as outward, for he must also read his own copy aloud to himself to make sure he has not transgressed. Like carving knives and icepicks, 'admit' and 'confess' have their right place and their lawful use (where men have admitted or confessed), but they become offensive weapons when a journalist tries to assassinate someone with them. Then again, a guerrilla is not always a 'terrorist', nor a separatist a 'rebel'. As he moves from news to interpretation to comment, guiding the reader through the deceptive maze of facts with qualifying signposts ('*surprisingly* violent reaction…with *unexpected* frankness…an *uncharacteristic* blush'), the path between bias and bias becomes ever narrower.

In consequence his opinions must be decently clothed, and immodesty give way to modesty whenever he puts prejudice to paper. An article in the Singapore *Straits Times* which begins loftily, 'I am amused by doomsayers who view every new height scaled by a stockmarket as moving towards a hair's breadth away from the precipice', also ends right there for me (and I am not referring to the syntax). The same applies when the reporter brings himself on stage. 'I saw them throw five grenades' is acceptable (eyewitness account); 'I watched as they threw five hand grenades' (which I once wrote) is not. The reporter is not a player, and even a columnist must forego the ego trip. For a financial journalist to inflict on her readers thirty-two column inches listing the programmes she likes and dislikes on the BBC World Service is an imposition. And that goes for another humorist who gave us her personal rating of current TV commercials in Singapore — as if we were not big boys now and able to decide for ourselves that (with rare exceptions) we loathed them all. When reading through copy, look for trouble, and if thine 'I' offend thee, pluck it out.

The nose of the journalist (sharp, predatory, the nostrils slightly flared) is not only a nose for news, but for news that has gone rotten — and not just because it has died on him. It discerns the point at which chequebook journalism, the hounding of a royal family, the clamour of doorstep reporters around the bereaved wife, the voyeurism of cameras greedy for grief, have gone beyond the public's right to know. Moreover, in a hard, ungiving face fashioned for brazening and ignoring knocks, the mouth reflects this sensitivity, for it is firm but full. A correspondent like Richard Hughes might be a master of trenchant Anglo-Saxon prose, but Dick was also a gentle and compassionate man. I have seen him weep unashamedly, less for the colleague who had been suddenly killed and whom he hardly knew, than for the wife the dead man had left behind and whom he did not know at all.

The jaw tells another story, however. The upthrust chin belongs to a resourceful joker who does not give in. When a story breaks he is exhilarated by the challenge, ready to put his head down and go for the deadline — swerving, bluffing, or meeting all obstacles head-on. The obstacles can be anything from a closed frontier to writer's block, for some of the most testing assignments are chairborne, not airborne. After three months off with TB I had to sit down and for the first time in my working life write a piece without smoking a single cigarette — and of all things it was a profile of Mao Zedong, the toughest possible task for a disused convalescent fresh out of confidence.

In 1973 I lunched with a leading Singapore pathologist while covering a mysterious murder that seemed worth a little extra trouble. I got it. 'It was a week old and stinking,' he said of the corpse, as I picked up my knife and fork, 'but you expect that, of course. In this climate the bacteria start eating away at the dead flesh in a couple of days, and the stomach goes green. The body becomes blackish, the skin blisters, and then the flesh flakes off.' He paused to dissect his medium rare steak with neat professional movements, and chewed on a morsel of red meat reflectively. 'The body swells,' he went on a trifle indistinctly, 'the veins marble with gas bubbles, the maggots get going from the outside, the eyes are eaten out and the whole body disintegrates. In three months you're down to bare bones. This is delicious. What's the matter? Not hungry…?' I got it all down along with my reluctant lunch, just as I had kept my ballpoint moving while a friendly American dictated an unusable scoop to me against the increasing clamour of the calculus in my kidney nine years before.

Pleased with myself? Hardly, after all these years spent blushing with shame when not flushing with pride. That dedication in the journalist's jawline is born of an ambiguous courage that itself is born of a sweating fear of failure ('BADLY OUTCLASSED BY SUN-TIMES…'), and can confront him with a moral dilemma a day. How far does he go towards hell fire — lying, cheating, picking and stealing — to get the story and beat the competition?

Playing the impostor to bluff one's way into a place (or out of it in enough of one piece to be able to file) is just the top of the primrose path. Held up at the Chinese frontier in 1958 by a security officer who rejected my passport because it was marked valid for Formosa, I heard myself yelling that I was the personal guest of Premier Zhou Enlai, who expected me in Beijing for dinner that Thursday. (He still kicked me out, but I made him carry my bags across the border to Hong Kong, and I was back — and in China — just twenty-four hours later). In 1980 I was shouting again, this time that I was a member of the personal entourage of the British Prime Minister, Mr James Callaghan (Maggie Thatcher was not within earshot), and already too late to join him in Beijing, where he was impatiently awaiting me before we had a personal meeting with Chairman Hua Guofeng, etc., etc. (That got me a seat on the only Boeing 747 in China).

Accosted by four Italian thugs well hung with hand grenades during anti-British riots in Trieste, I glibly betrayed my country by protesting that I was 'Canadese', and when a man in a fire-raising mob again asked me if I was English, I spat out '*Io*? Io sono Italiano come lei!' in tones of patriotic outrage that I hoped might cover any cracks in my accent. No cocks crowed. Nor did they crow when I decided I could not speak the language. Cloistered in the American lift of a Beijing hotel with half of a visiting team of Hungarian footballers, I did not disclose that I understood what they said, for in the days of Stalin's supposed communist monolith almost anything might be of interest. My unscrupulous eavesdropping was rewarded with a subversive exchange which ended with a neat one-liner as we reached my floor:

'The lift is a bit like the one in Lenin's Mausoleum in Moscow.'

'Yes, but this one works.'

The great thing about sinning is that it is easy to begin at the top and work one's way down, especially when money is involved. I never tried to bribe the telegraph clerks in Vientiane to send my cables first — too many of my rivals could outbid me anyway. Bribery is one thing, however, fraud another. Temptation was more insidious when Maurice Cavallerie, the owner of the Hotel Constellation, said at the end of a stay: 'Your bill is 18,000 kips. How much shall I write the receipt for?' Did you offend the excellent Maurice, lose a first-class source (and get yourself blackballed from the only rendezvous for reporters in Laos) by indignantly refusing to connive at his well-meant little fiddle? Most preferred to connive (and perhaps square accounts later).

Censorship was a flagrant invitation to cheat, of course. The best way to beat it was to smuggle copy out of the country, for as usual the simplest method was the safest — the more elaborate the machinery, the more numerous the gremlins. But that was not always possible. Before flying to North Vietnam in 1957, therefore, I arranged with the foreign news editor in London that he would cut out of my cables from Hanoi everything that lay between two semicolons. That would enable me to lace my otherwise critical copy with the sort of adulatory mush that the communists considered 'objective' reporting, with the certainty that while it would get me past the censors, it would never appear in print. Inevitably, the subs did not get the word, and the scheme went sadly awry. Without knowing it, however, I was in a great tradition.

During a crisis in the Spanish Civil War some twenty years before, the republican government in the besieged capital of Madrid put a clamp on all outgoing telephone calls and telegrams. Subsequently finding himself marooned with a first class scoop on his hands and no way of transmitting it to the *Daily Express* in London, the veteran foreign correspondent William Forrest successfully beguiled the censor with eleven carefully contrived paragraphs of anodyne guff which ended with the instruction: NOTE TO LATE SUB COLON PLEASE STRICTLY OBSERVE MY PARAGRAPHING. His cable was allowed to go. But alas the telegraphist who fielded it in London failed to add the instruction to the copy when passing it up to the sub-editors' desk. The late sub dutifully splashed the dead story — but nobody realised that the first letter of each paragraph spelled out its one vital message: GOVT HAS FLED.

As far as I know, government censorship led to larceny and forgery only once, when a correspondent who had been left alone for a moment in Souvanna Phouma's office filched the Prime Minister's rubber stamp so that he could clear his own copy for cabling, 'dashes' and all. But where a government robbed reporters (and everyone else) by imposing a fictitious rate of exchange for its feeble currency that turned a dollar into a dime, I had no compunction about robbing the government, and was on nodding (or head-shaking) terms with blackmarketeers from Saigon to Seoul.

When Keyes Beech and Pepper Martin and I set off to cover the civil war in Sumatra, the official rate of the Indonesian rupiah was ten times its real value. Accordingly, we bought a supply on the black market before leaving Singapore, and stashed a wad of notes that added up to money even in that crumbling currency under the felt pad of my portable typewriter, carefully screwing the machine back in place on top of it. We arrived at the port of Palembang as the customs house was closing, and the solitary officer present told us to take only what we needed for the night, leaving the rest of our luggage in the shed for inspection the next morning. Grumbling but meek, we pulled toothbrushes and razors and sarongs out of our bags, casually picked up our typewriters, and — 'Not the typewriters', he barked, and I can still hear the ugly words echoing around the empty building.

Some delicate fencing followed. We had to have the typewriters, we said; they were our tools of trade. Not tonight, he countered with a hideous wink; this is your first visit to Palembang and it's too late to start work, so you can look around, enjoy yourselves. But it's not our first visit, we parried, and we might need them at any…Well, then, you must be hungry and tired, he riposted, you need a good meal and rest before you write…However, we kept the duel going, wearing him down as reporters must, while the three typewriters stood on the counter in front of him, side by side and looking very prim. Finally he capitulated, 'All right,' he said, 'you can have one for emergencies.' He paused, his hand raised while we prayed — and then pointed suddenly: 'Take that one!' he ordered. It was mine.

Dedication makes a fastidious sinner, nonetheless, smiling on this misdeed, frowning on that. The path of the Far East correspondent is strewn with temptations, for even his legwork can lead him into bars, opium dens, and bordellos in the company of his more hospitable sources, and he may find himself succumbing to one or other of the pleasures they offer, or even all three the same night (oh yes he can — that's a myth). And if work does not seduce him, play always may. Yet while he may lie and wangle his way to the end of a story, his training and the exigencies of the chase tend to impose on him a measure of discipline and abstinence which, if not exactly calling for 'Jerusalem' as background music, usually preclude his taking time off to fornicate or drink himself insensible when his rivals may be one jump ahead of him. But his guardian angel is apt to disappear abruptly the moment he has filed.

The nicotine stains on the fingers will have been observed. This is a man who winds up as he works, until the membrane of his mind is screwed tight as a tympanum as he holds his breath and types his lead. But the moment he has filed the drum bursts, the discipline is blown to rags, and he is at his most vulnerable until duty calls again.

Reporters may drink to relieve the tension or to beat the boring hours of waiting for newsbreaks in anterooms or airports, and they may drink to get the facts when they have a bibulous source. But most of all they drink to unwind after their story has been despatched and there is nothing to worry about until the next one tomorrow. And not only drink.

All that is a matter for the individual conscience. There is only one rule that none must break: The correspondent must never get so incandescent that he sends an angry cable of resignation to his editor in the heat of the night before, even if he learns that his copy has been spiked. The hangover can last a lifetime.

The true professional can live with alcohol — at least until it kills him. He has a hard head, he is never too drunk to write, and even when stoned he can go through the other motions required of him as if he were sleepwalking. On one infamous morning Jim Robinson woke up in his hotel after a night out in Taipei to realise to his dismay that it was already ten-thirty and he must have missed his plane to the next story. He sprang out of bed, rang the bell, rushed into the bathroom to shower, and when the Chinese room boy appeared yelled, 'Quick, help me pack, I've got to get the next plane to Hong Kong.' 'But Mr Robinson,' protested the boy after a short, startled pause. 'But Mr Robinson, you *are* in Hong Kong.'

No single journalist can personify all, of course. The identikit may show the correspondent to be clear-eyed or blear-eyed, for more than the jaundiced observer would think ('they get all their stories in bars') do not drink at all. The mock-up I have put together cannot be a certified true likeness of you or me or anyone else, for if there are half a million reporters in the world, they have half a million faces. But the validity (or lack of it) of this study in the anatomy of the newspaperman and his job can be weighed on familiar scales. For it is exactly what we get every time we ask a prince or a pauper a question and scribble the answer in a 'reporter's notebook' — one man's view.

ABOUT THE AUTHOR

Dennis Bloodworth (1919–2005) was born in London in 1919 and lived in Singapore from 1956. After seeing service in World War II, he joined the London *Observer* in 1949, and until 1956, was successively based in Paris and Saigon. He was chief Far East correspondent of *The Observer* for 25 years, covering events in Vietnam, Hong Kong, Macau, Taiwan and China, until his retirement in 1981. He has also published four novels, and six books about China and the Far East—two of them with his Chinese wife, Ching Ping.